HAYAO MIYAZAKI

MASTER OF JAPANESE ANIMATION

FILMS

THEMES

ARTISTRY

HELEN McCARTHY

Stone Bridge Press • Berkeley, California

Published by
Stone Bridge Press
P.O. Box 8208, Berkeley, CA 94707
TEL 510-524-8732 • FAX 510-524-8711
sbp@stonebridge.com • www.stonebridge.com

Printed in the United States of America.

10 9 8 7 6 5 4 3 2
2004 2003 2002 2001 2000 1999

ISBN 1-880656-41-8

PICTURE CREDITS

Photograph of Hayao Miyazaki on part-title page 15 by Jun-
ichi Ochiai; background photograph of *My Neighbor Totoro*
stuffed toys © 1999 Helen McCarthy.

Copyright credits for the color insert on pages 17– 24
appear with their respective images.

CHAPTER 1 Part-title page 25 and page 29 from *Ponpoko*
© 1994 Hatake Jimusho • TNHG. Page 27 from *On Your Mark*
© 1995 Nibariki • Studio Ghibli. Cover of *Shuna no Tabi* on
page 31 © 1983 Hayao Miyazaki. Photographs on pages 33, 35,
and 36 by the author, © 1999 Helen McCarthy. Page 38 from
Only Yesterday © 1991 Hotaru Okamoto • Yuko Tone •
TNHG. Manga cover on page 40 © 1983 Nibariki. Video artwork images on pages 43 and 44, Buena Vista Home Entertainment Japan. Photograph of Studio Ghibli on page 47 courtesy
Tokuma International. **CHAPTER 2** Images from *Castle of
Cagliostro* © TMS-Kyokuichi Corporation • Monkey Punch,
used by permission of Manga Entertainment, Inc., with kind assistance from Rod Shaile at Manga's U.K. offices. **CHAPTER
3** Images from *Nausicaä of the Valley of the Winds* © 1984 Nibariki • Tokuma Shoten • Hakuhodo. **CHAPTER 4** Images
from *Castle in the Sky* © 1986 Nibariki • Tokuma Shoten.
CHAPTER 5 AND BACK COVER Images from *My Neighbor Totoro* © 1988 Nibariki • Tokuma Shoten. **CHAPTER 6**
Images from *Kiki's Delivery Service* © 1989 Eiko Kadono • Nibariki • Tokuma Shoten. **CHAPTER 7** Images from *Porco
Rosso* © 1992 Nibariki • TNNG. **CHAPTER 8 AND
FRONT COVER** Images from *Princess Mononoke* © 1997 Nibariki • TNDG. **CHAPTER 9** Part-title page 205 and stuffed
toys on pages 207 and 214, Sun Arrow Co., Ltd. Japan. Picture
frame on page 208, Benelic Co., Ltd. Japan. Video artwork
image on page209, Buena Vista Home Entertainment Japan.
Clock on page 210, Rhythm Watch Co., Ltd. Japan. Page 212
from *On Your Mark* © 1995 Nibariki • Studio Ghibli. Tea set
on page 213, Noritake Co., Ltd. Japan.

To the beloved memory of three much missed women:

My mother, Ellen McCarthy

Steve's mother, Rose Kyte

My "second mum," Bette Kitson

Contents

Preface

In the summer of 1989 I fell in love at first sight with the work of Hayao Miyazaki. An American friend and his wife, both anime fans, lent me some videotapes. One of them was My Neighbor Totoro, which became and remains my favorite film. I was captivated by its daring, its simplicity, its innocence, its beauty. That winter my local independent TV station screened Castle in the Sky, and showed me that the director whose courage was equal to telling a small child's story on its own scale could also unfurl an epic adventure with the old-fashioned panache of Robert Louis Stevenson, yet retain the delicacy and sensitivity of Antoine de Saint-Exupéry.

I've wanted to write this book ever since.

The Western world hasn't been entirely unaware of Hayao Miyazaki, in the same way that it hasn't been unaware of Japanese animation, but few outside Asia have really appreciated the depth and scope of either phenomenon. In conversation with Western animators and comic artists about the creative craftsmen they most admire, Miyazaki's name comes up again and again. My Neighbor Totoro had a U.S. video release in 1995 and won considerable critical acclaim. Academics and writers with a broad cultural perspective have long since acknowledged that the Japanese animation industry is not only the largest commercial animation industry in the world, but also a powerhouse of skills and inspiration. Yet most of us remained convinced of the hegemony of Western— read American—animation until America's animation giant Disney signed a deal for world distribution rights of a group of acclaimed Japanese theatrical releases with the Japanese production and publishing company Tokuma. These include movies by Miyazaki himself, his distinguished colleague Isao Takahata, and their colleague, the late Yoshifumi Kondo, who died at the tragically early age of forty-seven in January 1998.

"Manga movies" have become notorious in Britain and America for reasons that have little to do with the Japanese animation industry and much with the condition of U.S. and U.K. video markets.[1] Disney has chosen to avoid contentious areas of the Japanese industry altogether and go straight to the one production house that can demonstrate a record of commitment to artistic quality and integrity that equals, and in my opinion exceeds, their own. Studio Ghibli, the animation studio founded by Takahata and Miyazaki, has earned a reputation for an attention to detail and quality in every aspect of a production that borders on the fanatical: Miyazaki is one of the few directors in the industry who personally checks every key frame and redraws any he doesn't find suitable, a task most leave to the senior animators. Their productions are expensive in local industry terms, but every yen shows on screen. The quality of their animation work is matched in every area of each production, from writing to design and marketing. It was this commitment to a particular vision that captured my admiration while the seductive beauty of the on-screen images awakened the sense of wonder that lies dormant in all of us from childhood to life's end.

Some Western fans and journalists have called Miyazaki "the Disney of Japan" (a title previously bestowed on the late Osamu Tezuka, who died ten years ago). This says more about our need to label creative talents in ways we find acceptable than about Miyazaki or his work. Such comparisons give us a quick frame of reference, but they also prevent us from having to think too deeply about the content of the work or the individual views of the artist. If I had to label him in this fashion, I would prefer to call Miyazaki "the Kurosawa of animation." Not only does his work have the same rare combination of epic sweep and human sensitivity that the great live-action director possessed, but it also fails to fit into any of the neat, child-sized boxes into which the West still tends to stuff the animated art form.

The purpose of this book is simply to introduce Miyazaki and his work to a Western audience. For this reason it focuses primarily on the feature films being distributed by the Disney organization. It also sketches his earlier works and the careers of his colleagues, and briefly mentions his involvements outside directing and screenplays, but these areas are not covered in detail. There is so much to discover and enjoy in the work of Hayao Miyazaki and Studio Ghibli that many volumes by many writers could be devoted to the topic without exhausting it.

Think of this book as "Miyazaki 101." I hope it will be the first of many. I regard myself as privileged to have had the opportunity to write it. But reading is only a preliminary.

What you should do, as soon as you have the opportunity, is what I did on that afternoon in 1989 when I first watched *My Neighbor Totoro*. Go into a theater showing one of Miyazaki's titles, or rent one of his videos, then sit quietly and wait for the magic to start.

Seeing is believing.

ACKNOWLEDGMENTS

I want to give special thanks to a number of people without whose various contributions this book would never have been completed.

First and foremost, I would like to thank my partner Steve Kyte, who has helped me survive the realization of this long-held dream with love, patience, good humor, and his unerring sense of perspective. My friend and colleague Jonathan Clements has given invaluable assistance and encouragement.

Ten years ago Dafydd and Allyson Dyar sowed the seed for this book by sending me the movie that led me into Miyazaki's world; thanks for the acorns, and I hope you like the tree. Three years ago, a conversation with Jeffrey J. Varab convinced me that I not only could write this book, but *had* to write it, which finally persuaded me to badger more publishers—without that push I wouldn't have gone on trying to get it into print.

Stephen Alpert and Haruyo Moriyoshi at Tokuma International and Martin Blythe at Disney have been enormously helpful, going far beyond the call of duty in their kindness to an unknown and importunate writer. In January of 1999, over the course of two days, I was able to have extended sit-down interviews with both Hayao Miyazaki and producer Toshio Suzuki. During my visit, all the staff of Studio Ghibli were welcoming and hospitable, sparing valuable time to see me and answer questions—special thanks to Ms. Tai for her professionalism and patience, Ms. Itsuko for her wonderful studio tour, and Ms. Yasuda for her insight into the animation process.

The incomparable Frederik L. Schodt was, as ever, an inspiration. Tony Kehoe, Youri Foster, Mary Kennard, Fred Patten, and others provided much information and food for thought through their translation and writing. Steven Feldman, Atsushi Fukumoto, Ryoko Toyama, and other contributors to the Miyazaki Mailing List also provided a vast amount of very useful research material. Gordon O'Byrne and Kyoko Miyao gave invaluable assistance in Tokyo, as did Patrick Collins. Emmanuel Van Melkebeke, Nicolas Barbano, and Harry Payne helped to focus my thinking in several important areas.

My publisher at Stone Bridge Press, Peter Goodman, believed in this book enough to make it a reality, and I'll never be able to thank him sufficiently.

Finally, and most importantly, my heartfelt thanks to Hayao Miyazaki and Toshio Suzuki for their kindness and for their films.

Note to Readers

Each chapter in this book focuses on a particular title or aspect of Miyazaki's work. The information provided includes the origins of the movie; the main literary, film, or technical influences on it; character sketches; a story synopsis; a short staff list, including available details of English-language casting; and a critical appraisal or commentary. A brief section on how animated films are made is included among the pages of chapter 1. A Miyazaki filmography (which includes some of the manga he has worked on) and notes appear at the back of the book.

All transliterations of Japanese to roman characters use the standard Hepburn system, except that where creators' preferred romanized names are known they are used, even if the treatment is unorthodox. Names or references from Western literature or legend follow their Western form, and words in katakana— a syllabary used in Japanese to write "exotic" or "foreign" terms—are rendered as their Western equivalents where recognizable (so, for example, the katakana *na-u-shi-ka* is given as "Nausicaä" and *ra-su-ka-ru* as "rascal").

Dates follow Western rather than Japanese practice: 199X instead of Heisei X.

Individuals' names are given in Western style, family name last. In the same style, I have often referred to people and corporate bodies by family or corporate name only, without adding honorifics. No disrespect to any individual or body is intended.

Movie and series titles are generally given in their published Western form or, where they still await Western release, in the form by which the work is best known to me. The original Japanese title is given in transliterated form in the filmography listings.

SPOILER ALERT!

Throughout this book I give story synopses and discuss plot aspects in a way that gives away the endings and details of the titles. If you are one of those people who think the only point of watching a film is to find out how it ends, you should read no further. The story synopsis sections are clearly marked. Elsewhere there will be no specific spoiler warnings. I can assure you, however, that the works of Miyazaki, Takahata, and Studio Ghibli still delight and surprise me every time I watch them, no matter how often I have seen them.

HAYAO MIYAZAKI
MASTER OF JAPANESE ANIMATION

Captions to Color Pages

Castle in the Sky. A young girl falls from the clouds, buoyed up by the power of the glowing blue pendant she wears. Mineworker Pazu, coming back from an errand with his boss's supper, watches her float right into his arms, and together they embark on the adventure of a lifetime. This beautiful image was one of the movie posters for the original Japanese release

In olden days, there were many castles in the sky. They floated above the earth and were looked up to by ground-dwellers, but the secrets of their technology have been lost for ages.

Nausicaä of the Valley of the Winds. Pretty in pink, wearing the ornate headgear of a princess of the Valley of the Winds, Nausicaä listens to her father and the old Grandmother talking to Lord Yupa about the encroaching pollution of the world beyond their peaceful home. Behind her can be glimpsed some of the ornate Valley art that tells the story of the legendary savior foretold for her people, and perched on her shoulder is her new friend, Teto, brought back by Yupa from his travels.

Nausicaä fights desperately to stop the baby Ohmu from plunging into the Acid Sea, while Teto looks on. The acid might not kill the little creature, but it would cause terrible pain. It's not only her sympathy for the terrified baby that makes her act so bravely—she knows that unless she can save it, she won't be able to save her people from the Ohmu stampede.

Kiki's Delivery Service. Kiki flies along the coast toward Koriko accompanied by her black cat Jiji and some friendly seagulls. She looks the very picture of the modern young businesswitch out to make her mark in the world.

My Neighbor Totoro. Mei and Satsuki race excitedly toward the beautiful old house that is their new home. In the garden, wildflowers are in bloom and huge old trees stand sentinel. Old houses like this are now less common in the countryside around Tokyo, but they represent a traditional Japanese family home.

(*overleaf*) With Mei, Satsuki, and his own two siblings clinging to his fur, Totoro soars aloft and rides the night winds on his spinning top, roaring like the wind as he crosses the fields and woods of rural Japan. The scenery is based on a real landscape, but much of its beautiful woodland has been built over to accommodate the growth of Tokyo in the last thirty years. Japanese environmentalists are working to preserve the forests with Totoro's help.

Castle of Cagliostro. Lupin inches his way up an old stone wall, ignoring the dizzying drop below. This wonderful perspective background is worth studying in detail.

Porco Rosso. Marco Porcellino, the Crimson Pig, an ace airman with the head of a pig and the heart of a hero, takes to the skies in his beloved flying boat. The aircraft in Porco Rosso were designed by Miyazaki himself as an homage to the elegant Italian aircraft of the 1920s and their pilots, based on the technology of the time and using details and influences from real ships.

A deadly air ace and war hero is no match for a class of elementary schoolgirls enjoying an unexpected adventure. Marco has just rescued these little girls from the kidnappers who were planning to hold them for ransom, and plans to take them back to their families just as soon as he can fix the stalled engine of his flying boat. Meanwhile, who'll rescue him? The summery colors reflect the light-hearted mood of the scene, and the attention to detail gives visual depth.

Princess Mononoke. The giant forest god moves away from the world and into the mists of myth, already fading in the face of mankind's encroachment on its powers. The beauty of the sky and landscape makes this frame a work of art in its own right.

Ashitaka, riding his faithful steed Yakkle, shoots his deadly arrow. The pace of this dramatic sequence is reminiscent of the horseback action sequences in Kurosawa's seminal film *The Hidden Fortress*, which was an early influence on *Star Wars*. Costume details such as Ashitaka's straw cape and the style of weaponry were based on the best available research into this early period of Japan's history.

Whisper of the Heart. Poster art from the only feature directed by the late Yoshifumi Kondo, who died in 1998. The movie, which Miyazaki wrote and produced, is to be released by the Disney organization at an as-yet-unspecified date.

PREVIOUS PAGE AND THIS PAGE, TOP: Castle in the Sky.
THIS PAGE, BOTTOM, AND FACING PAGE, BOTTOM LEFT: Nausicaä of the Valley of the Winds.

TOP: Kiki's Delivery Service.
CENTER RIGHT: My Neighbor Totoro.
BOTTOM RIGHT: Castle of Cagliostro.

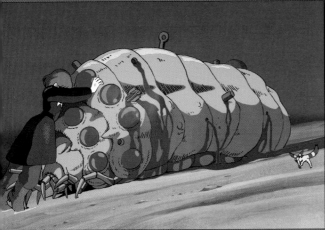

My Neighbor Totoro.

Porco Rosso.

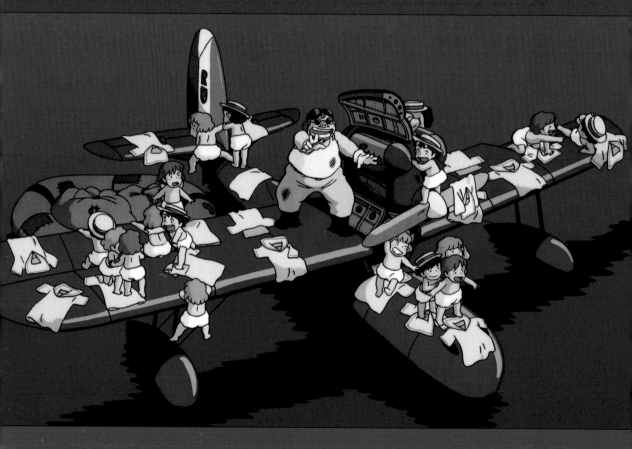

Princess Mononoke.

FOLLOWING PAGE: Whisper of the Heart.

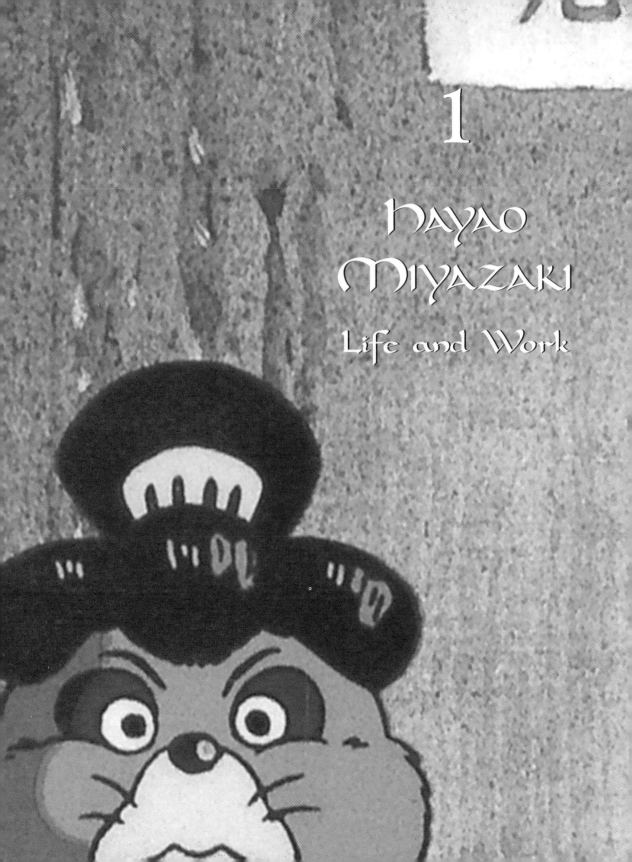

1

Hayao Miyazaki

Life and Work

Miyazaki grew up in the postwar years and joined the animation industry after graduating from the university, building on a lifelong interest in animation, film, and children's literature. He brought a considerable breadth of literary and political awareness to his chosen field, and during the early years of his career he began to explore the themes, ideas, and craft skills that would form the basis of his later works. Although much of his early work was in television, his ambition was to make feature films, and he gradually built up a circle of colleagues and collaborators who shared his dream.

EARLY YEARS

• •

Hayao Miyazaki was born into a well-to-do family living on the outskirts of Tokyo in January 1941. His father, Katsuji, who was then twenty-six years old, was a director of the family firm, Miyazaki Airplane. Headed by Katsuji's elder brother, the company was active in the war effort, making parts for Zero fighters. The war had an early impact on the young Hayao's life—he was three years old when the family was evacuated to safer districts, and he started school as an evacuee in 1947. It was another three years before the Miyazakis moved back to their old hometown, and then he changed schools again after only a year, moving to one of Japan's brand-new, American-influenced elementary schools.

But the biggest impact was probably the long illness of his mother, which commenced in the same year he started school. She was a woman of very strong character and intellectual interests. Although he says that he cannot trace his parents' influences on him, and that as a teenager he consciously sought to find his own path rather than follow his family's, the legacy of her powerful personality lives on in his work.[1] His youngest brother once commented that the determined, no-nonsense character of Ma Dola in *Castle in the Sky* reminded him of their mother.

Mrs. Miyazaki suffered from spinal tuberculosis. She was bedridden from 1947, two years after the birth of her fourth child, to 1955. The first few years of her illness were spent largely in the hospital, but she was able to be nursed at home thereafter and lived to old age.

Despite her absence from home and her long illness, she played a huge part in forming her son's view of the world.

Like many children in postwar Japan, the youngster decided he wanted to become a comic artist while in high school. His abilities at that time were limited—he couldn't draw people, having (like war babies all over Europe) only drawn planes, tanks, and battleships for years. It was an exciting time to be a young comic reader in Japan, and there was plenty of encouragement and inspiration. The teenage Osamu Tezuka had leapt to comic stardom in 1947 with his seminal manga *New Treasure Island* and started a powerful wave of enthusiasm. Established artists began to try new styles and techniques, and throughout the fifties there was an increase in comics consumption.

Miyazaki has taken issue with those who compare both his work and his role in the Japanese animation industry with that of Tezuka, pointing out that other artists such as Tetsuji Fukushima and Zohei Shiratsuchi were also

Soaring high above the contaminated Earth, an angel is set free to fly wherever she will, in On Your Mark *(1995). The two in the car are modeled on the pop stars who sing the song to which the video is set.*

important to his development. In an essay written for a Tezuka memorial collection, he describes the older artist's influence on his youthful work. As he grew toward independence, he consciously threw off this influence also, feeling he had to find his own path.

> To begin with, it's true to say that I was very heavily influenced by Tezuka. When I was in both elementary and junior high school, I liked his manga best of all the ones I read. The tragedies in his manga during the 1940s and 1950s—the early atomic era—were scary enough to make even a child shudder, they were so appalling. Both rock 'n' roll and the atom basically underpinned the tragedies, although the atom was to change toward the end of the era. . . . After that, when I passed the age of eighteen and felt that I just had to draw manga of my own, the question of how best to peel away the Tezuka influences buried deep within me proved an extremely heavy burden.[2]

Tezuka was named "the manga god" by his legions of devoted fans, but Miyazaki says that he preferred to regard him as a fellow artist against whose influence he had to struggle to find his own way, rather than an idol to be worshiped. He saw himself as a younger son who would be perceived by many as following his "elder brother," but regarded it as "bad form" to copy him, and destroyed much of his early work when he perceived it as too strongly influenced. Yet Tezuka's influence on the comics industry was so powerful that despite

his best efforts, it was not until he started work as an animator at Toei-Cine in his early twenties that Miyazaki was finally able to feel he had shaken it off, through studying the creation of movement and expression.

INTO ANIMATION

Like comics, animation enjoyed a peacetime renaissance. The experimentation of the early years of the century had brought Japanese animators into contact with their Western counterparts. Interrupted by war, this contact was now resumed with the active encouragement of the occupying American authorities, and Japan's animation industry once again began to produce entertainment for the cinema audience rather than overt war propaganda. From the 1960s this mass entertainment included material for the new medium of television.

Miyazaki's childhood interest in animation was rekindled by the first Japanese color animated feature, Taiji Yabushita's *Legend of the White Serpent*. He had been considering a career as a manga author, a path that he was not to reject entirely. Many years later, in an essay for a film journal, he recalled his feelings on seeing the film as a final-year high school student in 1958. "I have to make an embarrassing confession. I fell in love with the heroine of a cartoon movie. My soul was moved. . . . Maybe I was in a depressed state of mind because of the [university] entrance exams, or [maybe the cause was] my underdeveloped adolescence, or cheap melodrama—it's easy to analyze and dismiss it, but the meeting with *Legend of the White Serpent* left a strong impression on my immature self."[3] He realized the folly of trying to succeed as a manga writer by echoing what was fashionable, and decided to follow his true feelings in his work even if that might seem foolish.

It seemed his career path was moving away from the arts when he entered Gakushuin University, a prestigious institution with imperial connections, to study political science and economics. His final-year thesis was on the theory of Japanese industry. He could easily have been another pioneer of Japan's economic revival, but he wanted to find his own path in life and his interest in graphic entertainment and its possibilities was still strong. Among the many clubs and societies on offer at the university was a children's literature research society, which he joined. The group read children's books and comics, including many European texts. The young Miyazaki was exposed to a wide range of

In Ponpoko (1994), the tanuki (Japanese raccoons) hold a council. These normally peaceable, if mischievous, creatures are being driven to desperation by the encroachment of humans on their territory.

storytellers who used fantasy and legend in different ways. British writers like Rosemary Sutcliff, Phillipa Pearce, and Eleanor Farjeon, and Europeans such as Antoine de Saint-Exupéry, played their part in forming his views of storytelling and character development.[4] When he left the university in 1963, he did not take up an academic post or a business opportunity. Instead he joined Toei-Cine, the animation studio of the Toei Company, moved into an apartment near the studio, and after three months' training did his first professional work as an inbetweener on *Watchdog Woof-Woof* and *Wolf Boy Ken*.

An inbetweener is at the bottom of the animation ladder. He or she takes the key frames—the first and final frames of an action or movement, which are drawn by a senior animator—and produces the series of drawings in between. As might be expected, this work wasn't satisfying to someone of Miyazaki's intellectual intensity and passion. He was on the verge of giving up his new career in the same year when the animators' union hosted a showing of *The Snow Queen* (directed by Lev Atamatov, 1957). It reminded him of his first reaction to *Legend of the White Serpent* (which he had since dismissed as full of imperfections), and how the honest expression of simple, powerful emotions can strike people's hearts in animation as strongly as in any other medium.[5] Hoping that one day he would be able to express his own emotions in that way, he decided to keep going as an animator.

Miyazaki's intellectual and political background still influenced his approach to his work. A strong believer in union involvement in the workplace, he was active in the Toei labor union, leading a demonstration over a dispute soon after he joined the company. By 1964 he was Chief Secretary of the union, with his colleague and now friend Isao Takahata, with whom he had worked on *Wolf Boy Ken*, as vice-chairman. He moved up from being an inbetweener to handling key animation on the TV series *Wind Ninja Boy Fujimaru*. He was also dating a colleague, animator Akemi Ota, and a year later the young couple married.

Miyazaki's relationship with Takahata has been beautifully and playfully summed up in an essay by Takahata, *The Fireworks of Eros*.[6] Toshio Suzuki, longtime friend and colleague of both men, told me that Miyazaki considers this the best piece ever written about him and his work. Takahata contrasts his own supposed laziness with his colleague's energy, and acknowledges that their strong wills can lead to explosive confrontations, a truth that has been borne out by Miyazaki in a number of interviews, like the 1993 piece in *Animerica* magazine in which he said that though they had worked as producer for each other's projects, this role had to be a very "hands off" one to avoid clashes.[7] Despite the difference in their personalities and in the type of projects they choose, the enduring respect and admiration between the two is obvious, and their partnership was to form the foundation of one of the most respected studios in the world animation industry.

Around 1964, Miyazaki volunteered to help Takahata with his latest project, a new movie for Toei. TV production methods made the kind of expressive animation he wanted to produce difficult. Weekly production schedules that had to be adhered to at all costs and limited budgets meant that the number of cels used per episode of an anime series had to be kept as low as possible. This meant that movement often had to be restricted to the big, flashy, impressive sequences, and precious cels could not be "wasted" on the facial expressions or small gestures with which a live actor and director would develop a character. A shortage of skilled staff, aggravated by the long-standing practice of paying piecework rates and laying workers off between projects, meant that people with no training, background, or obvious talent were often hired at times of peak demand—not just as animators, but throughout the production process. With more and more TV series going into production, Miyazaki was concerned that chances to work on feature films might become scarce in the future, and saw the project as a golden opportunity.

Takahata already had directing experience on *Wolf Boy Ken* and other Toei projects. Now he was to direct *The Great Adventure of Hols, Prince of the Sun*, a new animated feature, with Yasuo Otsuka as animation director. Takahata and Otsuka wanted to make a much more expressive, realistic, and complex production than was possible in TV animation. Work started in 1965, and in a move that at that time was very innovative, Takahata and Otsuka opened their storyboard and planning meetings to the whole team, without regard for seniority or job title. Everyone was invited to contribute ideas, and Miyazaki was one of the most active participants, making major contributions to the style and story line of the

Shuna no Tabi (The Journey of Shuna) *is a Miyazaki comic that has elements in common with* Nausicaä of the Valley of the Winds *and* Princess Mononoke. *The delicate beauty of the artwork is a Miyazaki hallmark.*

film. The new Mrs. Miyazaki also contributed to the work as a key animator. (She continued to work on various animation projects until the birth of their second son.)

It took almost three years to finish *The Great Adventure of Hols*, which showed in

A BASIC GUIDE

Animation Technique

Because this book is about the work of an animation director and his colleagues, I thought it might be useful to give a brief outline of the process of cel animation, in order to provide a clear picture of the work involved in an animated movie or TV show. What follows is a very basic outline of the process; specific practices and timescales vary from studio to studio. If you are interested in finding out more, there are a number of excellent books on the market.[1]

WHAT IS ANIMATION?

There are, of course, many different kinds of animation. Cut paper can be animated with great success, and the making of cut-out puppets has been popular with children since the nineteenth century. The motion of cut-paper animation is crude, but some Russian and European studios have used the technique in films with considerable sophistication. You probably remember "flicker" (or "flip") books from childhood—a stack of paper with a little figure in a slightly different pose on each sheet. When you flicked through the paper fast enough, the figure seemed to move. It could be pretty jerky, but it was magical all the same. Claymation, the use of clay models whose position is changed in each frame to simulate movement, was developed to a high art by masters such as Ray Harryhausen, who made *Jason and the Argonauts*, and is still used by contemporary craftsmen such as the Oscar-winning Briton Nick Park. Glove puppets are another childhood favorite. Models can be animated in all kinds of ways, from the string-driven puppets of 1960s TV shows such as *Thunderbirds* to highly sophisticated and complex miniature vehicles in blockbuster movies. Until recently all major effects scenes were shot using models, but these days computer animation is accessible to most of the industry.

Cel animation is the form used by Miyazaki and Studio Ghibli for their work, so that's the form I'll discuss here. Cel animation is a series of images painted onto celluloid—hence the abbreviation. These images are then photographed in sequence and the film projected fast enough to give the illusion of movement. It's a little like those flicker books we used to play with as children, but on a much larger scale.

The general public thinks of an animator as someone who draws. That's not always the case. Anyone on the street would tell you that an animator is someone like Walt Disney, who makes a film based on drawings that are colored and run in sequence—but, except at the very beginning of his career, Walt Disney hired people to do this for him. He never drew or colored or photographed a single frame of any of his later hit movies. A more accurate term for such a person would be "key animator" or "inbetweener," someone who is a vital component of the huge team that is needed to make an animated film, but not someone whose name goes above the title. That place is usually reserved for the director or producer. Miyazaki is a di-

Studio Ghibli's works emerge out of a crowded, cluttered studio.

rector who is also an animator, and—unusual for the industry—he still corrects and redraws many of his junior colleagues' drawings himself. When you see a Miyazaki movie, you actually see the director's handiwork in the on-screen drawings, just as you would expect of an animator.

The whole process begins, of course, with an idea—a book the director or producer likes, an incident from daily life, a treatment pitched by a writer. At Studio Ghibli, the idea often comes from the directors or the producer Toshio Suzuki. It can be very vague at this stage; it doesn't need to be a full story outline with all the characters in place. Before it can go any further, it needs to be developed into a proposal: an outline of the story that gives details of the main characters, the mood of the piece, and the kind of audience it can appeal to. This may be supported by artwork to give an idea of the look the director has in mind, but this may change before the production is actually complete. The proposal is designed for one purpose only—to persuade backers to come up with the money to make the movie. To do this, a producer

must convince them that this show, with this director, will make money.

Relatively speaking, animation is cheaper to make than live-action blockbusters with big-name actors, but the key word is "relatively." The only cheap film-making is the sort you do at home on your video camera, and that's only cheap because you don't charge for your time. Making any kind of film is a labor-intensive process requiring high-tech equipment and a vast range of craft skills. Studio Ghibli employs a hundred full-time staff as well as another hundred outworkers for every production, and several hundred more people work on marketing the film and getting it onto screens across Japan.[2] When *Princess Mononoke* was released, it was the most expensive animation ever made in Japan. If it hadn't made enough money to cover its costs, the impact on its backers' balance sheets would have been serious. So once the funding is in place, director and producer have to work together to ensure that the movie can be completed on time, within budget, and to the best possible standard.

Studio Ghibli is unusual in that it employs a full range of staff and is able to carry out every part of the production process from conception to principal photography in-house. Many studios in Asia and the West, have to farm out much of the work to other companies, even companies in other countries. That American animated TV series your children are watching may have been financed and written in America, but the odds are it's been key-animated in Japan and the actual cel frames inked and colored in Korea, China, or Taiwan.

The process of placing the work starts very early once funding is in place, and is the producer's nightmare because if he or she can't get the right staff and meet his deadlines, he can't fulfill his commitment to the backers to make the film on time.

THE PROCESS

As soon as the money is in place and senior staff such as character designers, key animators, scriptwriters, and art directors have been signed up, a detailed timetable or flowchart for the progress of the work has to be prepared. Every element of the process must work together at the right time; the producer rides shotgun on this process. Meanwhile other, less concrete, decisions are being made by the director and key staff—what style should the production use? Is it to be very realistic, comical, fantastical, avant-garde? What's the overall mood of the production?

The script or screenplay is often revised right up to the last moment, but it will be substantially complete at this stage, and from it the storyboards are made. These are known in Japan as *e-conte*, short for *ei* (or "picture" in Japanese) continuity. These storyboards set out the whole picture, scene by scene, just like the storyboards for a live-action movie. Tiny sketches of the action will be made for each scene, usually in black and white though sometimes with a color indication, and alongside each one will be notes of any dialogue or sound effects and instructions from the director. Many directors like to draw their own storyboards, but sometimes a team of specialist artists, or the art director or one of the senior staff, will do them. The designers, senior animators, and key staff meet to fix the final look of the characters and their world, while the art director makes up the background boards, which set out the color range for the production. With all the planning and preparation in place, work can start on actually producing the cels.

The senior key animators, working from the storyboards, now decide, frame by frame, exactly what happens in each moment on-screen. The director, producer, and even the sponsors sometimes sit in on these meetings. Then the senior key animators get to work on the layouts, the basic drawings for each scene, and after a final check by the director the layouts go to the key animators, who draw the key frames—the most important parts of each scene. Usually, the key frames are the beginning and end of each action. The director checks the key frames and asks for any necessary changes. Miyazaki often corrects key frames himself, but on many productions the animation supervisor or animation director will draw the key frame corrections. All these checks are vital so that the inbetweeners can do their work correctly.

An inbetweener is at the bottom of the animation ladder. He or she takes the key frames and produces the series of drawings in between. These fill the gap and render the movement as smooth and fluid as the team's skill, the budget, and the production schedule allow. The inbetweener works from time sheets provided by the key animator that dictate how many cels will be needed for each scene and which cels make up each frame. He or she may clean up the key frames, removing stray lines and erasing unnecessary marks, though some studios have a separate department devoted to cleanup. Once the in-between drawings have been made and checked by a senior animator, who corrects any problems or faults, they are transferred onto celluloid. This is usually done via a mechanical copier, although in the early days of animation tracers used to trace each cel by hand, working over the original drawing.

USING COMPUTERS

The increasing use of computers in film-making has not yet affected the traditional animation inbetweener. Nowadays it's possible to handle certain sequences by programming a computer with the first and last frames and allowing software to morph through the required action linking the two. SFX director John Gaeta, talking in the May 1999 issue of *Empire* magazine about a complex sequence in *The Matrix*, described the process: "The computer looks at every pixel of every frame . . . and says that's a red pixel here on this frame and now that same red pixel is over here on that frame, so you have a huge file of information on every little pixel in every frame and you can do things with that information. It gives us the ability to create in-between frames that never existed."

The problem is, it costs a lot. The huge budgets of blockbuster sci-fi movies allow for this, but most animation directors just can't afford it. It's cheaper to animate character motion by hand. Until computers, software, and the skilled technicians needed to run both get cheaper, the inbetweener is likely to remain an essential element of the animation production process.

Some tasks, however, are being taken over by

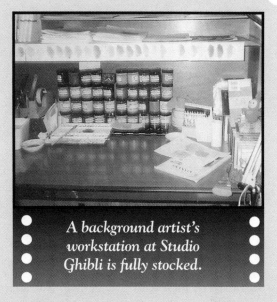

A background artist's workstation at Studio Ghibli is fully stocked.

sion are only made possible by the use of computers. Takahata's new film *My Neighbors the Yamadas* uses newly invented computer techniques as part of its highly original "wash fadeout" style. This allows the precise fading in and out of background watercolor washes. Even when suitable techniques exist, they aren't always perfect. The Toonshader package was already available when production started on *Princess Mononoke*, but it wasn't user-friendly and was further developed and customized by Ghibli staff for the movie.

Conventional background paintings remain a vital part of the animation process. They are started at the same time as the inbetweens, referring to the storyboards and background boards to get the colors and settings right. Every scene has its own background that may be seen from a number of different angles. A film with a historical background or a recognizable setting, such as *Porco Rosso* or *Princess Mononoke*, will also require many hours of research and perhaps some drawing at actual sites or in museums to get the details right. A good background painting is a work of art in its own

The Studio Ghibli conference room is lined with posters, books, and electronic gear.

right and makes a huge contribution to the success of a scene. Once the backgrounds are laid up under the character cels and any special effects being done on cel are added, the director, art director, animation director, and senior key animators can make their final checks to ensure that everything works together as it should, that the color balance of each scene is right and that all the timings work together to produce the overall effect desired.

Now the director and art director decide what lenses, filters, and other camera equipment will be needed for each scene to create the final effect and they make detailed notes for the cameraman. The whole package—cels, backgrounds, camera notes, and time sheets—is handed over to a photographic studio for shooting. The film is processed and checked, and the voice track, music, and sound effects added before final rushes are checked and film prints struck for projection.

All animation productions seem to have difficulty staying on schedule. This is partly because, with so many complex processes, it's easy for slippage to occur, and a delay in one part of the process holds up every other department that follows. To some extent Studio Ghibli has an advantage here—since all the staff work from one site and every process from concept to photography can be carried out there, some delays can be minimized. But even so, delays still occur. On his very first feature film as director, Miyazaki was still storyboarding long after production started; the staff began work on *Castle of Cagliostro* without knowing how it would end. When I visited the studio in January 1999 I was shown a flowchart for work on *My Neighbors the Yamadas* with two widely separated progress lines. The one furthest ahead, I was told, is "where we should be at the moment with the production" and the other "where we are." In-betweening was still going on for a handful of scenes as late as June 1999, with the scheduled opening date of 10 July fast approaching.

It's important to keep a clear perspective on the importance of computers in animation, but where deadlines are tight they can make a valuable difference. In *Princess Mononoke*, computers made a vital, but not a predominant, contribution to the movie. In time terms, only about fifteen minutes of the movie uses computer technology: ten minutes of digital ink and paint and five minutes of other techniques, including 3D computer graphics and morphing. Of approximately sixteen hundred scenes in the movie, the computer graphics team worked on about a hundred and fifty, or less than 10 percent. The huge god Didaribotchi was hand drawn, the particles inside its body computer generated on a wire-frame 3D computer model, and the body and particles digitally composited and painted. Ashitaka's arrows were hand drawn (except in the scene where he shoots Tatarigami through the eye) but some of the backgrounds they fly across were created in the computer or by texture-mapping artists' original background drawings. In the scene in which the maddened boar god chases Ashitaka and Yakkle across open fields, the five layers of the image were put together using digital composition: the outline of Tatarigami, his detailed shading and texture, the background of the fields, the path, and Ashitaka and Yakkle. The only shot which is one hundred percent computer-created is the one where the arrow hits the god's eye. The huge mass of tentacles writhing round his body were roughed out by computer using Toonshader on a CG wire-frame model, but the available technology didn't give the animators enough control, so the feelers were mainly animated by hand. In Tatarigami's death scene, and in the final moments of the film, after the great battle when the plants grow back to clothe the ravaged earth, some morphing techniques were used. In each case, the computer did not take over the traditional animation techniques Studio Ghibli excels in, nor was it subordinate to them. The two forms of animation coexist as part of the animators' tool kit, and the animators are working to find the delicate balance between the tool kit and the creative mind that allows art to grow.[3]

While Studio Ghibli was working on *Princess Mononoke*, its digitization facilities were relatively limited and its costs high—just before the film opened Miyazaki told *Asia Pulse* magazine that making a digital frame cost Ghibli three hundred yen, three times the cost of a similar frame in the U.S. Since then, the studio has invested its share of *Mononoke*'s profits in top-of-the-line systems that should help bring the cost-per-frame down,[4] but Miyazaki's wish that the Japanese government would provide the same level of support to its film industry infrastructure that other countries do has not yet been realized.[5]

Complex effects are possible with the help of the computer, but simpler methods have been used in the past to create movement and depth for specific purposes. For example, in *Nausicaä of the Valley of the Winds*, it was necessary to animate the giant Ohmu using overlapping layers of card for the segments of their bodies to depict the movements Miyazaki wanted.[6] The segments were manipulated with a lever to give the impression that the Ohmu's body was expanding and contracting as it moved forward or turned, and each movement was photographed to be laid over the backgrounds like a cel. This kind of cut-out animation has rarely been used in the West in recent years, being superseded first by multiplane cameras, which use layers of glass to lay elements of scenery one over another, and more recently by computer technology.

Most of the animation process is still labor- and energy-intensive as well as time-consuming. Good animation *looks* effortless but the stress on the staff is enormous. Andrew Simmons, a staffer at Disney, gave me the following humorous bird's eye view of the timescales of animation production and what they mean for the staff. He describes it as Animation Production Path 101:

Full day's work—a full eight-hour day, forty-hour week

Busy—forty- to forty-five-hour week

Very busy—forty-five- to fifty-hour week

Very, very busy—fifty- to sixty-hour week

Crunch time—sixty- to seventy-hour week plus some

Last week of crunch—living on Jolt soda and coffee

Done by Friday—getting the phone number for the Betty Ford Clinic

Done—coma

The next time you see an animated movie, remember how many people have been reduced to a coma to ensure it reaches your cinema screen on schedule.

Traveling to the country in search of her real aims in life, Taeko asks herself what it is she really wants. Only Yesterday *(1991), the story of a Japanese woman coming to terms with her past and making choices for her future, has relevance for women everywhere.*

theaters only briefly despite its critical and popular success. In stylistic terms, the film owes a debt to Miyazaki's earliest mentor at Toei, Yasuji Mori, whose clean and simple style of character design allowed for considerable emotional depth and flexibility. This style was to carry on in Miyazaki and Takahata's work on Nippon Animation's *World Master-piece Theater* series, and it remains a powerful influence on the work of Studio Ghibli even today.

Next Miyazaki made his first serious attempt at fulfilling his dreams of a comics career, producing a manga story under a pseudonym for a weekly children's paper in 1969. Fitting in the production schedule with his day job at Toei and the needs of a young family wasn't easy, but the serial ran for six months. Miyazaki has always been renowned as a perfectionist when it comes to his artwork—in a 1994 interview with comic superstar Masamune Shirow, both Shirow and interviewer Toren Smith commented on his habit of throwing away completed, painted pages, something Smith witnessed during the production of My Neighbor Totoro. (Smith described it as "enough to break your heart.")8 Still in search of a way to express his own ideas in his work, Miyazaki left Toei in 1971, following Takahata and another former Toei worker, Youchi Otabe, to A-Pro.

The studio contracted to work on a variety of projects and made an unsuccessful attempt to secure the rights to Astrid Lindgren's popular book Pippi Longstocking, which involved Miyazaki in a trip to Sweden with Tokyo Movie Shinsha president Yutaka Fujioka. The series was never made but the trip developed an important professional relationship. Also at A-Pro, Miyazaki and Takahata first made the acquaintance of a young animator called Yoshifumi Kondo. After two years the trio of Toei alumni moved on to Zuiyo Pictures, and Miyazaki went overseas again in the summer of 1973 to sketch locations and backgrounds for Alpine Girl Heidi, for which Otabe designed the characters. This was probably the first time any Japanese animator had gone overseas to sketch and research in preparation for a production. In 1975 Miyazaki went to Italy and Argentina for Three Thousand Miles in Search of Mother. Takahata directed both these series, and in 1972 and 1973 also directed Miyazaki's first short films as a writer, the charming Panda & Child and Panda & Child: Rainy Day Circus.

For some time, it appeared that fears about the decline of the animated feature might not be unfounded. Though Miyazaki and Takahata had a steady stream of work on TV series and individual episodes, and were increasingly respected in the industry as gifted craftsmen, feature film work was not readily available. Miyazaki directed his first TV series, the seminal Future Boy Conan, for Nippon Animation in 1978. From the bloated warplane, whose engines still reverberate in Nausicaä of the Valley of the Winds and Castle in the Sky, to the seaplane that prefigures Porco Rosso, we see Miyazaki's love of flight and steam technology sketched out for future development. Heroine Lana makes her own ethereal flight, setting a number of precedents for heroines from later works; she is an orphan, abandoned like San in Princess Mononoke, and Conan rescues her as Pazu does Sheeta in Castle in the Sky, and as Miyazaki later said he always dreamed of doing. Despite the contemporary success of Star Wars in Japan and its impact on writers of science fiction and animation, Conan made little or no reference to it. Miyazaki's literary and cultural influences are at work, and Fritz Lang's Metropolis is more significant than George Lucas's Empire. The growing ecological awareness that was to flower in later works pictures the terrible consequences of a world destroyed by war and rising sea levels in 2008. Conan also brought him back into contact with Yoshifumi Kondo, who worked on the series as an animator. He and Takahata were to work with Kondo on a number of projects in the following years; just a year later Kondo made his debut as a character designer on Takahata's series Anne of Green Gables.

Although Miyazaki was able to use some of his own ideas and influences in Conan, the structure of the series wasn't his to define. The constraints of time, money, and commercial sponsorship all hampered the standard of work that could be done in the TV series format. He was seeking work where his talent as both writer and artist could have free rein; but nevertheless when the chance to direct a movie arose in 1979, he took it despite the restrictions it imposed. The seemingly abortive trip to Sweden for *Pippi Longstocking* bore fruit at last when Tokyo Movie Shinsha

ANIMAGE COMICS ワイド判   定価340円

風の谷のナウシカ 2

宮崎 駿

The collected edition of the manga Kaze no Tani no Nausicaä, *also available in an American translation as* Nausicaä of the Valley of the Winds.

hired Miyazaki to direct *Castle of Cagliostro*, an action-adventure-romance starring Monkey Punch's renowned characters from the manga *Lupin III*.

MOVIES AND MANGA

Despite the constraints of working with another writer's characters and universe, Miyazaki produced a film full of charm, energy, and warmth, and was so successful that he was asked to direct two episodes of the second *Lupin III* TV series a year later. Both jobs gave him the chance to work with Yasuo Otsuka, who had become a Lupin regular, but on the series Miyazaki chose to use a pseudonym: Teruki Tsutomu. This name is also a wordplay; in Japanese it can read "employee of Telecom," the name of the company for which he was working part-time as an animation instructor. That would be enough to stamp his work for anyone in the industry, while not signaling to the world in general that he was going straight back to television work.

Early in 1981, still at Telecom, he began work with Italian animators, including Marco Pagott, who became a close friend, and with Kondo as character designer, on a series for the Italian TV channel RAI. *Great Detective Holmes* hit a preproduction hitch and was not finally completed and screened in Japan until 1984, but its charming and gentle reading of the Sherlock Holmes adventures in a world of clever canines proved very successful. The relationship with Pagott was enduring; Miyazaki's love of Italy and airplanes finally culminated in 1992 in *Porco Rosso*, with the hero named for his friend. He, Takahata, and Kondo started work on the U.S./Japan coproduction *Little Nemo*, based on the art of comics giant Winsor McCay, but Miyazaki and Takahata quit at an early stage for artistic reasons. Jean Giraud, the French artist better known as Moebius, a friend and admirer of Miyazaki, put the split down to personality clashes between Miyazaki and the president of Tokyo Movie Shinsha, Yutaka Fujioka, and commented that while *Little Nemo* took six years to finish, Miyazaki went on to make *Nausicaä of the Valley of the Winds* in nine months for "barely a million dollars."[9]

Miyazaki was soon hard at work on a second manga series that was to be published in *Animage* magazine starting in 1982. A monthly devoted to animation and related media, *Animage* was founded in 1978. It is still in publication and is widely respected as one of the most thoughtful and insightful journals on the subject, never hesitating to acknowledge the medium's low points as well as its highs, and treating animation as a mature and fully flexible art form. Its editor at the time was Toshio Suzuki, a founder member of its staff who had approached Miyazaki for a feature for the first issue and who soon became a close friend.[10] The magazine also formed an ongoing relationship with Yoshifumi Kondo, who provided illustrations for them.

The new Miyazaki manga was *Nausicaä of the Valley of the Winds*. It gave Miyazaki a chance to express all his ideas, dreams, hopes, and fears in the form of an epic story about a brave, beautiful girl and her fight to help her people and her world survive in a time of war and political wrangling.

The manga was a huge undertaking and did not see completion until March 1994, with many production breaks while Miyazaki worked on other projects. However, the appeal of the characters and setting was such that, despite Miyazaki's initial reluctance, plans to make a movie based on *Nausicaä* were soon under way. The ecopolitical consciousness of the seventies and Miyazaki's own passionate feelings about the oppression of small groups by powerful interests were influential in the development of the film story, but just as important was his awareness of the need for the film to stand on its own, independent of its origin as manga. With Isao Takahata as producer and Topcraft as the chosen production house, finance for the filming was secured through a joint venture between Tokuma and the advertising agency Hakuhodo, where Miyazaki's youngest brother worked. A month before detailed, hands-on animation work on *Nausicaä* began in 1982, Miyazaki's mother died at the age of seventy-one. The film opened in March of 1984; almost immediately it became a cult classic among animation fans.

With an eye on future possibilities and the need to protect their creative input, Miyazaki and Takahata formed a partnership to handle their works and copyrights, punningly christened Nibariki (Two-Horse Power), early in 1984. A year later, with another major feature film looming on the horizon, it was obvious to Takahata that they needed their own studio, and Studio Ghibli was founded in

Kichijoji, a western suburb of Tokyo. (Ghibli—pronounced *ji-bu-ri*—is a word for a strong Saharan wind and also the name of one of Miyazaki's favorite Italian airplanes.) As well as continuing to provide a vital link with Tokuma through his work on *Animage*, Toshio Suzuki was now working for Studio Ghibli, and former Topcraft production manager Toru Hara became studio manager at the new facility. Miyazaki set off on his travels again, this time to Wales, where he drew mining villages and explored the close-knit communities of the Rhondda in preparation for *Castle in the Sky*. Once again, his sympathies were stirred by a small group fighting for survival against a stronger power—this time by the Welsh miners' struggle to save their industry—but his main purpose in making the film was to create a classic boys' adventure story. Miyazaki outlined the problems caused by the film's tight schedule in an interview in June 1987:

> Usually, making animation means finishing off the storyboard, then giving it to the staff to do the rest, but because the schedule was so tight, I could do only half of each scene before it was time to give it to my staff. On the one hand, I had to touch-up my staff's drawings. On the other hand, I had to do the remaining scenes. It was a mess. My daily schedule went like this: I got up in the morning, I drew storyboards, I returned to the office. At the office, I touched-up my staff's material. At night, I went home and did some more storyboards. After that, I slept.

In Japan, I'm afraid the only one who makes animation this way is me, since no one else could take it.[11]

He added wryly, "I think this is something I feel proud of." He neglected to add that he also wrote the lyrics for the movie's end theme.

In 1986, the year in which *Castle in the Sky* premiered in Japan, the heavily edited English language version of *Nausicaä of the Valley of the Winds* known as *Warriors of the Wind* was released in the U.S. The cuts and changes in the structure of the original story destroyed much of its impact and took away a major strand of the plot.[12] Despite its clear artistic superiority to most of the children's movies available in the West at that time, *Warriors of the Wind* was severely maimed. Although what remained was still a visually stunning, powerful, and exciting movie, Miyazaki and Takahata were so horrified at the destructive nature of the changes that they refused to consider Western releases for their works for over a decade thereafter. If any further evidence were required to convince Miyazaki that, to ensure his vision was put across purely and clearly to audiences, every aspect of the production must be under the director's control, this travesty of his work supplied it.

With two successful features as writer and director under his belt, Miyazaki now turned to production for Takahata, and between them they made (despite the predictable clashes) a live-action documentary on the history of the Yanakawa Canal as a curtain-raiser to one of the most creatively remarkable years in any studio's history. In 1987 both men were directing new theatrical features at Studio Ghibli for Nibariki, with production finance and support from Tokuma. *My Neighbor Totoro* and *Grave of the Fireflies* were released on the same bill—surely one of the most moving and remarkable double bills ever offered to a cinema audience—in 1988.[13] Takahata's film, based on a semiautobiographical work by a survivor of World War II, is a heartrending testament of the child victims of war. Less than two decades separate its events from the ravishing vision of a childhood summer presented by Miyazaki. Both films were remarkable achievements, but *Totoro* was later to achieve an unexpected status as one of the greatest merchandising successes of Japanese cinema. Once more, Miyazaki tried his hand as a lyricist on the movie's ending theme.

UNDER PRESSURE

The young studio could not afford to rest on its laurels, so production began almost immediately on the next Miyazaki release. Based on a novel by Eiko Kadono, *Kiki's Delivery Service* involved the talents of everyone on the senior Ghibli team. Takahata acted as executive producer and general fixer, solving many of the preproduction problems with external companies and the novelist, while Kondo, fresh from his triumph as animation supervisor and character designer on *Grave of the Fireflies*, directed the animation. The director, character designer, and scenarist had combined work on the film with another new manga, which was to

Japanese video cover for Princess Mononoke. The art captures the movie's atmosphere of mystical beauty, but does not depict any action or the main characters.

provide the basis of his next film. By now Toshio Suzuki had joined the studio full-time, in time to help with one of the most visionary developments in the anime industry.

For a long time, Miyazaki and Takahata had understood that the kind of movies they wanted to make, and in particular the standards they upheld, were hard on the staff who worked with them. The Japanese animation industry operated on piecework payment—staff at the lower levels were paid on the amount of work they produced, and both they and senior staff were taken on a per-project basis and let go between contracts. Staff working to Studio Ghibli's standards were producing such fine, detailed work that, however much effort they put in, they could not produce enough work to make a living wage on a piecework basis. Many were receiving only half the average Japanese income. Directors and producers were also handicapped by this system. In boom times they had to compete for the best staff, while many skilled workers had to seek other employment when the industry was in decline.

Miyazaki wanted to create a team of permanently employed staff, on a monthly salary, with a proper career structure and training planned into their working life. In this way they wouldn't be disadvantaged by producing the kind of expensive craftsmanship that lifted the studio's work out of the ordinary run of the Japanese animation industry, and he and Takahata would always be able to rely on a pool of talented staff who knew their way of working. With the support of Tokuma, he was able to implement his plan in 1990 and Ghibli began its policy of annually hiring new permanent staffers and planning their training and integration into the existing team. But with regular monthly salaries to pay, downtime at the studio was now an unaffordable luxury, and the Ghibli team was soon back at work on not just one, but two overlapping productions—*Only Yesterday* and *Porco Rosso*.

Overlapping the productions was not ideal. The schedule meant that Miyazaki had to

Japanese video cover for My Neighbor Totoro. This scene never actually appears in the film, but sums up its whimsical charm perfectly.

start work on *Porco Rosso* with no assistance at all, because the rest of the team was tied up on the demanding final stages of work for the Takahata-directed, Miyazaki-produced *Only Yesterday*. The film looked at childhood in sixties Japan through the eyes of a young woman at a crossroads in her life in the eighties, and premiered in 1991 to critical acclaim. Meanwhile Miyazaki, perhaps to take his mind off the stress of having to produce, direct, and assist himself on *Porco Rosso*, had dreamed up a new project. He wanted to build another studio.[14]

It was really not so much a crazy daydream as a logical extension of his attitude toward animation and animators. To produce the best work, it was necessary to recruit, train, and keep the best people. This meant not just paying them regularly, but giving them a safe, decent environment to work in. It would also minimize ongoing costs and deliver greater creative control to have the entire team working together under one roof.[15] Ghibli couldn't afford the outlay required, but Mr. Tokuma, president of the Tokuma corporation, was supportive of the plan and underwrote the construction costs. The new studio meant not only a huge additional expense—for a studio that had already doubled its production costs at a stroke with its revolutionary hiring policies—but a vast extra workload for Miyazaki. Despite his complaints about having to kickstart *Porco Rosso* single-handedly, he undertook the design and supervision of the building project himself. He drew the first blueprint, chose materials, met with builders, and checked every detail personally.

Studio manager Toru Hara had character-ized Ghibli's production strategy as one of high costs, high risks, and high returns, but the latest risks—a hugely expensive production and a hugely expensive new facility at the same time—had proved impossible for a pragmatic manager to contemplate, and Hara left Ghibli as work started on both undertakings.[16] A year later, *Porco Rosso* played out a sunlit dream of politics, romance, and drama over the Adriatic in the 1920s on screens all over Japan. It became the highest-grossing film of the year.

The new studio in Koganei, another western Tokyo suburb located a little further out of town than Kichijoji, was finished at around the same time as the film, and staff were able to move in just after release. Despite the great risks and costs, Miyazaki and Takahata had created something remarkable at Studio Ghibli: a team of dedicated artists and craftspeople with security of employment, in a purpose-built environment, working toward a single goal—the production of animated theatrical films of a quality that was rarely equaled and never surpassed by any studio in the world.[17] It was time for Miyazaki to return to the challenge that had, in a way, started the actual process of his studio's development. He decided to finish the manga version of *Nausicaä of the Valley of the Winds*.

While Miyazaki did battle with the final chapters of the manga—he was recorded as saying he wished he'd never started the work, which had become both a huge creative triumph and a leech of his time and energy—Studio Ghibli made further technical progress. By setting up its own photography department with the purchase of two computerized cameras, the studio had now moved the entire creative process in-house. With a level of control over every stage of production that was unique in the industry, the team at Studio Ghibli could achieve something quite remarkable. Not only could they produce wonderful films, but they could bring their high standards to television productions. Their first TV special, *I Can Hear the Ocean*, directed by Tomomichi Mochizuki, was screened in 1993, and at the same time the studio made forays into the world of TV commercials with two identity slots for a Japanese TV network's anniversary, and worked on Takahata's next picture, the ecofantasy *Modern-Day Raccoon War Ponpoko*. At this stage they began to use computer graphics images (CGI), at first with just a few shots in *Ponpoko*, but later with increasing confidence.

Takahata's film appeared in the cinemas in 1994 and was Japan's nominee for the Oscar for Best Foreign Film a year later. In the same year, Miyazaki's father died at almost eighty years old and Yoshifumi Kondo started work on his debut movie as director, *Whisper of the Heart*. The delicate romantic fantasy premiered in 1995.

Alongside it on the bill was a short film, *On Your Mark*, animated to music by Chage and Asuka and directed by Miyazaki. Kondo was already being talked of by fans and critics as the heir-apparent to the Studio Ghibli tradition, and this seemed to fans to confirm his status.

For some time, Miyazaki had been saying to various interviewers that he did not intend to continue the pace of his work at Studio Ghibli forever. His immense creative involvement at every stage of the studio's work as well as his own writing, art, and design had left him little time for family or any other pursuits, and he felt that the time was coming when he would step down from such active involvement with the studio's projects. In 1993 he told *Animerica*: "Bear in mind that I'm a director who actually draws animation. Maintaining my current level of involvement can't possibly last much longer. . . . And I'd like to retire before someone suggests it to me. My particular Achilles' heel is my worsening eyesight. It all comes down to how far you can push yourself."[18]

He was at work on an idea that had first occurred to him twenty years ago and that he had decided would be his final movie as director for Ghibli. Various ideas as to what he would do after this were mooted—he might remain involved in the studio's work on a different level, devote more time to his teaching work, or produce a different kind of animation in a new, smaller studio. Takahata had not discussed his own retirement publicly, but he is of the same generation as Miyazaki: the war babies who helped shape the new Japan.

Kondo was a perfect choice to take the studio ahead into a new millennium, because he was born in 1950 and grew up through Japan's rise to world influence but was rooted in the powerful traditions and craft skills that Miyazaki and Takahata had learned in their early years at Toei. Before that, the whole of Ghibli's creative talent was devoted to the next, and possibly last, Miyazaki movie—the hugely powerful, mold-breaking *Princess Mononoke*.

FUTURE PERFECT?

Princess Mononoke, with its dark and dazzling story, its harking back to Japan's misty past, and its use of computer graphic imaging as an extension of the traditional animators' toolkit, was a mammoth hit, the highest-grossing Japanese movie to date. (Until the massively promoted *Titanic* hit Japan, it was also the highest-grossing movie ever released in that country.) Its unprecedented success at the box office seemed the icing on the cake of the 1996 distribution deal between Tokuma and Disney, which was set to bring the works of Miyazaki, Takahata, and Kondo to worldwide audiences from 1998 onward. An American theatrical premiere for the new movie was already being discussed for 1999. Miyazaki had designed a new building to house his private office, a short walk from Studio Ghibli, where his farewell party was held in mid-January 1998. Tragedy struck just a short time afterward, when Yoshifumi Kondo died of an aneurysm in the early hours of 21 January.

The sudden and unexpected loss moved the animation world deeply, and both Takahata and Miyazaki delivered touching eulogies to their younger colleague. He did not live to see the success of his work on *Kiki's Delivery Service* in the American market, nor was he able to work with translators and scriptwriters on the English-language version of his *Whisper of the Heart*. Within days of his death, Tokuma had announced that Miyazaki would return to Studio Ghibli to direct a new movie, while Takahata's next production, a theatrical version of the successful manga *Our Neighbors*

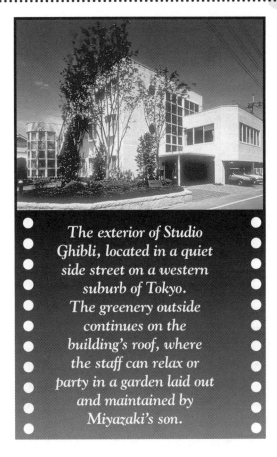

The exterior of Studio Ghibli, located in a quiet side street on a western suburb of Tokyo. The greenery outside continues on the building's roof, where the staff can relax or party in a garden laid out and maintained by Miyazaki's son.

the Yamadas, was already on schedule for a summer 1999 release.

Studio Ghibli's development as a creative powerhouse has been secured by two important elements—the genius of its founders Miyazaki and Takahata, and the constant support of Tokuma and its president. Audiences around the world have seen on countless occasions that no matter how much money you pour into its production and marketing, a bad movie is still a bad movie. Yet without a solid financial foundation, no studio that sets its standards as high as Studio Ghibli's can hope to continue its work with the degree of independence necessary to make enduring creative decisions.[19] The deal with Disney promises to make the work of Studio Ghibli known all over the world and may well help secure its future. The studio is even slated to have its own museum, scheduled to open in 2001.

Ghibli and Miyazaki are now in the same dangerous position as Osamu Tezuka—some fans and critics have elevated them to godhood. In an interview in 1995 Mamoru Oshii, director of many Japanese animated hits including *Patlabor* and *Ghost in the Shell*, pointed out the injustice of imposing that status on both the studio and Miyazaki himself. "You shouldn't make him a god, since he's the one who has to carry that burden." Humorously, he likens the studio to the Kremlin, with Miyazaki as chairman, Takahata as party chief, and Suzuki as head of the KGB, and goes on with more seriousness to say that Ghibli's highly organized structure produces work of a quality that can be found nowhere else, but would not suit every creative individual. "I think that for them, making a movie is still a kind of extension of the union movement."[20]

Miyazaki constantly refers to the fact that he would like to see talented new directors in the Japanese animation industry, and is trying to foster them, but so far with the exception of Kondo, Ghibli has produced no heir to its traditions. The future may be secure in terms of prestige and finance, but without dynamic new directors Ghibli's work will eventually come to a halt.

Miyazaki continues to work in diverse fields as illustrator, manga author, artist, and director. He seems to have come to terms with filmmaking's physical demands. When I met him early in 1999, he said that he works hard while making a project but is able to take a long break between each one, so he doesn't find the labor too arduous. He is also planning his next movie. Interestingly, although he had at first planned to follow the unprecedented success of *Princess Mononoke* with another film for young adults, Toshio Suzuki feels that Ghibli should no longer make such movies, and convinced Miyazaki to make something for children instead. He is working on a story that will feature the ten-year-old daughter of a colleague as heroine. It will be released sometime in the year 2000.

Miyazaki now stands at the pinnacle of Japanese artistic achievement. He has helped raise two mass entertainment media, animation and comics, to the status of artistic and literary excellence, and with his gifted colleagues has created a body of work of great depth, beauty, and honesty. What he will do in the next millennium is not yet known, but movie lovers around the world, and several generations of children and their parents, may be selfish enough to hope that it won't involve too many long retreats to the peace and quiet of his mountain cabin. We haven't seen nearly enough of his work yet.

2

CASTLE OF CAGLIOSTRO

The Princess and the Thief

Miyazaki's directorial debut is a romantic action-adventure tale that combines an appreciation of slapstick comedy with a sophisticated sense of characterization and pace. Many of the themes he would develop in his later movies are sketched out in this light-hearted caper set in a European never-never land of ancient castles and modern intrigues. It stars a princess in distress and a lovable rogue who steals hearts as easily as jewels. The dramatic finale has a satisfying sense of retribution and a bittersweet twist, without souring the movie's overall sense of fun.

ORIGINS

The characters of Lupin III and his partners in crime were originally created by manga writer and artist Monkey Punch and remain among the longest-running and best-loved characters in manga and anime.[1] New theatrical and video releases continue to the present day. A lovable rogue, Lupin was based in part on another literary ancestor, *Arsene Lupin, Gentleman-Thief*, the brainchild of French novelist Maurice LeBlanc. Lupin senior's exploits on the Riviera and elsewhere in high society kept French readers gasping at his daring and chuckling at the incompetence of the police in the 1920s; the Japanese artist read the books, loved them, and decided to make his own character a Japanese descendant of the legendary Frenchman.

This has caused a good deal of com-plication for fans of the manga and anime ever since. Although the character of Lupin III is Monkey Punch's own creation, the Arsene Lupin name and the original story are the property of the LeBlanc estate, which has asserted its rights on several occasions. For this reason, the Japanese criminal genius has used a nom de guerre in two American editions of his adventures on video. Anim-Eigo called him Rupan III, following the Japanese pronunciation of his name, and Streamline Pictures chose to call him Wolf (the Latin word for wolf is *lupus*) in their releases, *Tales of the Wolf* (the Miyazaki episodes from the TV series) and *Castle of Cagliostro*. A 1980s French release of *Castle of Cagliostro* renamed our hero Vidoq the Fourth and was entitled *Vidoq vs Cagliostro*. Aware of the difficulties over using the Lupin name in Europe, Nippon TV renamed character and series *Cliff Hanger* when they offered rights in the series for Western markets in the 1980s.

Monkey Punch's characters had a well-established screen history before Tokyo Movie Shinsha asked Miyazaki to make *Castle of Cagliostro*. A TV series had been made in 1971, and Miyazaki and his colleague Takahata had codirected a number of episodes. Another had started in 1977 and was still running when *Castle of Cagliostro* went into production, and in 1980, after *Castle of Cagliostro* was released, Miyazaki wrote and directed two episodes of this series under a pen name. An earlier feature film, *The Mystery of Mamo*, had enjoyed box-office success in 1978. Miyazaki had all the problems facing any incoming director of a well-established

Crackshot Jigen takes aim at the goons chasing the beautiful young woman, while Lupin steers straight ahead. Notice the simple yet accurate depiction of the European car.

Lupin and Clarisse prepare to make an unorthodox exit from the autogyro. Flight is a recurrent motif in many works by Miyazaki, and in this movie it's used both to create tension and lighten it with humor.

franchise. Most of his characters were already set up. Fans of *Lupin III* expected to see Lupin, his sidekicks Jigen and Goemon, his would-be nemesis Inspector Zenigata, and his on-again, off-again lover and rival Fujiko; they would accept nothing less than a story that gave all these well-loved characters some part to play. However, he was to write and storyboard the film, which gave him a certain freedom of action within the characters' established boundaries. The challenge was to take the franchise and put his own stamp alongside that of its creator: to make not only a *Lupin III* movie, but a Miyazaki movie.

To do so, he made use of LeBlanc's and Monkey Punch's mythology as well as historical sources. There was a real eighteenth-century rogue named Guiseppe Balsamo who used the title Count Alessandro of Cagliostro and who was actually a con artist at the court of Louis XVI of France. LeBlanc published a book called *Countess Cagliostro* in 1924; it features a mysterious woman who is the granddaughter of Cagliostro the conman, just as Monkey Punch was to make Lupin the grandson of LeBlanc's gentleman-thief. The heroine of *Countess Cagliostro* is called Clarisse, and later marries Lupin. The idea of a drowned treasure also occurs in a LeBlanc Lupin novel, *The Girl with Green Eyes*, and there are moments reminiscent of Edogawa Rampo's *Clock Tower Mystery*. The huge royal wedding in a tiny European state is reminiscent of many a pulp romance, but also has echoes of the media hoopla around the wedding of film star Grace Kelly to Prince Rainier of Monaco. The opening sequence, with its spectacular getaway after a casino robbery, and the rooftop chases later in the film call to mind one of Kelly's most enjoyable films, *To Catch a Thief*, in which costar Cary Grant played a charming gentleman-thief at play on the Riviera.

The other major influence on Monkey Punch's manga was the James Bond movies, but in my opinion this is less evident in *Castle of Cagliostro* than elsewhere in the Lupin canon, although it does open with a casino heist on Bond's beloved Riviera and features a tense yet comical sequence with a small car catapulting down precipitous slopes and through woodland, like the one in *For Your Eyes Only*. It's as if Miyazaki has gone back a little further in cinema history, to a time when wacky caper movies with dastardly villains could still offer laughs as well as explosions, and romance held its own rather than being completely submerged by sex. This range of influences and the careful tying-in of

his original story to the Lupin canon attests to Miyazaki's breadth of cultural awareness and enriches a film that is very much his own.

ART AND TECHNIQUE

Work on *Castle of Cagliostro* started in May 1979 with the preparation of the story and storyboards. Animation work started at the beginning of July, with the storyboards only a quarter finished; Miyazaki finished them while animation was going on, a nerve-racking process for the entire crew. The film was completed at the end of November and released in theaters on 15 December 1979—an astonishing seven and a half months from commencement to release, with under five months of production time (though Miyazaki has commented that he wished he could have had another month).

Although no specific research trip was undertaken for this film, Miyazaki's Heidi sketchbooks must have come in useful for some of the mountain and lakeside vistas, and he also cites a book he saw in a shop window and snapped up, *Italian Mountain Cities and the Tiber Estuary*, from Kagoshima Publishing.[2] Monkey Punch's love of placing his characters in exciting foreign settings was magnificently exploited by the director and his team, who created a European wonderland as exotic as any Hollywood fantasy. Miyazaki also took the chance to acknowledge, very elegantly, the influence of French animator Paul Grimault. The palace of the king of Takicardie in

Grimault's *Le Roi et L'Oiseau* looks like a sketch for the castle of Cagliostro, and as the film unfolds we see even more similarities, from the dizzying, soaring spires and turrets and the vertiginous rooftops all the way down to the dungeons, trapdoors, and oubliettes.[3]

The wedding scenes in both films also have some points of similarity.

Miyazaki's longtime colleague Yasuo Otsuka had been on the *Lupin III* animation team from the very beginning, working on the pilot film in 1969. The character design and gener-

Who knew European cars were so tough? Lupin and Jigen defy the laws of gravity in their attempts to foil the Count's goons as they enter the tiny country of Cagliostro. The summery color palette of the movie adds a light-hearted element to the comical yet action-packed chase sequence.

al direction of the film's style are a tribute to his skills. As a Lupin regular, he was well aware of the path the character designs had taken in the past, but as a colleague of Miyazaki he knew the style and feeling the director wanted to put across. The characters in *Castle of Cagliostro* are softer, younger, and more romantic in sensibility and in design than in any of their earlier incarnations. Otsuka had made a number of appearances as an extra in the first TV series, and in *Castle of Cagliostro* he can be glimpsed at the wheel of a huge truck in the opening scenes. Guest roles for the crew are a fairly common practice in Japanese animation; Miyazaki's home was one of the settings for a *Lupin III* TV series episode.

At a very early stage in preproduction, Miyazaki plotted the layout of the castle itself with great care. A plan of the interior with its many levels was used to work out complex action sequences and character movements throughout the film. This detailed plotting and layout allows the audience to suspend disbelief and accept the castle as a real location, as solid as the French chateaux settings for Cary Grant's capers in *To Catch a Thief*. The pace is also beautifully handled, with an upbeat, action-packed opening sequence followed by a series of beautifully linked set pieces leading to the classic ending fight.

The color palette of the film is predominantly summery, in line with both the setting and the characters. Lupin is a cheerful kind of guy, a happy-go-lucky optimist at heart; Clarisse's youth and innocence demand a setting of sunshine and flowers. Where darker colors are used they emphasize the film's subplot of the struggle between the dark and light

sides of the ruling family of Cagliostro. Most of the Count's plotting and the machinations of his underlings take place either at night or in artificially lit, stuffily furnished rooms. Lupin's first meeting with Clarisse takes place in a sunlit garden, and they say their final farewell in a sunlit meadow. By contrast, the Count keeps her locked in a painted chamber heavy with occult symbols. The final battle between good and evil is at night, in the shadowy spaces of the great clock tower, and the resolution of the mystery comes with the dawn, as the light gleams off the long-hidden beauty of a treasure greater than anything our heroes had imagined.

The music is evocative and rich. Yuji Ono, in fine form, draws on a wide range of influences, from the jazz beloved of Lupin's creator and used in some form in all his moving picture incarnations, to the romance and majesty of the classic orchestral form. Lupin's familiar TV theme is vividly reworked and the soundtrack powerfully supports the action. Although composer Jo Hisaishi has become almost synonymous with Miyazaki's films since *Nausicaä*, Ono does a fine job and the soundtrack is a pleasure to listen to in its own right.

The Lupin franchise is still going strong, with TV and theatrical features, and has even broken into the world of computer games, where the *Castle of Cagliostro* incarnation seems to be the favorite. A laser disc–based arcade game called *Cliff Hanger* used footage from *Castle of Cagliostro* and *The Mystery of Mamo* in the early 1980s, and a Playstation game based on *Castle of Cagliostro* was released in January 1997.

Japanese animation fans took the film to their hearts immediately. Readers of *Animage* magazine voted it their favorite animation of all time, and Clarisse their favorite heroine, until the appearance of *Nausicaä of the Valley of the Winds*. It was still in their top ten animated films in 1995, more than fifteen years after its debut, and continues to be well regarded by Japanese viewers today. In America it has been well received on limited theatrical release as well as on video. New audiences will find it very rewarding.

THE CHARACTERS

Arsene Lupin III is around five feet, ten inches tall, weighs a lean 138 pounds, and has black hair with sideburns and dark eyes. His appearance can change almost miraculously—he is known as a master of disguise, and has even foiled Interpol with his daring impersonations of their own personnel. His origins are shrouded in mystery, but like his renowned French ancestor he is intelligent, agile, brave, and a great romantic. He is very kindhearted under a cool, hard-boiled veneer, and always does his best to help children, animals, and those in trouble. He is also a complete sucker for a pretty face and will take the most absurd risks in pursuit of a girl. His other faults are greed—he can eat anything, and frequently does—and a certain slobbishness. Yet when he's working he is a

meticulous planner and produces gadgets and devices of incredible ingenuity.

Fujiko Mine's surname means "peak" or "summit" in Japanese. Whether this is a reference to her supreme professional skills or to her most prominent physical assets is left to the audience to decide. She is a lissome brunette from an old Japanese family of thieves, and diversifies into spying when the need arises. Her chief passions are gold and men, which she tries to combine by dating and robbing as many rich men as possible. She especially likes Americans, Englishmen, and the French. She is as clever and agile as Lupin, and far more ruthless and single-minded. They have an on-again, off-again affair and their business relationship sometimes has them working with each other, sometimes on opposite sides. In *Castle of Cagliostro* she has dumped him and masquerades as a governess to get into the Count's castle and look for the precious counterfeiting plates. Her role is less prominent than in other movies or the TV series, but her relationship with the innocent Clarisse provides an interesting comparison with the later relationship of Gina with Fio in *Porco Rosso*.

Daisuke Jigen was originally inspired by James Coburn's gunslinger in *The Magnificent Seven*. He is a taciturn, beer-drinking firearms expert who is rarely seen without a cigarette drooping from his lower lip and always wears his hat pulled low over his eyes. He's spent some time in the

U.S., having offended a few dangerous people in Japan, and this has heavily influenced his style of dress. He is reputed to be the best marksman in the world. He's known Lupin for many years, and although he has left the gang to work alone on occasions he is very loyal to his old friend and always shows up when needed. He deplores Lupin's laid-back attitude and his addiction to women, since he himself mistrusts the opposite sex—especially Fujiko.

Goemon Ishikawa XIII

Goemon Ishikawa XIII looks like a figure from another era with his long black hair and traditional samurai dress. His beliefs and attitudes match this image—he is a fighter of the old school, reserved, proud, and stoic, with great courage and loyalty. Goemon is a swordsman of unmatched skill and never uses firearms, relying on his ancestral sword, Zantetsuhen, which can cut through any object, even solid steel, as if it were paper. He comes from an ancient family of Japanese warrior-thieves and has vowed to preserve the traditional virtues of bushido in the changing modern world.

Inspector Zenigata

Inspector Zenigata is ninth in a dynasty of detectives stretching back to Japan's Edo period (1603–1867). He is a good cop whose life is dominated, and often ruined, by his self-imposed mission to arrest Lupin III and bring him to justice. As a member of an international police force he can chase his nemesis all over the globe rather than being confined to Japan, but he never quite succeeds in clicking the cuffs around Lupin's wrists. Creator Monkey Punch said that he had Tom and Jerry in mind when setting up the relationship between Zenigata and Lupin, and certainly their encounters can be as crazy as anything between that cat and mouse duo!

Clarisse

Clarisse is a beautiful young lady who has been away from Cagliostro completing her education until just before the film opens. She returns to her homeland to make an arranged marriage with the Count, a distant relative, following the death of her father in the fire that destroyed the old royal palace. She is a gentle yet courageous girl, with no experience of the world but with a sweet and giving nature, an archetype that Miyazaki was to develop in his later heroines. Clarisse is from the "light" side of the family, while Cagliostro's branch has followed the path of "darkness"—but she knows the two sides must be united if the secret of her family is ever to be revealed. The talents of Sumi Shimamoto, Clarisse's voice, made such a deep impression on Miyazaki that he used her again as Maki, heroine of the final episode of the second *Lupin III* TV series, and entrusted the central role in *Nausicaä of the Valley of the Winds* to her.

Count Cagliostro

Count Cagliostro is as black-hearted a villain as ever menaced an innocent heroine. He is modeled on such classic rogues as

In the painted chamber at the top of the tower where she is kept prisoner, Count Cagliostro tries to wrench the ancestral ring from Clarisse's finger. The family resemblance between the two is clear.

Rupert of Hentzau, archvillain of the novel *The Prisoner of Zenda*—an urbane and cultivated creature with a heart of ice to match his nerves of steel. He has absolutely no conscience, and ruthlessly exploits his title and social position to conceal the activities of the family counterfeiting business that he and his ancestors have run from the castle cellar since the early Middle Ages.

THE STORY

The casino, Monte Carlo: the security guys are in pursuit of a couple of daring thieves who have just turned over the joint. As their big black pursuit cars literally fall apart around them, Lupin III and his sidekick Jigen can hardly see the road for banknotes. Their little

Fiat is stuffed to the sunroof with money, enough to make them rich for life . . . except that, with the notes so close to his eyes, Lupin suddenly realizes that they're fake. As the friends pitch handfuls of seemingly perfect counterfeit dough out of the windows and sunroof, his agile brain starts to puzzle over who, how, and why—and digging back into history, he starts to make some connections that will lead him down a road to the past.

Soon he and Jigen are heading for Cagliostro, Europe's smallest country. Everything looks very rural, very peaceful, and picture-postcard perfect. As they fix a flat on the road—having decided who has to work the jack by a quick game of scissors, paper, stone—all that changes. A small car driven by a very young woman in a bridal gown and veil races past, pursued by a group of big goons in a large sedan. Unable to resist the chance of a good fight and a pretty girl, Lupin sets off in hot pursuit. Jigen's marksmanship skills are in demand as they come under fire from the men in black, but thanks to some crazy driving— up the side of a mountain, through a little wood, and almost under a huge truck—they manage to see off the bad guys and catch up with the girl. She has fainted at the wheel, and things get even crazier as Lupin leaps from one car to the other, tries and fails to avoid going over the edge and into the lake, and, despite his best Batman utility belt line, ends up out cold, in a heap with the girl at the bottom of the cliff. As she bathes his face with her glove, trying to revive him, a boat comes around the headland and she flees into the woods. By the time Lupin comes round and Jigen joins him, she's on board and heading across the lake toward the ancient castle that dominates the town. But she's left her rescuer a souvenir—inside her glove is a silver signet ring with the image of a capricorn, a half-goat with a fish's tail.

Lupin and Jigen get back on the road and stop off at a ruined palace. It used to be the royal palace, but it's obviously suffered a massive fire. An old caretaker finds them on the grounds and tells them to go away, but Lupin leads Jigen through the ruins to a beautiful water garden opposite the castle of Cagliostro, where he reminisces about his first visit to Cagliostro, long ago, when he was just starting out on his life of crime. As they talk, the Count's autogyro airplane lands at the castle and he makes his way across an extending bridge to the lonely turret where the young girl, Clarisse, is held. Her governess, whom we later learn is really international crime goddess Fujiko Mine in disguise, is dismissed and the Count looks down at his drugged prisoner, still in the wedding gown she was trying on when she escaped. We see the family resemblance; they have the same short nose and the same auburn hair. He reaches for her hand to compare their heirloom rings, his gold, hers silver, and sees that hers is gone, obviously to the meddling tourists who helped her. The rings somehow form part of the key to a great treasure hidden long ago by their mutual ancestor. He's determined to get it—and get rid of the meddlers.

Meanwhile Lupin and Jigen have made their way into town and found a friendly inn where Lupin indulges his twin passions of shoveling down food and sweet-talking the waitress. He learns that Clarisse has come home to marry the Count, a union of light and shadow that the old legends foretold. Of course, they're being spied on, and later that night their room is invaded by a deadly force of ninja and some of the old weapons on the walls are put to more than decorative use. A frantic escape over the roof follows, with the ninja giving chase, and they finally shake off their attackers by car. Meanwhile Fujiko, still disguised, sneaks through the huge rooms of the castle to a secret vantage point where she can listen to the Count discussing the latest batch of counterfeit plates with his manservant. As the servant turns to leave, we see

Deep in the dungeons of the castle, Lupin waits among the debris of ages for Zenigata to turn up. The Inspector is determined to be the one who finally puts the cuffs on the renowned master thief Lupin III. Whatever scrape Lupin gets into, Zenigata won't be far behind.

that Lupin's calling card is fixed to his back. Now the business is becoming personal.

In the early morning rain, a figure out of Japanese history gets down from a European farm cart—Goemon has arrived to join Lupin and Jigen in the camp they've set up at the old ruined palace. Other people are starting to arrive for the wedding, including Zenigata and an Interpol detachment, to offer their protection to the Count, an old "friend" of Interpol, from the notorious criminal believed to be in the area. The Count feels he's in no need of protection, and a tour of his perimeter defenses seems to prove the point, while Jigen wonders how Zenigata tracked them to Cagliostro, and Goemon guesses that Lupin made sure he knew where they were. Leaving him to cover them from the hideout, Lupin and Jigen make a perilous journey into the castle through the only route not covered by lasers and cameras—the underground water tunnels.

The prewedding banquet is in full swing as Lupin and Zenigata carry out an elaborate game of chase and impersonation through the castle. The hapless Inspector drops out before too long, falling victim to one of the Count's countless oubliettes, and his host tells his men he's been called back to Paris and left word for them to follow. Meanwhile Lupin catches up with Fujiko and learns that Clarisse is in her isolated turret with no way across. With his usual love of a challenge, he scales the highest point of the castle, checks the wind, slides down the ancient tiled roof, and prepares to launch himself across the void with the aid of a rocket and a grappling line. The lighter fails to light when it should, the rocket fails to perform as it should, and he's left sprinting frantically down a near vertical slope, just about building up enough momentum to carry him over the gap and arrive with a bone-crunching thud on—but not yet in—the turret.

Clarisse is sitting in a room painted with the most seductive and beautiful colors of darkness—a combination of the night sky and the fantasies of astrology—despairing of her future, when down through the ceiling comes her rescuer. He returns her ring and vows to save her again, and when she doesn't believe him, he rustles up some party tricks to make her smile—producing flags of all nations and a paper flower like a conjurer at a child's birthday party. The Count's arrival interrupts this tender scene, and after he retrieves the silver ring Lupin is dropped down a hidden trapdoor to the very bottom of the tower, miles below. The Count tells his young relative that a family prophecy five hundred years old foretold their union, and she can't fight it—then Lupin's voice comes from the transmitter he put in the counterfeit silver ring, before a smiley face pops up to taunt the Count even further. But the manservant, Jodo, says there's no way he could have survived the fall, and goons are dispatched to find the body and retrieve the real ring.

Lupin and Zenigata are reunited in the dungeons below the tower and make plans, agreeing to put aside their differences until they can escape. Running rings around Jodo and the goons in another hilarious sequence, they do manage to escape, and find the counterfeiting factory, which is also under the castle. Counterfeiting is apparently not illegal in

LIVERPOOL JOHN MOORES UNIVERSITY
LEARNING SERVICES

Cagliostro, and this accident of law has enabled the Count's dynasty to manipulate history for the last half millennium. Zenigata agrees to help Lupin expose the fraud.

Fujiko, still disguised, is saying her farewells to Clarisse when they see smoke rising through the floor of her painted chamber. Over the lake at the old palace, Goemon and Jigen see it too and realize it's their signal to move. Lupin and Zenigata are burning the presses. They escape the Count's men again and steal the autogyro while Fujiko and the Princess watch. To Zenigata's horror, he finds he's having his first flying lesson and his first solo flight at once, as Lupin leaves the little ship to get into the turret. It's time for Fujiko to show her true self as she tries to blast them out, then produces a rope when that fails. As Lupin hauls Clarisse up, Fujiko holds the attackers at bay with a handy machine gun, but after an epic battle Lupin is wounded on the roof and the Count threatens to kill him unless he gets the silver ring. He plans to shoot him anyway, and when Clarisse throws herself across him he makes it plain he'll shoot her too, so Fujiko, with all the familiarity of an old love, tells them where Lupin will have hidden the ring, and proves to be right. As the Count is about to exact his revenge Zenigata comes clumsily to the rescue, crashing the autogyro, and Lupin and Fujiko escape with him. She takes off on a previously concealed glider, the hapless Zenigata ends up in a tree, and Lupin is picked up by his faithful henchmen, Goemon cutting him out of his burning clothes with a single stroke of his sword while Jigen drives.

Back at Interpol, Zenigata finds the politi-cal will to deal with the Count surprisingly lacking, and the whole debacle is written off as a kidnap attempt by Lupin on Clarisse. The Chairman orders the case closed—there will be no further action on the counterfeiting matter. Zenigata's good policeman's instincts are outraged, but what can he do? Meanwhile in Cagliostro, Lupin lies seriously injured in the little cottage to which Jigen and Goemon brought him, where the gruff old palace care-taker and his faithful dog are hiding them. Lupin's miraculous powers of recovery are helped by his massive food intake, and the others hear the full story of how the young Clarisse and the dog rescued him all those years ago, when his first caper went so badly wrong. With the wedding next day, he has little time to repay his debt to her and keep his promise. Meanwhile Fujiko intervenes again, making sure Zenigata knows Lupin will be at the wedding. She's already got her invi-tation, as part of the team reporting the event for the television network NBK.

Huge traffic congestion caused by crowds traveling to the wedding is made worse by an avalanche that blocks the route. Even the Archbishop coming in to perform the cere-mony is held up, but that evening the ceremony begins with a candlelit procession of chanting monks. Clarisse, dressed all in white like a spirit of pure light, waits in a candle-lined room for the Count, who is decked for his wedding in a goat mask and a huge dark cloak with a lining red as blood. She seems to be almost in a trance. The couple walk side by side under an arch of swords, reflected in the blades by the light of many candles. But as the Archbishop begins the ceremony, Lupin's voice rings out from the altar, and the huge cross is shattered by a flying sword. Darkness descends. A bizarre procession echoes the bridal party of moments earlier as a bandaged figure speaking in Lupin's voice is carried in. As the figure is speared through, Clarisse's trance breaks, but it was only a dummy—

Lupin is impersonating the Archbishop. With Goemon and Jigen covering their escape, Lupin takes Clarisse and heads for the clock tower. Meanwhile Zenigata asks Fujiko to bring her camera crew down to the basement and help him expose the Cagliostro counterfeiting setup.

Back off, Rambo, Fujiko is going into action! Lupin's beautiful and treacherous sometime-girlfriend spends much of the film disguised as a prim governess, but her final scenes demonstrate the full range of her skills.

Lupin looks at the beautiful gardens of the old palace, now destroyed by fire, and remembers his first visit to Cagliostro many years before. He knows that the little country hides a mysterious secret, but not until the end of the movie will we find out just what a treasure is waiting to be discovered.

As Lupin joins the two rings to read the inscription on them, the Count gives chase. An epic fight ensues inside the huge workings of the tower's ancient clock. Lupin and the Count circle each other like tiny toys on the ancient cogs and gears, each fighting to avoid a fall to his death as well as to defeat the other. As the hands move toward midnight the Count snatches Clarisse, but Lupin tells him he has the rings and has worked out the riddle. The key to finding the ancient treasure of Cagliostro is the carving of the goat looking east, above the face of the clock. The rings are his two eyes. He offers to trade them for Clarisse. Needless to say, the Count tries a double cross, but Lupin catches her as she falls and they plummet into the lake together.

The Count claws his way up the clock face to the goat carving and clicks the two rings into place in the figure's empty stone eye sockets. Inside the tower, the great gears suddenly change motion and the whole fabric of the building shakes. The hands of the clock finally close on midnight, crushing the Count between them with a satisfying squelch, and bells peal out as water bursts the aqueduct and brings down the tower. As the water rushes back into the lake around the castle, bursting its elaborate system of floodgates and tunnels, the dungeons and cellars are filled, the counterfeiting presses are destroyed, and the castle of Cagliostro is marooned at the center of the huge new lake.

As dawn breaks, Lupin carries Clarisse, still in her wedding gown, down a passage formerly under the lake to the ruins of her old home and they see the treasure of Cagliostro at last. A beautiful Roman city, perfectly preserved by the protecting waters of the lake for centuries, stands shining in the morning light, a treasure for the whole world to share. But it's time for him to say good-bye, before Zenigata can get reinforcements from Interpol and capture him. He kisses her tenderly on the forehead and leaves her with her faithful old retainer and his dog, while he, Jigen, and Goemon head off in their trusty little car. As Zenigata pauses before taking up the chase, he tells Clarisse that Lupin is still a thief—this time he's stolen a young girl's heart.

Things are the same as ever at the end of a caper. Zenigata is trying desperately to catch the trio. Fujiko, ever practical, has managed to salvage the plates and waves as she races away on her motorbike. The last shot in the film is of a sunny Mediterranean coastline. It's a beautiful day for another madcap chase.

COMMENTARY

Castle of Cagliostro is an astonishingly assured debut feature. The thirty-eight-year-old Miyazaki had already directed for TV, but was ready and eager to show what he could do with more screen time, higher production values, and a bigger budget. For Miyazaki fans it also has great interest as a sketch for several of the themes he was later to develop in *Porco Rosso*, but its value for its own sake is firmly established in the first few scenes.

The story takes place in the never-never land that is the Japanese dream of Europe, a rustic paradise of crumbling yet infinitely sophisticated cities and castles; ancient titles and even older secrets; lakes, mountains, and high flower-strewn meadows; and mystery and romance. There is a Japanese phrase that sums up this yearning for the beautiful, mysterious fantasy otherwise—*akogare no Paris*, the Paris of our dreams. In *Castle of Cagliostro*, Miyazaki gave Japan the Europe of its dreams, shining and perfect, with all expectations of adventure and romance fulfilled and no language problems. It's a honeymoon movie, the delicious consummation of a young director's passion for the big screen. He has been creating travel guides for dreamers ever since.

The film's charm and humor are easily assimilated by the casual viewer, yet it has enough density of plot to please film buffs. The plot walks the fine line between comedy and suspense with nonchalant ease, its set pieces and action sequences dazzling and its tender romantic moments unforced. Moments like the slapstick chases, the swimming and dungeon sequences, and the wacky opening with pursuit cars falling apart and banknotes streaming all over the highway are balanced by gentler jokes such as Lupin's little magic trick to make Clarisse smile and are thrown into relief by the terrifying rooftop shoot-out and the final fight between Lupin and the Count.

Tied to a well-established character set, Miyazaki does each regular justice. As with all imported casts, some of them have to be moved to the fringes of the action for much of the time. In some movies (for example, the disastrous *Streetfighter II* live-action version) such characters are mere ciphers thrown in to fill airtime with a pointless reiteration of their well-known characteristics, but Miyazaki gives each a place in his story with meaning and purpose. The most important relationships he takes from the manga are those of Lupin with Jigen and Lupin with Zenigata. Jigen is there to be the old buddy, the point man and confidant to whom Lupin can unfold the vital background information the audience needs when setting up the story. Zenigata fulfills his usual function as the foil for Lupin's ingenuity and also provides, on behalf of the audience, the unsophisticated reaction of an honest man

confronted with corruption in high places. Zenigata, like the old retainer who cares for Lupin twice, is the film's everyman, the decent sort whose plain, plodding exterior can blind us to his essential goodness, the salt of the earth in the midst of all these charming crooks.

Fujiko has an essential function in the plot—to anchor Lupin in his own reality. In the midst of his memories of starting out on a life of crime, when perhaps he could have taken another road, and his romantic wish to protect and help the princess in distress, Fujiko reminds him that he can't go back there. The boy he was has changed, and the life he has chosen is one that has more to do with unreliable, hard-nosed, gun-toting bitches who know the score than with innocents only just out of a convent school. Although her role in the film is fairly short it has considerable impact, and Miyazaki gives her one of the greatest escape scenes of her career. He was later to develop the same theme—the relationship between an older, sophisticated woman and smitten ingenue—in *Porco Rosso*. As for Goemon, his function is the same as ever, to bring a touch of old-fashioned loyalty and an awareness of what it means to be your own man to this world of greed, deceit, and shifting certainties.

But it is in the relationship between the three principals, Lupin, Clarisse, and Cagliostro, that Miyazaki's character-building truly excels. If Clarisse and Cagliostro are the light and the darkness, Lupin is the twilight—on the shady side, but still not totally consumed by the dark, a halfway house between the heaven of complete innocence and the hell of absolute amorality. In other words, he's just another fallible human who hasn't yet given up hope in the face of experience. He must balance between these two polar opposites, doing his best to protect the innocent but recognizing his tendency toward the dark side.

The dark side, as presented in the person of the Count, has a certain repellent fascination. He exudes the accumulated authority and style of centuries of wealth, breeding, and complete selfishness. Miyazaki's later films move away from this direct, simplistic personification of darkness. *Porco Rosso*, closest in spirit to *Castle of Cagliostro*, lacks individual focus for evil. Its "villains" are buffoons, but

Inspector Zenigata is hot on Lupin's trail, backed up by a contingent of Interpol's finest. But is that really the Inspector—or is it Lupin himself, proving yet again that he's a master of disguise?

FILMOGRAPHY AND PERSONNEL

Lupin III: Castle of Cagliostro

Lupin III: Cagliostro no Shiro

Theatrical release, 15 December 1979

RUNNING TIME: 1 hour, 40 minutes

Based on the manga by Monkey Punch and the original stories of Maurice LeBlanc

DIRECTOR, COWRITER, STORYBOARDS: Hayao Miyazaki

COWRITER: Haruya Yamazaki

CHARACTER DESIGN, ANIMATION DIRECTOR, ART AND DESIGN SUPERVISION: Yasuo Otsuka

ART DIRECTOR: Shichiro Kobayashi

ART AND DESIGN SUPERVISION: Kazuhide Tomonaga

MUSIC: Yuji Ono

© Monkey Punch/Tokyo Movie Shinsha

U.S. theatrical release 3 April 1991 in New York City by Streamline Pictures.

U.S. video release October 1992 by Streamline Pictures.

U.S. re-release on video planned for 1999 on Manga Video as *Lupin III: The Castle of Cagliostro*.

U.K. video release in 1996 by Manga Video.

the State, sidelined as a collusive force in *Castle of Cagliostro*, has become more important than the individual as the source of oppression and violence in the later film. As the twentieth century moves on, the menacing shadow of Rupert of Hentzau or Sherlock Holmes's criminal arch-enemy Professor Moriarty dwindles in comparison to the ill will of nations as expressed at Nuremberg or in Tiananmen Square. In *Castle of Cagliostro* Miyazaki is able to work within the conventions of romance and convince us that if evil can be defeated on an individual basis all will be well.

Even though the focus of the forces of light, the innocent Clarisse, is trapped by her duty to her family and the ancestral legend, the common man, imperfect and weak, will rally to her aid and mine the sources of good in his own heart. Yet Clarisse is even more securely bound by her own innate helplessness. Like all very young things, she is unable to cope in the big, frightening world without help. That doesn't mean she lacks courage—far from it, as Miyazaki shows—but unlike Fujiko she doesn't have the skills or contacts to protect herself, let alone shape life closer to her wishes. At the end of the film she is still the ingenue; we are left wishing we could know the woman she might grow to be, and to look for traces of that woman in the later films.

The sequences in which these three elements—the night, the light, and the half-light—come into conflict are among the most dramatic and beautiful in the film. The night chase as Lupin and Jigen fight to evade destruction at the hands of Cagliostro's ninja is masterly, the perilous (and hilarious) skid across the rooftops to the princess's dark tower equally so. Perhaps the most memorable image in a film packed with memorable images is the moment when, as the polar opposites meet to walk to their wedding, the masked Count unfurls his great cloak like a dark wing and frames, but does not engulf, the white-clad, almost nunlike figure of his bride.

The final fight inside the workings of the huge clock is both powerfully symbolic and a perfectly staged action sequence, rarely equaled for tension and drama in the live-action format. It has disturbing echoes of Hitchcock both in its imagery and its pacing though Disney fans may also note a somewhat lighter resemblance to the clock scene in *The Great Mouse Detective* (1986). As the hands crunch closed on midnight and the bells chime the end of the Count's life, they also signal the end of Clarisse's rite of passage and the beginning of a new Cagliostro—quite literally, since even the familiar landscape will be changed. Something wonderful will emerge from all that has gone before, but some things will be unchanged. In the real world, love and friendship can last forever but the thief rarely marries the princess.

Miyazaki returns Lupin and company to their familiar paths as they leave the fairyland of Cagliostro for the no-less-artificial—but more familiar—world of international crime. He knows, as does the audience, that he has been able to subvert the pattern of their screen lives only briefly, that he is playing in someone else's universe. Yet the film confirms his promise as a director and pushes open the door into his mind for an intriguing glimpse of what was to come. *Castle of Cagliostro* is a rare thing: a film that allows the audience to accept the possibility of beauty and magic without compromising their intelligence or sinking into sentimentality. With its technology twenty years out of date it is unlikely to get another theatrical release, but if you ever get the chance to see *Castle of Cagliostro* on a large screen, be sure to take it. Like Miyazaki's later movies, its breadth of vision deserves to be viewed on the grand scale.

3

NAUSICAÄ OF THE VALLEY OF THE WINDS

Princess Messiah

Considered by many fans to be Miyazaki's most significant work, this movie tells the story of a beautiful young princess growing up in a near-feudal world in the distant future, after war has destroyed most of mankind's technology and polluted the environment seemingly beyond repair. Her love for all living things and her passionate determination to understand the processes of nature lead her into terrible danger, and she learns that the dark forces of the world beyond her homeland are matched in intensity by her own feelings of rage, pain, and loss. Can she lead her people beyond survival to reconciliation with nature and with each other?

ORIGINS

"There has never been a work of art created which didn't somehow reflect its own time. . . . *Nausicaä* comes from the new world views regarding nature which came about in the '70s." So Hayao Miyazaki summed up his seminal movie in *Animerica* magazine in 1993, almost a decade after its release. Yet in the same interview he confided that the huge manga on which the movie was based was a fill-in job, pure and simple. "I started drawing the manga only because I was unemployed as an animator, so I'll stop drawing it as soon as I find animation work."

He had stopped and started several times since 1982, but the remaining chapter of his epic story finally appeared a year after that interview.[1]

The movie would never have been made without the manga, yet in some senses the manga is an albatross around the neck of the movie. The reason lies in the differing nature of the two media. In a comic, especially a long-running comic, the writer can explore story lines, develop characters, and build relationships in ways not available to the director of a two-hour movie. And if a picture is worth a thousand words, the huge number of frames in a comic of *Nausicaä*'s length allows room for more story than the scenes of even a two-hour movie. Many critics have made the mistake of looking at *Nausicaä* the movie as a poor relation of *Nausicaä* the manga.

To avoid that trap, I won't offer any critical opinion on or comparison with the manga. This is a book about movies. If you want to read Miyazaki's big and beautiful comic book, it's available as a five-volume edition from San Francisco–based publisher Viz Communications.

The *Nausicaä* story originated in a movie proposal. After directing *Castle of Cagliostro*, Miyazaki had been approached by the editors of *Animage* magazine to cooperate on an arti-

cle about his work. During discussions he showed the team some drawings for movie projects he wanted to develop, and in 1981 *Animage* took some of these ideas to its parent company, Tokuma. All were rejected, but several later made it to the screen. One was set on a flying island run by robots and developed into *Castle in the Sky*; another introduced the character of Yara, queen of the Valley of the Winds.[2] Since there was no film prospect in

Surprised by Yupa in her underground laboratory, Nausicaä is worried and frightened by the terrible events around her. The glowing colors and strange forms of the plants give the scene an exotic beauty.

the near future and Miyazaki was looking for work, *Animage* proposed that he should do a comic strip for them. He agreed on the condition that he could do whatever he chose in the story, that he could suspend or end it whenever film work came up, and that the project would not be used as a starting point for animation. Perhaps with the latter condition in mind, Miyazaki created a world that was to prove very difficult to animate.

In conversation with the American novelist Ernest Callenbach, author of *Ecotopia*, in 1985, Miyazaki said that there was "one big event" that led to the creation of *Nausicaä*: the pollution of Japan's Minamata Bay with mercury.[3] Because the pollution levels rendered the fish inedible, people stopped fishing there and within a few years there was a huge increase in fish stocks in the bay, far in excess of anywhere else in Japan. Miyazaki said that the news "sent shivers up my spine." He admired the toughness and resilience of other living creatures, that they could absorb the poisons humans create and continue to thrive.

However, the roots of Nausicaä's character and her world go even deeper, back into Miyazaki's reading as a child and young man. In childhood he read a traditional Japanese folktale called *The Princess Who Loved Insects*, the story of a medieval princess who was fascinated by all living things, especially insects. Even when she was considered too old to play in the fields and was urged by her family to start putting on fine clothes, painting her face, and thinking of marriage, she preferred to be out of doors watching a chrysalis transform into a moth. Years later, browsing through Bernard Evslin's *Dictionary of Grecian Myths*,

he encountered the Phaeacian princess Nausicaä, who rescued Odysseus in Homer's epic poem. Evslin's image of the fleet-footed, brave, and merry Greek princess merged with that of the Japanese heroine and became the princess of Miyazaki's rural kingdom.

The ecosystem she loved and studied so eagerly in Miyazaki's story was based on Japanese historical and scientific writings into which the young man had dipped over the years. Her kingdom and the political and social pressures of the world around it also evolved from Miyazaki's wide reading on history, sociology, and politics. An article in *Asahi Journal* in April 1987 records that "parts were based on Sasuke Nakao's *Origins of Plant Cultivation and Agriculture* and Eiichi Fujimori's *The World of Jomon*. . . . The Russo-German war depicted in Paul Karel's *Operation Barbarossa* and the Yunnan operation in *Dansakusen*."[4] In the same article he discusses his admiration for the pragmatic environmentalism of Akira Miyawaki, author of *Plants and People* and a pioneer of the urban greening movement, which urged people to go out and plant trees as a first step toward improving their environment. Elsewhere he mentions his distaste for military superpowers, engendered by reading Caesar's *Gallic Wars* and Howard Furst's *Spartacus*, and his admiration for the bravery of the Celts.[5]

So, gradually, his princess became even more involved in study and defense of the environment than her Greek and Japanese inspirations, and the world he created around her became more and more complex. The Celtic influence would be deployed with greater force and awareness in *Castle in the*

Sky, and the Jomon period (10,000 B.C.–ca. 300 B.C.) became one of the foundation stones of *Princess Mononoke*; in his manga and his first film as writer/director, he was able to sketch out a range of ideas and concerns that would continue to occupy him for years to come.

Within a very short time, *Nausicaä of the Valley of the Winds* attained such popularity with readers that pressure for an animated version began to build. To begin with, *Animage* suggested just making a fifteen-minute short film; Miyazaki, who had said he absolutely would not use the manga as a basis for animation, came back with the suggestion that an hour-long video animation would be better, and finally Tokuma agreed to make a full-length feature film.

ART AND TECHNIQUE

Work started on the movie on the last day of May 1983. Animation commenced at the beginning of August, and the film was released in March 1984. From the beginning, Miyazaki had put himself in a difficult position. Having set out to make his story complex and hard to animate, he now had to animate it. With sixteen chapters of the manga completed when he started work on the animation, he was faced with the problem of making a complete, self-contained narrative for the film without creating conflict with the existing manga story line. It's a problem faced by any screenwriter with a text source and a deadline. "First of all,

we can't start unless there's an image. Abstract theory and commonsense notions don't turn themselves into pictures." [6] Miyazaki the film writer amalgamated several elements of Miyazaki the manga author's story, telescoped some details, altered the character emphasis here and there, and shifted the narrative focus to the invasion of Nausicaä's homeland by the Tolmekians; he had his screenplay.

Although the story is set millennia in the future, it is not aimed solely at a science fiction audience. Its apocalyptic elements are undeniable but they owe little to sci-fi sources; Japan has had its own twentieth-century apocalypse, and no one who lived through World War II or studied its history needed the inspiration of science fiction to imagine the Seven Days of Fire. In an interview with the Japanese magazine *Comic Box* in November 1982, soon after the *Nausicaä* manga began publication, Miyazaki said that though as a young man he had read a range of science fiction material from hard sci-fi to sword and sorcery, he generally preferred nonfiction. Isaac Asimov's *Nightfall* had made a strong impression on him as a student, and among more recent titles he cited Brian Aldiss's *Hothouse* (saying the plant life was interesting but the human characters less so), Ursula Le Guin's *Earthsea* books, and J. R. R. Tolkien's *Lord of the Rings*.

Despite extensive fan and critical speculation as to the influence of Frank Herbert's *Dune* on *Nausicaä*, I have been unable to document any confirmation of this apart from a reference to the naming of the Ohmu. ("Ohmu" derives from the Japanese syllabic rendition of the English word "worm," as in "sand worm." The sand worms are gigantic

In a flashback to her childhood, Nausicaä remembers how she tried in vain to protect a baby Ohmu from her father and his warriors. People kill the Ohmu because they fear them, but Nausicaä has always believed that if one tries to understand living things, one will find they are not our enemies but our neighbors.

burrowing insects in *Dune*. It is also the first two syllables of the word *o-mushi*, meaning big insect or King Insect.) Miyazaki's interest in tales of interplanetary travel and galactic political strife is limited. He feels that nature is the source of interesting and involving stories. He told the Hong Kong magazine *A-Club*, "Only if nature exists can mankind exist, so only nature makes wars and all those other moving stories possible. Because of this,

I don't feel interested in outer space movies, since there's nothing much in space but darkness. So all my animation and comics involve land, sea and sky—they all revolve around what happens on Earth."7

The production schedule was tight—French comic giant Moebius contrasted *Nausicaä*'s nine-month schedule and million-dollar budget admiringly with the much more protracted and expensive *Little Nemo* coproduction, from which Miyazaki had withdrawn.[8] Matters were further complicated by the fact that Tokuma was a print publisher with no studio facilities. Topcraft, a production studio whose work Miyazaki and Takahata knew, was brought in to handle the studio side of the project, and as a result of this cooperation Topcraft's Toru Hara, producer on the film, was later to join Studio Ghibli as chief executive officer.

Isao Takahata is credited as executive producer, but came on board reluctantly. As Miyazaki told YOM magazine, "Our thoughts about movie making are completely different. If we discuss a production plan, we definitely won't reach an agreement." His involvement came at Miyazaki's own request, very early on in the process before Topcraft was involved. Knowing that Tokuma didn't have a production facility and that he couldn't handle everything himself, he asked them to persuade Takahata to be producer and commented, "I heard that Takahata-san said yes after he used up an entire notebook to sort his thoughts out, but I know he didn't want to do it. In truth, a director can't produce another director's film. If two directors have a one on one argument, there will be bloodshed." [9] However, Miyazaki respected his colleague's tenacity, determination, and problem-solving abilities, and his contribution was a valuable one. In particular he was instrumental in persuading young experimental composer Jo Hisaishi to put his efforts into full-length film scores.

Before *Nausicaä*, as Takahata told *Anime-land* magazine, Hisaishi was composing "minimalist music" consisting of isolated notes continually repeated.[10] Takahata's persuasive

powers, which were to prove vital on a number of future occasions when productions hit snags, in this case ensured a moving soundtrack that draws on European and Asian orchestral and vocal traditions to create a unique impression. Hisaishi has gone on to work with other animators and live-action directors, notably "Beat" Takeshi Kitano, but his work for Miyazaki is widely regarded as outstanding music in its own right. The rest of the soundtrack links superbly with the music; the strange yet convincing noises of its natural world, the splintering of wood, crashing of metal, and roar of explosions are all well balanced with dialogue and silence to create an aural picture that supports the images on screen. The first five minutes of the film, as Nausicaä walks through the luminous depths of the poisoned forest, convey wonder, beauty, awe, and magic with no need for words.

The plant and animal life of the film is based firmly on the natural world and creates a sense of solid reality despite its initial impression of strangeness. The insects are especially interesting, perhaps as a reminder of the heroine's link with the Japanese princess who loved insects. The Ohmu are splendid embodiments of raw power, yet their great size and strength is driven by intelligence that manifests in an evolved social system, communication over distances, and extended care of the young, calling to mind that other huge and endangered creature, the whale. The huge dragonfly-like creatures inhabiting the poisoned forests are accompanied by wonderful, evocative sounds of flight and movement. The fungus-like plants glow, shimmer, and shed spores like gleaming snowfalls. Nausicaä's fierce little fox-like pet evokes the predictable response accorded to small fluffy mammals before reminding us that they have teeth. Miyazaki's complex designs presented some challenges that could only be overcome by developing new animation techniques. In general he prefers to stick to traditional methods of animation, but *Nausicaä* demanded inventiveness. For example, to depict the movement of the giant Ohmu as Miyazaki wanted, it was necessary to animate the creatures using overlapping layers of card for the segments of their bodies. [11]

The scenery of the lush, peaceful Valley of the Winds and the devastated lands nearby create a fascinating contrast. In the dead village where we first see Yupa, layers of dust and decay give the aura of death and desolation, yet in the poisoned forests, once the hallucinogenic strangeness of shape and color has been accepted, there is light, growth, and life everywhere. Like the oysters and fish of Minamata Bay, the nature of Nausicaä's world has absorbed the poison man created and is adapting to it and getting on with the business of living. Throughout the film, Miyazaki uses design and color to emphasize the subtext that human life, highly specialized and individuated, may be at risk from man's stupidity, but life has a broader definition than just humanity. The right of every living thing to cling to life is unquestioned; Miyazaki said that *Nausicaä* itself was "inspired by a kind of animism."[12]

The technology of the human world is clumsy by comparison, driven by expediency and availability rather than planning and innovation. The Tolmekian war machines and flying ships are big and ugly, and even the windmills and cottages of the valley dwellers can't compare with the structures nature builds. Although craft skills are valued, as is shown in the complex tapestry-inspired montage that is used for the opening credits, art styles and modes of expression are very similar across the movie's civilizations. Because the huge war that ended in a disaster called the Seven Days of Fire has reduced most of humanity to the same near-feudal technological level, there is little variation in style or shape to most man-made objects, whether they are clothes, vehicles, or weapons. A few notable exceptions are the scraps of a higher technology preserved by the larger, richer countries. The leader of the Tolmekian army has an artificial arm to replace one taken by a giant insect; the Pejiteians manage to unearth one of the terrible biological weapons of the ancient war. The two great nations are trying to fight the poisonous growths that are choking their world; only Nausicaä, by studying the plants calmly and fearlessly, is able to reach the understanding that nature is actually regenerating land and water by using plants as living poison filters.

Sadly, most of this subtle subplotting was removed from the previous American edition of the film, available on video in the 1980s as *Warriors of the Wind*. The film was subjected to a devastating series of cuts. Almost half an hour of exposition and character development was removed to make a "feature-length" version emphasizing only the action-adventure aspects of the story. Both Miyazaki and Takahata were appalled. Takahata said of the edited version: "It's absolutely horrible! They cut Hisaishi's pieces of music, changed dialogues. . . . We haven't given broadcast rights to foreign countries since and we'll never again give such rights without careful examination of the conditions beforehand. All these movies are grounded strongly in Japanese culture and are not made with an eye to export. Censoring them is worse than betraying them."[13]

A version of the original, full-length film was shown in London in August 1995 with subtitles personally approved by Miyazaki, as part of the No More Hiroshimas festival marking the fiftieth anniversary of the dropping of the atom bomb.[14] I was asked to introduce the screening, and felt privileged to be able to share the uncut version with an English-speaking audience. It was almost as if the movie, like its world, had grown past a devastating, destructive attack and back to wholeness. Hopefully, the deal between Tokuma and Disney will enable many more American and British film-lovers to enjoy the movie as its director and producers intended before too many more years have passed.

THE CHARACTERS

Nausicaä

Nausicaä is a young princess who lives with her father, King Jhil, in the Valley of the Winds. Her mother has been dead for some time but we know her daughter can remember her because she is present in a flashback sequence that shows Nausicaä's memories of early childhood. Nausicaä is a happy, outgoing young woman but she has a more serious side—she is deeply interested in all living things, and even has a secret room under the castle where she studies the plant life of the polluted lands and tries to understand its evolution. She is physically tough, able to handle a sword, and very athletic. She is a very gifted aviator on her little jet-powered glider, called the mehve in the film; the name derives from the German word for gull. The story shows us many instances of her agility and endurance. Brave in small things as well as big ones, she has the courage to let a frightened animal bite her so as to win its trust, and she has the courage to die for her people. The film shows her developing through her teenage years, learning to master anger and the desire for vengeance and becoming more confident in her opinions and beliefs.

Young magazine interviewed Miyazaki to promote the movie and asked him why the protagonist was female. He said that he could only create the kind of character he wanted as a girl. "Nausicaä is not a protagonist who defeats an opponent, but a protagonist who understands, or accepts. She is someone who lives in a different dimension. That kind of character should be female rather than male."[15] He also acknowledged the exhilaration of seeing a woman in such a role, referring to the protagonist, played by Gena Rowlands, of one of his favorite action movies, *Gloria* (1980). Later he expressed concern that making a young girl the heroine of the film might play into the hands of those who saw animation as antifeminist or simply as another chance to drool over young girls, but felt that a male lead imposed too many conventional ideas on the story. "If we try to make an adventure story with a male lead, we have no choice but to do *Indiana Jones,* with a Nazi or someone else who is a villain in everyone's eyes."[16] He didn't feel, as a film-maker, that he could end with all problems solved and all loose ends tied up, but wanted to create a character who could get over the immediate danger and convince the audience that this person would be able to cope with whatever happened next.

Teto is the name Nausicaä gives to the fierce little creature that Yupa brings as a gift for her at the start of the film. Looking like a cross between a fox and a squirrel, the little animal becomes devoted to its gentle mistress.

Jhil is Nausicaä's father, a good king who cares for his people and a brave man. However, he lacks his daughter's vision and believes the conventional wisdom that the Ohmu and forest creatures must be destroyed and that man should fight nature rather than work with it.

Yupa is Nausicaä's mentor and has taught her much about flying, about the world, and about human nature. He has known her since she was a little girl and is deeply fond of her. He is a skilled fighter but it is his wise advice that holds her back from killing in blind rage to avenge her father.

Grandmother The blind sage who tells Nausicaä the legend of the valley savior. Grandmother is another woman of great courage. She defies the invaders and is not afraid to tell them that their plans are foolish.

Kushana is the villain of the piece, but a villain with motives and feelings of her own. The powerful warrior leader of Tolmekia, she comes to the Valley of the Winds solely to secure possession of the Pejiteian secret weapon, the God Warrior. She has no malice toward its people but she is determined not to permit them to stop her from carrying out her objectives. She will sacrifice anyone or anything to fulfill her objectives and has no compunction about crushing those who get in her way. Yet she is secretly driven by a need to revenge herself on the creatures that destroyed her limbs.

Kurotawa is Kushana's second-in-command, a brave general who knows that he will stay in second place as long as his brilliant leader is alive. His indolence (and perhaps also his knowledge of his ability) stops him from challenging her, but he has no particular loyalty to her and will grasp the opportunity of her disappearance to take her place. He has no discernible morals and, like her, thinks the end justifies the means.

Asbel is the Prince of Pejitei, the brother of the Princess who is killed when the airship in which she is a prisoner crashes in the valley. His thirst for revenge drives him into battle and Nausicaä rescues him. They are the first to see the pure, clear space below the poisoned forest and the first

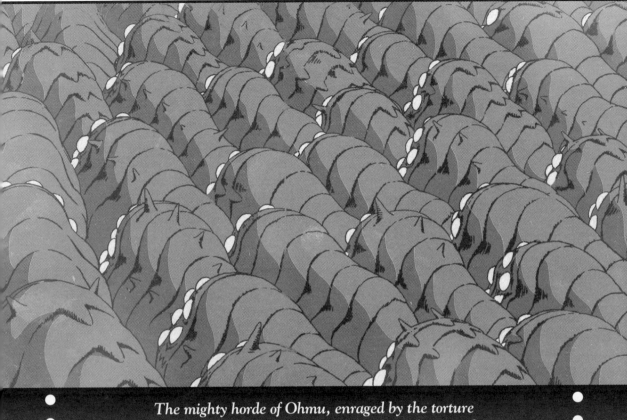

The mighty horde of Ohmu, enraged by the torture
of their young and the humans' attack on them, rush
toward the Valley of the Winds, eyes glowing red with rage. Only
Nausicaä and one baby Ohmu, both badly injured, stand
between the herd and her loved ones.

to understand that nature is healing the world, not destroying it.

THE STORY

An old warrior, leading two huge birds, enters a deserted village completely consumed by poisonous fungus and gases. As he surveys its desolation, huge insects fly across the sky. He knows that soon the village will be consumed by the poisoned forest.

The opening credits roll. We see Earth's future, and almost see her doom, in the scenes of a primitive wall decoration. Technology ran out of control and developed huge weapons in the form of gigantic biochemical warriors that unleashed fire and destruction on the world.

The poisons used in war and science enabled huge insects and plants to infest our world, killing mankind, releasing poisonous gases, and allowing a poisoned forest, a sea of pollution, to spread and grow, its glowing rotwood a sign of impending doom. But just as it seems the story must end, history becomes prophecy. An angelic creature in a blue robe appears and becomes the savior of mankind.

The war took place a thousand years ago. As the credits fade, Nausicaä appears on her jet-powered glider, soaring amid the clouds over the poisoned forest.

She wanders fearlessly through the polluted forest, astounded by the beauty to be found even in death. The shell of a giant Ohmu, a great insect that can grow more than thirty feet tall, fills her with awe and wonder, and she takes shelter under a clear lens from one of its huge eyes as a deadly rain of spores falls from a nearby plant. Without her breathing mask she would be dead in minutes; with it, she is safe under the crystal lens. Then as she rests, she hears a shot and takes to the air again. The old traveler we saw in the opening moments of the film is under attack from a living Ohmu, its many eyes red with rage. Using flares to stun the giant insect, Nausicaä sees the traveler to safety then wakes the Ohmu again with the sound of a small whistle, which leaves it calm, its many eyes glowing a peaceful blue instead of their earlier angry red. Blue is the color of peace for more than just the humans of the valley. As the Ohmu returns to the poisoned forest, Nausicaä greets the man, her beloved "uncle" Yupa. He's brought her a dear little pet, and after she overcomes its fear and nervousness with her gentle acceptance,

Nausicaä names it Teto and takes it back to the Valley of the Winds with Yupa.

In the village in the valley, Yupa tells King Jhil and his trusted friend, the blind Grandmother, that the spread of poisoned fungus seems to be affecting more and more of the land. The breezes that blow into the valley are pure, even though they blow across the deadly Acid Sea to reach the land. The pure winds have protected the valley and its people from many airborne poisons, but the King, like many other people, has breathed in too much polluted air and is now sick and bedridden. Grandmother tells Nausicaä the story shown in the mural on the chamber wall of the legendary blue-robed savior who will come to them across a field of gold to lead mankind back to a clean, peaceful world. But that night, peace is shattered when a Tolmekian battleship crashes into the mountains near the valley. It has been attacked by a swarm of giant insects from the poisoned forest. Even more shockingly, Nausicaä finds a young girl dying in chains in the wreckage. She tells her that she is Princess Lastelle of Pejitei, and her last words are a plea to destroy every bit of the aircraft's cargo. When Nausicaä tells her the crash has destroyed everything, she dies smiling.

One of the swarming insects has survived the crash, and Nausicaä calms it with her whistle and leads it to the boundaries of the poisoned forest to make its way home. In the distance, a huge Ohmu stands watching. . . .

Next day, as the villagers work to destroy any fungal spores left by the creatures that would otherwise infect the valley's pure soil and vegetation, they find a huge creature, a

When Yupa gives her a tiny creature as a gift, Nausicaä is thrilled.
The little thing, a cross between a fox and a squirrel, is very badly
frightened, and bites her when she tries to make friends, but she
manages to win its trust and names it Teto.

ball of pulsing life, that has survived the crash. Only Yupa suspects what it is. Legend says that one of the ancient God Warriors, fire-breathing demons that unleashed the Seven Days of Fire, was buried alive under the city of Pejitei. A Pejiteian princess was a prisoner on the Tolmekian ship, and she begged them to destroy all its cargo. Soon his terrible suspicion is confirmed as Tolmekian warships invade the peaceful valley, knocking over the windmills that provide its power

and tearing up the green pastures and crops.

Nausicaä is helping to dig graves for those who died in the previous night's crash when she sees the ships arrive. As she races to help get everyone to safety, she is suddenly afraid for her father King Jhil. She arrives just too late to prevent the soldiers from killing him, but as she rushes at them in a rage, bent on revenge, Yupa blocks her path and tells her that it is time for the killing to stop. She has a duty to her people now. She must act for their good, as her father would have wished. As she sees her people under the guns of the invaders, she passes out from shock.

Kushana, princess of the Tolmekian Empire, tells the villagers why her army has invaded. She has a plan to wipe out the poisoned forest of fungus before it destroys the whole Earth, and wants the people of the valley to unite with her in fighting it. Grandmother tells her that her efforts will be futile, and when Kushana's second in command, General Kurotawa, tells her to be quiet or else, she simply laughs and says that he can kill her just as he killed the king. The people didn't know about this, and are shocked and angry, ready to attack the Tolmekian guns with anything to hand. Nausicaä averts tragedy, just as Yupa did at her father's deathbed, by convincing them that there must be no more killing. Revenge would only lead to their deaths, as it would have led to hers. Reluctantly, they cooperate with the invaders and work to bring the huge creature that survived the crash back to the castle. But Kushana doesn't trust them. When she needs to return to Tolmekia, she decides to take Nausicaä as a hostage for their good behavior, along with a group of her father's trusted old friends.

The evening before they are due to leave, Yupa can't find Nausicaä, but the little pet he gave her is scratching at a wall in her room. Yupa finds a secret tunnel leading into the depths of the rock on which the castle is built, and in which Nausicaä has concealed her laboratory. Here she is growing plants from the poisoned forest, and has learned that with pure water and clean soil, the plants offer no danger to man. The forest is not the source of the poison—it is man's devastation of the soil and water that has caused it. She hoped to find a way to cure her father and all the others affected by the poison gases, but now the Tolmekians have invaded, her father is dead, and her research will be destroyed if her water source is polluted by their activities. Her dream is finished, like the peace and safety of the valley. Next day, she and the old men leave in two Tolmekian battleships and a small valley craft on tow behind one of them.

Their fleet is attacked by a tiny Pejiteian craft that proves more than a match for them. In a terrifying aerial battle, most of the big ships are destroyed and the little valley ship is cut adrift. Nausicaä climbs out onto the ship's frame in a dramatic attempt to try to stop the pilot of the Pejiteian craft from attacking again and taking more lives; as he hesitates, he is attacked in his turn and his plane damaged. Nausicaä's battleship is also damaged and she and her old friend Mito decide to try to reach one of its escape craft. They are almost ready to take off when Kushana appears. Despite her feelings toward the woman who was responsible for killing her father and destroying her homeland, Nausicaä can't leave her to die, and the three take off together.

They look for the valley craft, find it, and eventually land together on a lake in the poisoned forest. Kushana tries once again to take command by pulling a gun on her rescuers, but when she fires she rouses a swarm of Ohmu from below the waters of the lake. Their eyes are blue, not red, so Nausicaä thinks she can communicate with them and tell them the humans mean them no harm. Spreading her arms toward them, she is enfolded in a forest of glowing golden tentacles. Suddenly, she sees herself on a golden pasture, staring at a glorious blue sky—but the dream ends abruptly as the Ohmu retract their tentacles and swim away, their eyes turning an angry red. Nausicaä tells the valley men to fly home and make sure everyone is safe, then takes off in her glider, which was aboard the ship, and follows the swarm. Kushana, in shock at the strange events, does not resist when Mito takes her gun and leads her away with them.

Deep in the forest, the pilot of the Pejiteian craft is trying to kill an attacking army of forest creatures. He is trapped on the edge of a cliff and when he runs out of ammunition he can either jump or be eaten. He jumps, and finds himself pulled from the mouth of a huge flying insect by Nausicaä. The creature chases them and knocks them out of the air, and they and the glider sink slowly into a patch of quicksand.

Nausicaä is dreaming of when she was a little girl in the fields with her mother and father nearby. She's trying to save a baby Ohmu but her father tells her she must give it up. She watches in tears as soldiers take it away, begging them not to hurt it but knowing they won't listen to her. When she wakes, she and the pilot are lying on the huge flat surface of an ancient tree trunk. The boy, Asbel, tells her he is a prince of Pejitei and that they have fallen right through the poisoned forest and are in a cavern deep below it. The air here is pure and clear. As she walks through this strange underground world, Nausicaä realizes that nature has done just what she was trying to do in her laboratory. Here below the poisoned forest, filtered through its roots, the air and water is purified of all the chemicals man pumped into them centuries ago. She is crying when Asbel catches up with her, but they are tears of joy.

Back in the valley, the ambitious Kurotawa learns that Kushana is missing, and sees the gigantic Fire Demon open its eyes for the first time. Yupa is told that the valley men are back without Nausicaä, and goes to find them and their captive Kushana hidden on the outskirts of the valley. She is completely fearless, telling him they must free her because they need her to avert the anger of her people, and that the Fire Demon Tolmekia stole from Pejitei must be kept alive because only it can destroy the poisoned forest. She reveals that an Ohmu attacked her when she was a child and destroyed her arm and leg. Destroying the Ohmu and the poisoned forest will be her revenge, as well as freeing mankind from its threats. But for the valley, it may be too late. A boy comes to report to the elders that there are spores all over the land and the trees are covered with fungus. The only way to save the rest of the valley is to burn the whole forest. Yupa and Mito set off to find Nausicaä, the others go off to help the forest-burning effort, and, left to herself, Kushana escapes.

Meanwhile Nausicaä has learned that Asbel is Lastelle's twin brother and had attacked the Tolmekian fleet for revenge. Next morning, they take off in her glider for his homeland to tell his mother that she has lost one of her children. But Pejitei has been destroyed by two enemies—the Tolmekians and the creatures of the poisoned forest. An airship brings some of the survivors to meet

FILMOGRAPHY AND PERSONNEL

Nausicaä of the Valley of the Winds

Kaze no Tani no Nausicaä

Theatrical release, 11 March 1984

RUNNING TIME: 2 hours

Original story by Hayao Miyazaki

DIRECTOR, SCREENPLAY, CHARACTER DESIGN:
Hayao Miyazaki

ANIMATION DIRECTOR: Kazuo Komatsubara

ART DIRECTOR: Mitsuki Nakamura

MUSIC: Jo Hisaishi

MUSIC DIRECTOR AND SCRIPT: Shigemaru Shiba

PRODUCER: Toru Hara

EXECUTIVE PRODUCER: Isao Takahata

PRODUCTION: Yasuyoshi Tokuma, Michitaka Kondo

© Nibariki, Tokuma, Hakuhodo

Edited U.S. theatrical release in June 1985 for one week in New York City by New World Pictures under the title Warriors of the Wind.

Edited U.S. video release in December 1985 by New World Video under the title Warriors of the Wind.

This 95-minute edition was released in Britain in the late 1980s on Vestron Video, re-released 1993 on First Independent Video with a further 1-minute cut. Rights for both releases have now lapsed and these edited versions are no longer available.

Uncut and subtitled U.K. theatrical screening in August 1995 as part of the Building Bridges film festival at the Institute of Contemporary Arts, London.

them, and to her horror Nausicaä learns that they plan to lure a swarm of Ohmu to attack the valley and catch the Tolmekians there. They too want revenge and to control the God Warrior. Her people will be unfortunate casualties of someone else's war. They are embarrassed to tell her this because she has saved their Prince's life, but they are determined. They don't believe her when she tells them the poisoned forest is cleaning the air and water, not destroying it, and despite Asbel's attempts to help her they take her prisoner on their airship, just as their own Princess was taken by Tolmekia.

Back in the valley, mayhem reigns as the people revolt against their invaders and the old men steal a tank and help them escape to the outskirts of the valley. Kushana's return ends Kurotawa's brief dream of glory. On the airship, Lastelle and Asbel's mother helps Nausicaä escape in disguise and she reaches her glider just as the airship comes under attack by a Tolmekian battleship. Nausicaä doesn't want to leave Asbel to fight alone as the ship is boarded, but he pushes the glider off and she heads for the valley. The battleship follows and tries to shoot her down, but just as it looks as if she and the Pejiteian airship are doomed, Yupa and Mito fly in and save the day for both. As Yupa takes command aboard the Pejiteian ship, Nausicaä and Mito head back to the valley, her glider slung onto the plane, to try to save their people from the Pejiteian stampede plan and the Tolmekian troops with their God Warrior.

The valley folk are gathered on the edge of the Acid Sea, and are in a panic—not because Kushana's troops are all around them and about to attack, but because the winds that have protected their home for so long have dropped completely. It's dark. From the air, Nausicaä and Mito can see a huge swarm of Ohmu, their eyes glowing red with rage, rushing toward the valley. It doesn't take long to see why they are so angry. Up ahead, Pejiteian soldiers are torturing a baby Ohmu as they fly above the Acid Sea. The young creature is hanging from wires, its body pierced with metal spears and bullets, blood flowing down from many wounds. The Pejiteians start to shoot at Nausicaä and Mito, but she orders him not to return fire for fear of hurting the little Ohmu even more. She takes off in her glider and sends Mito back to warn the valley folk while she tries to save the baby Ohmu, just as she tried so long ago when she was a little girl. Kushana is concerned for Nausicaä's safety when Mito arrives, but when he tells her about the oncoming Ohmu swarm her nerve falters. Ohmu are the thing she most fears, but she steadies herself and tells her troops not to be afraid while they have the Fire Demon on their side. Kurotawa tells her the creature is only half evolved and can't be used in battle, but she tells him that they can't wait.

As Nausicaä circles in her glider, trying to persuade the Pejiteian soldiers to release the Ohmu, one shoots her despite her pleas for a peaceful solution. Bleeding from several wounds, she manages to jump into their craft and it crashes onto a tiny patch of land in the middle of the Acid Sea. Badly hurt, she struggles to her feet and tries to stop the frightened young Ohmu from rushing into the acid waters. As she tries to push it back, its blood soaks into her clothes and dyes them deep blue. When it keeps pushing in its panic, her feet slip into the sea and the acid waters burn her terribly. As the little Ohmu calms down at last, she falls to the ground in pain and the baby reaches out gently with its golden tentacles to comfort her. The Ohmu sense that their young one is now safe; Nausicaä thinks her people will be safe as well. Then the Tolmekians open fire on the Ohmu swarm, and they rush toward the valley once again to trample this new threat.

With no other choice before her, Nausicaä threatens the Pejiteian soldiers with a machine gun and tells them they must take her and the baby Ohmu to the valley. It's the one chance to save her people, because the Tolmekian tanks seem to have no effect on the onrushing mass of huge animals. Then Kushana unleashes her Fire Demon, the last of the God Warriors that destroyed the world in the Seven Days of Fire a thousand years ago. This demon is only half ready, in some ways still a baby himself, but he goes into battle at Kushana's command. Not even his huge beam of fire can stop the onrush of the Ohmu, and he collapses and withers to a skeleton without slowing their murderous stampede. The army

*Badly damaged by its huge effort at destruction, the God
Warrior falls, already disintegrating. Kushana's attempt to use
the technology that destroyed the world so long ago to
solve its new problems has failed.*

panics, and the people of the valley wait for
death.

Then, out of the skies, the Pejitei aircraft
appears and lowers Nausicaä and the baby
Ohmu straight into the path of the swarm.
They look tiny before the huge creatures, and
as the swarm rushes onward Nausicaä is tram-
pled and her body flung high in the air before
disappearing again. As a terrible wail of grief
goes up from the people of the valley, the sun

is rising. The Pejitei craft carrying Yupa,
Asbel, and the rest of his people flies in above
the Ohmu swarm and Yupa suddenly sees that
the creatures' eyes are changing from red to a
deep, calm blue. Suddenly, the whole swarm is
still. It has stopped on the very threshold of
the valley.

The Ohmu make a circle around their baby
and the still body of Nausicaä. Her sacrifice
saved her people and their home. As the on-

lookers weep for their princess, and even Kushana is moved, the Ohmu stretch out their glowing tentacles. The body is lifted on a forest of golden fronds and a shower of golden flakes shimmer to the ground. Slowly, Nausicaä is lifted higher. Then she sits up. Smiling at the baby Ohmu she saved, she runs joyously across a field of gold to thank the Ohmu for saving her and bringing her back to her people. Grandmother, who cannot see, asks the children to describe the scene for her. The princess is dressed in deep, pure blue and is coming to them across a field of gold. The legend has come true. And suddenly, to complete their happiness, the villagers look up and see Nausicaä's lost glider floating toward them. The wind has lifted again.

Amid much rejoicing, Asbel whirls Nausicaä high into the air and the people of Pejitei rejoice to see that their desperate plan didn't cost the valley people their lives. The Tolmekians head back to their empire, but as Pejitei has been destroyed, its people stay to help the folk of the valley rebuild their world. The Ohmu, too, return home. The closing credits show Nausicaä, Asbel, and Yupa in the poisoned forest, which is no longer a threat but a promise of a renewed world.

COMMENTARY

It has been said that this is an antiwar movie, a pro-ecology movie, a feminist movie, even a political movie. Miyazaki says otherwise. While acknowledging that a director can do nothing to influence how an audience perceives his films, he says that all he wants is to entertain. When *A-Club* asked him if he wanted his films to inspire people to protect nature, he was very direct: "I don't make movies with the intention of presenting any messages to humanity. My main aim in a movie is to make the audience come away from it happy."[17] So how far does he succeed here?

For Japanese audiences, *Nausicaä* has been a favorite ever since its release. Both the movie and its heroine still place in "fan favorite" polls and its sales on video have held up well. I think English-speaking audiences will react just as favorably. Despite the change in technical standards in the last fifteen years and despite some passages of limited character movement and weak drawing, the movie holds up magnificently as a work of art, the beauty of its background paintings supported by a breathtaking scale of vision. The original soundtrack is compelling and the characterization powerful, though of course much will depend on the choice of voice actors and the force and subtlety of the English script. This is a rip-roaring adventure with all the trimmings—a sparky and sympathetic heroine, a powerful and deeply motivated opponent, warmth and humanity, creatures great and small, fight and flight sequences with a real kick, a little comic relief, terminal tension, and a full-scale three-handkerchief happy ending. There are messages galore for those who want to look for them and a solid story for those who don't. The ending of the film takes a huge risk, moving away from the chaos and drama of a massive battle to focus on Nausicaä's martyrdom and rebirth in a sequence of unashamed and almost overpowering sentiment, which is saved from spilling into sentimentality by its unmistakable sincerity. The thunderous climax of the battle and death scene puts us through an emotional wringer to pull off a massive cathartic release.

Not every critic approves of the messages they see in the film. Opinion is split in Japan and the English-speaking world. Some find the excursions into messianic mode offensive, while others object to the deus ex machina effect of the happy ending. Writing in *Anime U.K.*, Julia Sertori comments that the story promises a blue-clad messiah to save the world, only to let us discover that the world doesn't actually need saving; the message she reads is that environmental crises are best solved by complete inaction, and she concludes that message and film are completely lacking in credibility. [18] Her view is supported by Kenji Sato in his book *Godzilla, Yamato and Our Democracy*; indeed, he goes further by pointing out that the "villains" of Pejitei and Tolmekia are motivated by good sense in trying to deal with the crises as best they can on the basis of the information available to them.[19] Despite Miyazaki's comments that he finds stories about Earth more interesting than those about space, *Patlabor* director Mamoru Oshii commented that *Nausicaä* is "*Space Cruiser Yamato* Miyazaki-style . . . filled with the emotion of a kamikaze attack . . . a powerful film made out of ideology itself."[20] French artist Moebius describes Miyazaki as "a narrative and graphic genius" and names *Nausicaä* as his favorite Miyazaki movie. "Miyazaki

claimed his autonomy with *Nausicaä*, which is a great movie, a masterpiece. The work he did after continues at the same level, in the fineness, in the beauty."[21]

But there is more to *Nausicaä* than debate about its supposed messages, especially when the movie is considered in the context of Miyazaki's other works. In July 1984, just after finishing *Nausicaä of the Valley of the Winds*, Miyazaki was asked by Japan's *Heibon Punch* magazine what he planned to do next. He said, "Fujimori and Nakao have taught me that there was a different Japan from the sterile and beautiful Japan of Kabuki and Noh. I'm convinced that, if I look upon Japan in this way, I can create something new."[22] His "something new" grew backward.

The seeds that germinated in fire and destruction in the Valley of the Winds were to grow back, in Miyazaki's movie time frame, through the terror of the Seven Days of Fire, back into present-day Japan through the perfect summer of *My Neighbor Totoro*, to burst into life in the morning of Japan's history in the forests of *Princess Mononoke*. His princess out to save her people now has a wilder, fiercer face, but still the face of a young woman capable of change, growth, and self-determination. The conventional hero "like Indiana Jones" who could not credibly plead for peace and kindness and had to move down well-worn paths of narrative expectation learned understanding in *Castle in the Sky*, lost his innocence yet regained his faith in *Porco Rosso*, and finally matured into *Princess Mononoke's* Ashitaka, a hero with a strength and sweetness to match Nausicaä's own. Where many artists travel away from their original innocence, Miyazaki has circled back toward it. In his end is his beginning.

The striking beauty of his scenery, especially his skyscapes, is even more pronounced here than in *Castle of Cagliostro*, and the weird beauty of the poisoned forest creates a powerful impression. Despite some deficiencies in the drawing and occasional static backgrounds, such details as the cloud of dust that puffs back from the glider's jets as Nausicaä lifts off lend powerful solidity to the action. The contrast between light and dark and interior and exterior is used to good effect, and the contrast between the crude weapons of mankind and the power of nature, whether subtle or simply overwhelming, is particularly well played. The artistic deficiencies of the movie are not failings of invention or of ability, but of time, money, and the ability to recruit enough staff at the right level—all problems Miyazaki was to address with increasing determination throughout his career. Were he inclined to revisit old haunts (and a reading of his movies to date shows that he can be), a modern epic along the lines of *Nausicaä*—but made by the staff he and Takahata have trained over the past decade and with the studio facilities provided from *Princess Mononoke*'s huge profits—would be an overwhelming experience.

The psychological contrasts are well stated too. The audience is left to make its own connections between the helplessness of young Lastelle, young Nausicaä, and the two young Ohmu; the blindness of Grandmother and the far more limiting spiritual blindness of Kushana and Kurotawa; the closed minds and hearts of those who will not look at nature

without fear or prejudice versus Nausicaä's sense of wonder and curiosity; and the selfishness of the Pejiteians and Tolmekians versus Nausicaä's willingness to put herself at risk to save them. The particular contrast between Kushana, who sets out to be a savior by deciding on her preferred solution and imposing it on the problem, and Nausicaä, who observes and seeks to bring all sides together in harmony, is very well drawn; the idealistic, innocent young girl and the dynamic, practical leader are both not as they seem, with Kushana's own revenge motive and Nausicaä's moments of darkness linking them closely together.

The characters of *Nausicaä*, from the princess herself to the bumbling old codgers who are her fellow hostages, are all human. They have flaws, problems, and sides we'd rather not see. Their heroism is admirable precisely because of those flaws. Nausicaä will let a tiny animal gnaw through her skin without complaint, but she's still capable of blind, murderous rage. She keeps trying to get people to come together and solve problems in peace, but she knows despair as well as optimism. The Pejiteians and Tolmekians are not cardboard villains, but people struggling with their own problems. The Ohmu are not a ravening swarm bent on mindless destruction from some cheap monster B flick, but creatures with as credible a place in their world as the humans, whose needs and motives are just as credible. There is tenderness and kindness in the way Miyazaki draws his characters that shows a genuine warmth toward human frailty.

Nausicaä of the Valley of the Winds shows all the passions and obsessions that Miyazaki was to develop in his later works, and reveals the weaknesses in the production system that he was to spend the rest of his working life striving to overcome. It lays out his major themes and the character archetypes he would develop with such success. Above all, it gives us a clear view of the gentleness at the heart of his work, a gentleness that does not duck tough questions but that counsels a spirit of realistic optimism, reminding us that the world has moments of great beauty, and the only way to appreciate them is by living. It is a beautiful and moving film, but more, it is a film without which the rest of Miyazaki's work could not be fully understood. While achieving his aim of providing an audience with two hours of pure entertainment, it provides those who love his work with a great deal more.

4

CASTLE IN THE SKY

Flight to Adventure

Set in an alternate nineteenth century where steam is still the main source of power, this thrilling adventure tale takes a boy from a tiny mining village on the journey of a lifetime. Pazu begins with a dream of proving his dead father's theories right, and finds himself caught up in piracy and political intrigue on a grand scale when a young girl with a mysterious pendant falls out of the sky and into his life. Taking their lives in their hands, the pair must soar above the clouds to find the lost remnants of an ancient civilization whose terrible powers built castles in the sky. But can they prevent those powers being loosed on the world?

ORIGINS

• •

After the success of *Nausicaä of the Valley of the Winds*, Miyazaki and Takahata set up their own production office and studio. *Tenku no Shiro Laputa (Laputa, Castle in the Sky)* was not the first production by Studio Ghibli, but it was the first in the style we have come to associate with the studio.

In his book *Shuppatsuten*, Miyazaki says, "The motif for *Laputa: Castle in the Sky*, which was released last year, is the island floating in the sky in the third section of *Gulliver's Travels*, by Jonathan Swift."[1]

Inspired by a long line of heroic sagas, Miyazaki's original scenario gives a twist to Swift's future and our past by postulating an industrial revolution scenario far below the technological levels of the flying islands, the "castles" of the title, which have now assumed the status of myth.

His literary interests show strongly in the epic adventure format, reminiscent at times of *Treasure Island*, with the hero and heroine torn from their quiet lives by forces outside their control or understanding, and forced to grow, develop, and eventually take control of their own destiny if they are to survive. His understanding of the lives of ordinary workers is also echoed in the sympathetic portrayal of a poor yet warm-hearted and honorable mining community, based on a study trip to Wales in 1984 at an early stage of planning for the film. His skepticism about science and technology as tools of progress is often inferred from the way in which escalating levels of technological control equate with escalating levels of violence, greed, and injustice in his work; yet this is not a comment on technology but on man's inability to use it wisely.

The Welsh dimension is one of the film's strongest influences. In an interview in 1999, Miyazaki said,

> I was in Wales at the time of the miners' strike. I really admired the way the miners' unions fought to the very end for their jobs and communities, and I wanted to reflect the strength of those communities in my film. I saw so many places with abandoned machinery, abandoned mines—the fabric of the industry was there, but no people. It made a strong impression on me. A whole industry with no work. There was a huge pit I visited, that had been turned into a kind of theme park where people could study the history of the industry. As I was walking round the mine I could see these great lumps and seams of coal—

Pazu's father took a picture of the flying island of Laputa from an airship many years ago. He was accused of faking the picture and died a disappointed man, unable to convince anyone except his son that one of the ancient castles in the sky still existed.

On top of the chimney alongside his little cottage, Pazu prepares to welcome the new day and give the mining village its wake-up call with a tuneful melody on his trumpet.

in Japan we'd have to go down 1500 feet or more to get anything like that. I thought what a pity it was that the industry was dead, but on the other hand there's nothing that could be done about it. Like the explosion of the Hindenberg—after that happened the whole technology [of airships] was discarded. Events had just gone too far to continue with it, so all the pilots and staff lost their jobs.[2]

It seems that *Castle in the Sky* also contains echoes of the struggle of the Welsh people for nationhood and freedom, with roots in Celtic culture. Miyazaki had a friend who presented the director with a book of photographs to use as a reference. The book was *Land of Our Fathers* (by Tatsuo Kurihara and others). One chapter, which spoke of a childhood and hometown in Wales and a grandfather's pride as a Welshman, made a deep impression on Miyazaki.

Although Welsh people carry the mixed blood of various races, they are at bottom Celts. The Celts were conquered by the Roman empire as barbarians, and were continuously conquered thereafter . . . my anger at the military superpowers when I read Caesar's *Gallic Wars* and Howard Furst's *Spartacus*, and the courage of the king of the barbarian Celts that comes out of Sutcliffe's *Mark of the Horse Lord* come gushing forth all in a jumble and, moreover, whilst the year-long struggle of the British miners mixed with impressions of the Miike [coal mine] struggle of 1960, these were all imposed on the faces of the Welsh miners in the photographs. I went to Wales to scout locations, and made the film's protagonist a young boy miner just before the mines were shut down. Although the film has been completed, the interest [in the Celts] continues to dog me.[3]

The film did not do as well as its precursor at the Japanese box office, earning around two and a half million dollars, but its mix of epic action-adventure and techno-ecological theme has since earned it cult status.[4] When Disney decided to release the story on video in 1999 as the second tape in their Miyazaki series, there were some concerns regarding the translation of the title. Many Americans' first language is Spanish, and in that language *la puta* is not simply a reference to a classic novel but a highly derogatory word signifying a woman of easy virtue. Obviously parents

might hesitate to show a film with such a title to their children. The studio was aware of this at an early stage; in an interview in a French magazine in July 1992, Isao Takahata commented that the original *Laputa* was "an island which was floating in the air and wasn't receiving sunshine because it was too evil—which explains the negative connotation of its name which is derived from the word 'bitch' (*puta* in Spanish, and *pute* in French)."[5]

The problem was easily resolved. The Japanese word order of the title puts *Castle in the Sky* first, and so it was decided that this should be the release title for the English language video. In fact, the word "Laputa" was not included in early working titles. Since this is very much a boy's adventure story, some of the titles originally proposed included Pazu's name as well as a reference to flying castles, but the need to find a recognizable cultural hook for backers and distributors led to the inclusion of the city's name from Swift's novel instead.

ART AND TECHNIQUE

Miyazaki's world-building talents, already displayed in magical detail in *Nausicaä of the Valley of the Winds*, were used to similar effect in this film. In *Castle in the Sky*, he turned for inspiration to the history of man's dreams of flight, and the opening credits present a panoply of magnificently dotty eighteenth- and nineteenth-century flying machines rendered in a graphic style and gentle color scheme reminiscent of antique prints. All these were designed by Miyazaki himself, and despite their extravagant appearance, all are workable according to the technology on which they are based. The flying islands themselves are also represented in detail that indicates their true function, letting the audience know that the long-lost power in the film might not be the unmixed blessing that the young hero and many others imagine. The airships hark back to *Nausicaä of the Valley of the Winds*, cattle-cars in which people are ferried like so much cargo through the skies. The city of Laputa itself at first looks like the ideal combination of science and nature as it might have been dreamed by Verne or Wells—a series of tranquil gardens unfolding around a hidden core of crystalline power. Only as the film progresses do we see that the city shows only its harsh and threatening underside to the world below, reserving the tranquillity and beauty above for its own elite. Nature has gentled the city's cold crystal heart not through man's agency but by simply taking over once he has gone, cloaking the symbols of oppression in greenery and flowers and tangling the machinery of domination in the roots of a mighty tree.

Fans of Japanese animation will be aware that another production about the conflict between lesser and greater technologies and the political struggle to control resources appeared in the same year as *Castle in the Sky*, with its story also centered on a huge tree. *Windaria: Legend of Fabulous Battle*, directed by Kunihiko Yuyama and with designs by Mutsumi Inomata, has been available in the U.S. on video for some years. Large trees, especially camphor trees, play an important role in Japanese tra-

dition and it's not uncommon to see them even in very recent titles for young audiences not as familiar with folklore (for example, the recent TV series *Revolutionary Girl Utena*). Windaria's central tree, with an almost shamanistic persona of its own, is treated as a guardian spirit by the people who live in its shadow. Laputa's central tree is invested with a less superstitious significance; it serves as a metaphor for the reviving and life-giving power of nature, but its seemingly miraculous ability to save what is best and most beautiful about the flying city is a direct result not of magic but of its proper place in the ecosystem.

Most of the design detail is drawn from the eighteenth and nineteenth centuries. The costumes are based on nineteenth-century fashions. The mining village where the story opens is entirely typical of the small industrial dormitories dotted across northern Europe, the valve-and-turbine machinery is of a piece with its settings, and the charmingly wacky railroad mingles nineteenth-century technology with cartoon Westerns. The huge iron dreadnought in which Pazu and Sheeta are taken to the capital and the government train that captures them earlier are ugly, self-important expressions of the iron fist of power—very like the much more elegant black dome beneath Laputa that is revealed when its weapons systems are activated.

Although the technology used is antique, its scale and scope are sometimes breathtaking. The railway in the mining community and the fortress in which Sheeta and Pazu are held have bridges, ramps, and depths as vast as anything in the classic SF film *Forbidden Planet*—that other great fable of faith in techno-

In the peaceful gardens of Laputa, Sheeta and Pazu encounter a war robot like the one that fell to earth. But this robot is a gentle guardian of the wild creatures in the garden and seems completely uninterested in doing anyone harm. The design of the robot is closely related to one that appears in a Miyazaki-directed episode of the Lupin III TV series.

logy run mad—and the sense of scale adds enormously to the epic feel of the adventure. Interestingly, most of the technical engines shown in human hands in *Castle in the Sky* are heavy-handed and ungainly—the cattlecar airships, the dreadnought, the elevator that brings the miners up after their shift. Only tiny, individual craft like Pazu's skeletal glider, or the quirky collection of junk that is the Dola ship, have charm and personality. Technology that works for the individual is more interesting and ultimately more useful than technology that merely organizes and channels his labor.

In *Castle in the Sky*, the natural world seems more under man's control than in any of

Miyazaki's other films. The only animals and birds we see are tiny creatures in the exquisite parklands of Laputa and Pazu's caged doves. Most land is either covered in houses and mines or farmed. The crashing waves of the sea are no obstacle for the huge government dreadnought. The wildest and freest thing in the film is the sky; even though man sends his airships across the heavens, clouds and storms can toss them about and hamper their progress and the smallest slip can kill. Meanwhile the mines are shown as another country, a world that man can exploit but not destroy. Once the miners have gone, the silent passages and underground lakes remain. On the ground, man's works seem to rule the world, but above

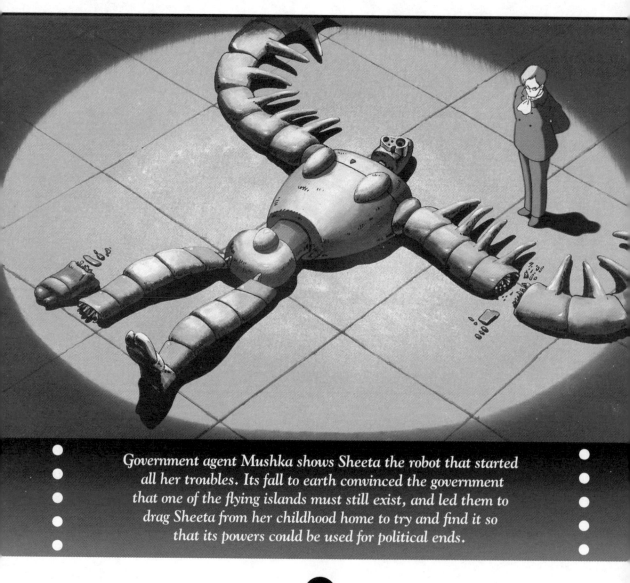

Government agent Mushka shows Sheeta the robot that started all her troubles. Its fall to earth convinced the government that one of the flying islands must still exist, and led them to drag Sheeta from her childhood home to try and find it so that its powers could be used for political ends.

and below the ground he is still subject to forces beyond his control. The skies and the enduring rocks speak of a history in which mammals have made only a brief appearance, and their technology seems a puny thing alongside such grandeur.

The story might seem to have an anti-technology message, but this is far from true. Miyazaki isn't against technology, but he is against blind faith in technology and the belief that it can solve all our problems. As we enter the twenty-first century, the challenge is not how to recapture the old world, as Mushka tries to do in *Castle in the Sky*, but how to build a new world in which humane values can flourish. When I put this to him he said,

> I'm not really optimistic about the next fifty years because we're going to face more human tragedy as we human beings start to do more and more stupid and dangerous things. After that time, when we've tried them and they have failed, maybe we'll move on to try better ways of doing things and things will improve. The danger of the increasing acceptance of computers in our world right now isn't that they are bad things in themselves, but rather that people think you can conquer the world using computers. We'll probably find that's not true. Literature and so on was limited to a very few rich educated people until this century; then it started to get really widespread and common and people began to get tired of books. That's going to happen

to computer games, animation, and all our current fads, and that's when we'll learn what will be there in the next century. On a personal level I'm not pessimistic, because I think if I can find a way to help the children I know learn what makes them feel good and what will make a better world, I can help them to deal with the future through my work.[6]

THE CHARACTERS

Sheeta

Sheeta, an orphan girl from a remote farming community, is about thirteen years old. She knows that her family is a very old one, with many legends and secrets in its past, but is completely unaware of her ancestry as a member of the ancient royal house of Laputa and heir to the city's incredible powers. Her pendant, an heirloom, holds the key to these powers but she doesn't know that when the story begins. Although she is very quiet and shy, and often seems uncertain of what course of action to take, Sheeta has great courage and is very loyal. At the beginning of the film she is a frightened little girl, grieving for her parents and torn away from everything she knows, but by the end she has matured into a warm-hearted, brave young woman with a wonderful sense of fun.

One of the most interesting arguments of early 1999 on nausicaa.net, the Internet discussion group of Miyazaki fans, centered on

Castle in the Sky as an example of Miyazaki's views on feminism and the benign power of matriarchal societies. I can follow the line of logic that says that since the power of the stone is passed down in feminine jewelry, because it's Sheeta's nurse who teaches her the charms, and because Mushka can't use the stone's full power without Sheeta, there may be reasonable grounds for advancing the theory. Still, I have to point out that there is no firm evidence in the film that the power of Laputa or any other flying city passes down the matriarchal line. Further, given that the power of the flying cities seems to have been used exclusively to oppress the earthbound and keep the skyborne elite in their position of privilege, a Laputan matriarchy would have been a corrupt and evil system inclined to exploitation and violence by the use of weapons of mass destruction. I prefer to think of the gentle Sheeta as the last inheritor of a line whose abilities, faults, and virtues were not gender determined, and of the film as having no ax to grind for any particular political system, but rather for a humane and responsible society.

Pazu

Pazu is about fourteen and, like Sheeta, is an orphan. He lost his mother when he was very young and his father died a disappointed man, ridiculed by many because he believed the ancient flying cities were not myth but fact. He photographed Laputa once, but everyone except Pazu believes he faked the picture. Pazu is determined to follow his father's dream and is building his own flying machine so that one day he too can take to the skies and search for evidence of the cities'

existence. For the present, he lives alone in a small cottage above the mine and works as an assistant to the chief engineer, fetching his lunch, passing tools, and helping to maintain the complex but aging machinery that keeps the community in work. He is well known and liked in the village for his cheerful nature and happy-go-lucky enjoyment of life, but when tested by circumstances he shows great courage, far beyond the unthinking rashness of childhood.

Mushka

Mushka is an agent of the government, but for years he has devoted his entire life to a secret dream; his work is merely a means to give him the power to pursue it. He too comes from the old royal house of Laputa, and only Sheeta stands closer than him in line to the ancient throne. He is cold-hearted, calculating, and entirely evil, wanting the power of Laputa only for his own ends and with no interest in the good that it could do for mankind. He is young, tall, and not uncomely, but his face and demeanor are cold and contemptuous even when he is trying to impress.

The General

The General is not so much evil as stupid—he is typical of the unthinking, arrogant type of soldier parodied in so many books and newspaper cartoons, and is designed to look and dress like a typical Prussian officer. He wants the power of Laputa for his government, but also to bolster his own prestige and increase his chances of promotion. Deeply conventional, he is not the sort of person to seize that power and re-

Sheeta is terrified as the tower in which she was held burns around her. The robot that scared her at first is only trying to defend her, but she still doesn't understand why.

sponsibility for himself, and he is too stupid to realize that Mushka is using him and his men.

The Chief Engineer

The Chief Engineer, known to everyone as The Boss, is a huge ox of a man with a warm heart and a big fist, always ready to fight if his friends are threatened. He is doing his best to help keep the mine afloat, but times are hard and there are very few minerals left to be brought up. His wife is a red-haired lady who's also formidable in a fight, and who is very fond of Pazu and helps him and Sheeta escape.

Old Pom

Old Pom is an old miner who now lives the life of a hermit in his beloved caves and tunnels, away from the confusion and danger of the surface

After the terror of their flight from their pursuers, Pazu and Sheeta float down a deep shaft into the mines, borne up by the power of Sheeta's pendant. The walls of the shaft are lined with old workings and mining equipment.

world. He meets the children underground and tells them a little more about Sheeta's mysterious pendant and the secrets of the levitation crystals.

Ma Dola

Ma Dola is the head of the family business—the Dola Gang of sky-pirates—a widow who lives her life independently. Outwardly she's a no-nonsense, all-action, treasure-hungry harridan who is twice as tough as any of her sons, but in reality she is a tender-hearted woman who admires the courage of the two young orphans and promotes their romance.

The Engineer

The Engineer, also known as Pa, is a very quiet man who appears to be under the thumb of his outspoken partner Ma Dola. Yet he's the one who keeps the pirate ship and small planes in the air, and in their scenes together it's clear how she respects and relies on him.

The Dola Boys

The Dola Boys are hulking great brutes with sweet hearts, and unlike the Engineer they really are completely under the thumb of their formidable mother. They try to appear as tough and determined as she is, but they've all inherited her tender heart—they're just not so good at concealing it. They're not very clever, but they have good natures and great courage. They all fall madly in love with Sheeta, but it's an innocent devotion mixed with protectiveness and shyness, not the predatory attention of a sophisticated elder to a child.

THE STORY

Sheeta has been arrested by government agents and is being taken by airship to the capital, far from her home. She isn't sure why she has been arrested and is very alone and very afraid. During the night the airship is attacked by pirates, who also seem to be after her. In desperation, she seizes her chance to stun her captor and crawls out onto the airship's skin. Buffeted by the wind, and with pirates making a grab for her, she loses her grip and passes out, falling thousands of feet through dense cloud.

Down below, in a small mining town, Pazu is working late, going to the cookshop, the nineteenth-century equivalent of a hamburger stand, to fetch meatballs for the boss's supper. As he returns he spots a bright speck falling through the sky, a mysterious blue star—and sees it's a girl, floating to earth as smoothly as if she were being lowered. She's about to fall into the open mine shaft, and as he races to catch her he sees that the blue light is coming from a jewel around her neck. At first she is light as a feather in his arms, but once he has caught her the light dies and she suddenly weighs exactly what you'd expect a girl her size to weigh, with nearly disastrous results. Pazu has to get back to work, but later he takes her, still unconscious, back to his home to sleep.

Sheeta wakes the next day and finds that Pazu is a friend, willing to help her when she tells her story. He has been building an aircraft in the hope of proving that his dead father really did see the legendary city of Laputa, even though everyone else believes he was lying. He tells her how the jewel she wears seemed to help her float to safety—but when he tries to test its powers by falling off the roof while wearing it, all he gets is a sore head. She knows nothing about its history, just that she was told never to show it to anyone or give it away. The only other thing she knows about her family history is that her nurse taught her a few old spells and charms, including one she must never use except when all is lost. She has no idea what any of this means.

Before the two young people have time to think about it further, the pursuit begins. Both the pirates and the government are on Sheeta's trail, and with the help of the villagers and a friendly train driver the pair try to escape. At first Sheeta urges Pazu not to get involved, anxious to avoid putting him in danger, but he insists that they have a pact—he'll help her escape, she'll help him look for Laputa. In a thrilling railroad chase across track bridges spanning dizzying drops, Ma Dola, the head pirate, and the government men under agent Mushka slug it out for possession of Sheeta and her jewel, destroying huge portions of the railroad and its equipment until the children are left clinging to a broken timber and finally fall. Then, once again, the stone wakes and Pazu and Sheeta, hand in hand, float safely down into a huge pit and out of sight, while Mushka and Dola look on.

Pazu and Sheeta are in the mines, where they take refuge to rest and eat the food Pazu stuffed into his bag as they fled, and where they meet his old friend Pom, an elderly recluse who lives mostly underground. He tells them that Sheeta's jewel is a levitation crystal of the purest sort. Most of the rocks in the region contain some of the strange mineral, but in such small quantities that when mined it pulses briefly with light and then dies, and is useless for commercial purposes. Only levitation stone crystals work as power generators, and only the old inhabitants of the floating cities had the secret of synthesizing crystals from levitation stone ore. The rarity and value of Sheeta's pendant might account for the in-terest of the pirates, but what can the government want with it? As Old Pom says, it's a very serious matter.

Emerging from the mine, Sheeta is troubled and concerned for Pazu's safety, but he reminds her that they have agreed to help each other. Just then a government force surrounds them, and although Pazu tries to help Sheeta he is hit on the head and knocked out. The pair are taken to a fortress in the capital and Pazu is thrown into a deep dungeon, while Sheeta is taken to a huge room in a high tower, given beautiful new clothes, and kept a prisoner. Only by agreeing to cooperate with the government can she secure Pazu's safety and freedom. Despairing for herself but determined to keep Pazu safe, she agrees. When she says good-bye to him, he is furious that she can "forget" their promise to each other, but he is ejected from the castle with a handful of gold coins and sets off for home, confused and feeling betrayed.

When Mushka finally shows Sheeta what he wants her to do, she is terrified. A huge robot has fallen to earth, and he recognized it as one of the legendary robot soldiers of Laputa. On its casing is the same symbol as on Sheeta's pendant. She is to wake the robot and help them use it to find the location of Laputa so that the government can seize its power. Meanwhile Pazu is seized by the Dola gang, and Ma tells him in no uncertain terms what she thinks of a boy who doesn't even have the wit to realize when a girl is sacrificing herself to keep him safe. Finally understanding why Sheeta had to work with the government, he agrees to help the Dola gang rescue her and seek the legendary treasure of

After their fall into the mines, Pazu and Sheeta meet an old miner in the deep underground caverns. He tells them more about the mineral from which Sheeta's pendant is made, the rare and precious levitation stone, and shows them the beauty of the caverns.

Laputa. As the robot wakes and devastates half the castle, Pazu and the gang fly in to snatch a terrified Sheeta from the roof of the burning tower. But thanks to the sudden, brief appearance of a beam of light pointing from Sheeta's pendant into the sky, Mushka now has what he wanted—a fix on the direction of Laputa—and he has the pendant itself, dropped during the rescue. The government prepares an airship to take Mushka, the General, and a picked force to conquer the castle in the sky. The pirates are headed in the same direction with Pazu and Sheeta aboard.

The journey is long and has moments of danger, but as everyone gets to know each other Pazu and Sheeta come to love the pirates as the family they have both lost, and the Dolas take them to their hearts. Sheeta cleans

FILMOGRAPHY AND PERSONNEL

Castle in the Sky

Tenku no Shiro Laputa
(literally, Castle in the Sky Laputa)

Theatrical release, 2 August 1986

RUNNING TIME: 2 hours, 10 minutes

DIRECTOR, WRITER, EDITOR: Hayao Miyazaki

ANIMATION DIRECTOR: Yoshinori Kanada

MUSIC: Jo Hisaishi

SOUND: Shigeharu Shiba

PRODUCTION DESIGN: Toshiro Nozaki, Nizo Yamamoto

PRODUCERS: Tatsumi Yamashita, Hideo Ogata, Isao Takahata

EXECUTIVE PRODUCER: Yasuyoshi Tokuma

ASSOCIATE PRODUCER: Toru Hara

© Nibariki, Tokuma Shoten

U.S. theatrical release, March 1989, in Philadelphia by Streamline Pictures. Streamline had U.S. theatrical distribution rights for one year only. The dubbed version it released was provided by the producer, Tokuma, which had commissioned it for screening on Japan Airlines flights.

U.S. video re-release tentatively scheduled for 2000 from Buena Vista Home Entertainment.

Final information on the American cast is not available as I write, but Anna Paquin, star of *The Piano*, is to play Sheeta, with James Van Der Beek of *Dawson's Creek* as young hero Pazu. Respected TV and movie actor and singer Mandy Patinkin is down for a role. Former Jedi Knight Mark Hamill, widely respected for his voice work on the animated *Batman* series, has also been mentioned for the role of Mushka.

---

the filthy galley and cooks and washes for the crew, with unexpected and somewhat sheepish help from her new band of overgrown admirers, while Pazu helps Pa keep the ship aloft and takes his turn at night watches. As they near the predicted position of Laputa, there are skirmishes with the government craft, and in a fierce storm Pazu and Sheeta find themselves cut adrift in the ship's reconnaissance glider. Pazu's flying skill keeps them in the air somehow, and as they finally pierce the eye of the storm they find Laputa floating in the calm at its center, an oasis of peace and beauty inhabited only by small animals and a few

robot guardians. Even the robots are gentle—they look like the one that so terrified Sheeta in the castle, but seem to have lost the programming that enabled them to do harm. An enormous, beautiful tree dominates the city, and its roots have grown through the entire structure, right down into the mysterious engines far below the surface that keep Laputa running. Tall flowers blossom underground in the heart of a supercomputer so complex no one alive can understand it.

The government has also landed, and Dola and the pirates are captured just as Mushka captures Sheeta and tells her that they are related. Both are descended from the ancient Laputan ruling house, though Sheeta is the rightful heir. He reveals his true colors as he uses the pendant to wake Laputa's army of battle robots and arm its weapons systems. As Pazu tries desperately to come to Sheeta's rescue, Mushka threatens to kill them both and shoots off her pigtails to reinforce his threat. Reunited for a brief moment, the two young people agree that since they cannot allow Mushka to use the power of Laputa to dominate and enslave the Earth as his ancestors had once done, they must use the final, terrible spell Sheeta learned from her nurse. It is perfectly clear that they don't expect to survive it; they are willingly signing their own death warrant to save their world from Mushka's madness. For Pazu this is an especially courageous decision, since he is also saying good-bye to the dream of Laputa, which has sustained him since his father's death. Holding hands, they say the spell together. It releases Laputa's central levitation crystal, which crashes through its man-made restraints and carries on rising through the core of the city. The machinery of Laputa begins to crumble, all its weapons and robots crashing to earth.

But the roots of the great tree cradle the crystal and prevent it from flying into space. Gradually, as the debris of the weapons system falls, all that remains of the mighty civilization of Laputa are its gardens with the great tree, their tiny creatures, and the gentle robots. The beautiful remnants of the city soar far above the reach of mankind, their peace and beauty safe from greedy hands. Pazu and Sheeta recover consciousness to find that the gar-

den is rising higher and higher, propelled by the crystal whose forces are now uncontrolled by any man-made systems. All the men of war and their dreams of dominion are gone, but Dola and her family, with their human greed for treasure and love of freedom, have survived and even managed to show a profit on the trip. The friends are reunited in the sky before Pazu and Sheeta set off for her old home, where they plan to live a peaceful life together. Pazu's dream of adventure in the skies and his promise to his father's memory are finally fulfilled.

The film's closing credits show images of the peaceful rural life that awaits them, but the final image of the film is of Laputa, the castle in the sky, orbiting peacefully above the Earth.

COMMENTARY

Nausicaä of the Valley of the Winds looked at the dangers of allowing science to run wild while ignoring the balance of nature. *Castle in the Sky* takes a slightly different viewpoint. Technology isn't just about war and industry; technology is fun and games. We don't really understand it, but we want it at almost any price. The only problem is, we haven't taken time to check the bill.

Miyazaki has frequently stated that he doesn't want to make films with a moral or a message, but they seem to emerge anyway. Sheeta is ignorant of her heritage and its implications in the same way that mankind has lost the

Pazu and Sheeta are aloft in the pirate vessel's glider, sailing into dangerous skies in search of the fabled flying island of Laputa, the Castle in the Sky.

knowledge of the great flying castles. Pazu wants the adventurous and enjoyable side of technology but hasn't thought past this to the implications of what he might discover. These are very widespread viewpoints in our society—most of us in the "developed world" can't actually make or repair the stuff we use every day, and most of us don't think about where technology is taking us. We are also largely ignorant of the limitations of our technology. We can send pictures around the world in microseconds for the benefit of people chatting on the Internet, but can't get food to people in the flooded deltas of Bangladesh in time to stop them from starving. We can give ourselves more and newer kicks with designer drugs but haven't yet eradicated leprosy. We can tinker with the genes of the unborn, but millions of children still die of entirely preventable ailments like diarrhea.

If Miyazaki were making the film now, the impact of the computer and the growth of telecommunications over the past decade might have led him to change his views, but it seems unlikely. Human ignorance and selfishness have not been conquered by the greater availability of information, and the vast majority of the world's population is still excluded from access to the benefits of technology for purely political or commercial reasons. Just like Mushka and the General, we can put our faith in technology; just like Pazu, we can think of it as a superb adventure or a game. But if we do not begin, as a people, as a world, to think through the implications and costs of our actions, we will find ourselves in trouble.

Every time I see *Castle in the Sky* I am struck again by its power as a polemic, but also by the strength and delicacy that prevent the story from being overwhelmed by the ideas and opinions it provokes. It is easy to read the film as a passionate yet balanced plea for a new look at the purpose of technology, but impossible to ignore its power as a masterpiece of storytelling and film-making.

Some commentators have criticized the plot as unnecessarily long-winded and complex. It may be that to anyone without a grounding in classic literature, any plot that takes over two hours to unfold seems cumbersome. I view the structure of *Castle in the Sky* in the same light as that of a classic adventure novel. The pacing and plotting of the film en-

able Miyazaki to develop his ideas fully while giving the audience plenty to see and think about. Just like the doctor in *Gulliver's Travels* or Jim in *Treasure Island*, Pazu and Sheeta fall into a wide range of situations and adventures that are linked by their personal growth and the growth of their relationship. All these situations also play their part in moving the adventure along. Like chapters in a book, some move fast (the rescue from the tower) but others are more reflective (the sequence in the deep mine) so that the viewer can draw breath and ponder what's gone before. My view is supported by *Ghost in the Shell* director Mamoru Oshii, who said in an interview for the *Kinema Junpo* special issue in 1995 that *Castle in the Sky* is his favorite Ghibli film because of its strong structure as a boys' adventure story.[7]

There are no extraneous scenes or characters in *Castle in the Sky*, no wasted imagery or dialogue. Everything contributes to the building of a coherent world and a social structure that the audience accepts immediately because no line or frame seems out of place. Pazu and Sheeta's fall from the railway tracks, like Sheeta's fall from the airship, is perfectly paced and allowed to take its own time, and the repetition of the scene helps emphasize the change in Sheeta's world brought about by her friendship with Pazu. Where earlier she was unconscious and unable to help herself, now she is floating safely to solid ground, holding the hands of a friend she can trust. When Mushka tells Sheeta how the robot soldier fell out of the sky onto a farmer's land, the way he tells the story is revealing of his nature and his world. If this level of detail and involvement is long-winded and complex, I'd like to make a plea for more long-winded and complex films and more directors strong-willed and gifted enough to make them.

The design and art direction of the film is close to faultless. The scene in the underground cavern where Old Pom shows the children how the traces of levitation stone ore in the rock come to life in the darkness is one of breathtaking beauty, the still lake in the cavern rendered with as much care and detail as the skies in the action sequences. The flying island is revealed through the vortex of a storm so powerfully rendered that you could almost believe the old legends of storm-dragons without the sketchy suggestions of dragon-shapes which are, for me, the film's only false artistic note.

Laputa itself is an amalgam of everything gracious in ancient architecture, wrapped around a core of pure fifties science fiction—great blocks and symbols sliding through infinite space, manipulated by the power of thought. Its concentric circles of terraces and pools, spreading out like ripples from the great tree, sometimes reflect the sky and sometimes reveal it through gaps in the massive masonry. The city's design blurs the boundaries between sky and water, playing with form and substance like a print by that master of bizarre multidimensional imagery, M. C. Escher. The same level of devoted precision is lavished on the design of the small details of piping and valves in the mine, or the tiny animals and birds that provide a flash of movement in Laputa's surreal stillness, as on the might of its war machinery or the robots.

The other matter of great interest in the design area is Miyazaki's tendency toward recycling. For the robot he reused a design from his work on the *Lupin III* TV series, and he had already established the "Miyazaki girl" look that Sheeta was the latest example of. The simple yet expressive facial styles developed by Miyazaki and Takahata allowed a wide range of emotions to be depicted, but the face itself was becoming a shorthand for a certain type of heroine—young, thoughtful, attractive, but with as-yet-unrevealed depths of courage and character.[8] To begin with, shy, pigtailed Sheeta seems as unlike Nausicaä as a heroine could be, but by the end of the film the resemblance is so marked that when Mushka shoots off her pigtails it's not merely a threat but the final stage in a transformation ritual.[9] It's entirely fitting that the ragged ends of the hair give Sheeta a style not too far off the Nausicaä bob.

The music in the film deserves special mention. Jo Hisaishi's remarkable original score draws on the orchestral traditions of great cinema composers such as Korngold and Bernard Hermann and provides a suitable dramatic background for moments of tension and excitement, with tender and romantic themes for more reflective moments. Hisaishi also uses a wide range of vocal and musical resources—the choral statement of the main theme that cuts off so abruptly when Pazu and Sheeta speak their terrible spell is particularly noteworthy. As this book goes to press, a rescoring of the film to bring the soundtrack up to the required standard for American movie theater projection has just been completed.[10] If it goes ahead, audiences will be able to enjoy

Hisaishi's artistry via a full-scale state-of-the-art theatrical sound system.

Castle in the Sky isn't my favorite Miyazaki film, but I never fail to enjoy it to or find something new and thought-provoking on every repeat viewing. It would certainly be in my top-ten animated films; its many strengths reveal themselves more with long acquaintance.

If parents who lament the lack of suitable entertainment for children buy a copy of the video, they'll discover something wonderful. Here is a film that treats boys and girls equally without trying to pretend that they're identical. It allows heroism and goodness to exist without being stereotyped. It revels in the joys of action and fun but emphasizes the need for life and relationships to be built on more solid ground. It even spells out, in a way that the computer-game generation won't find too preachy, the age-old message that it's not how many expensive toys you own that matters, but how you play with them.

The only thing parents can do to make the experience even more rewarding is to take the children to the cinema and let them revel in the vision of those enormous skies and that fantastic floating city spread across a big, big screen. *Castle in the Sky* is, above all else, a breathtaking adventure on the grand scale. It deserves to be appreciated as its maker intended.

5

MY NEIGHBOR TOTORO

The Beauty of Simplicity

Not so very long ago, two little girls and their father moved into a beautiful old house in the Japanese countryside. With their mother ill in the hospital and their father busy at work, Mei and her big sister Satsuki soon find themselves in a world of wonders, where cuddly creatures called Totoros can soar on spinning tops above the world, tiny seeds can turn into huge trees, and buses shaped like cats bound across the countryside completely unseen by grownups. Nature and imagination work their magic for Mei and Satsuki when they most need help and comfort, showing them how powerful and how precious the beautiful world around us is.

ORIGINS

As with the projects that were to become *Castle in the Sky* and *Princess Mononoke*, the idea that was to grow into *My Neighbor Totoro* was first pitched to Tokuma in the early 1980s but was rejected. However, Miyazaki places the origins of the story long before then. He said in an interview in *Animerica* magazine that, "*Totoro* is where my consciousness begins," and told his friend, the famous novelist and cultural historian Ryutaro Shiba, that the central figure of Totoro was a figment of his imagination, inspired by his childish imaginings of fearsome creatures living in the forest.[1]

It was a struggle to get the green light on the project in 1987. Producer Toshio Suzuki says that when he first showed the sketches for the character of Totoro to the finance and distribution executives, the men in suits didn't think the furry giant could take off, literally or figuratively. He thinks this is because Totoro's appeal doesn't wake until you see him in motion, animated on the screen.[2] (Ryutaro Shiba agreed with him, telling Miyazaki that he had been struck by the way the big Totoro's belly ripples as he sleeps, just like a living creature's.)[3] Suzuki, an expert at surmounting obstacles, came up with a unique pitch. He proposed that the film should form a double bill with a production for publisher Shinchosa. If a film were made of their book *Grave of the Fireflies*, a novel of childhood suffering by a survivor of the fire-bombings in World War II, school classes would be taken to see it because of its historical content, and that same audience would then stay on to see another movie on the double bill. Shinchosa wanted to break into movies and was not too worried about losing money to do so; this was an ideal opportunity for them. *Grave of the Fireflies* would be di-

rected for the screen by Miyazaki's colleague Isao Takahata.

It was far from an ideal pairing; *Grave* is a dark, demanding piece aimed at somewhat older viewers, and Suzuki was worried about the impact each film would have on the other's intended audience. There was also the

Satsuki, with Mei dozing on her back, waits at a woodland bus stop to meet their father on his way home from work and meets Totoro himself, waiting for a very different kind of bus. In this shot she has lent their furry companion the umbrella she brought along for Daddy, and his surprised look as he listens to the sound of the rain bouncing off the stretched fabric is just the start of a wonderful—and very noisy—game.

problem that animation based on Japanese contemporary experience wasn't exactly big box-office at the time. Distributors simply didn't believe there was an audience for a story about two little girls and a monster in modern Japan. [4] And the pairing meant that two feature films had to be completed at the same time. Studio Ghibli was breaking new ground in a number of directions. Suzuki simply hoped for the best.

As it turned out, things went better than he could have dreamed. At first, My Neighbor Totoro performed respectably but not superbly at the box office. A little merchandise was generated, but there was no hint of the tidal wave to come. In 1990 Studio Ghibli yielded to persistent requests to license a range of cuddly toys based on the film, opening the floodgates for a massive merchandising success. Profits from subsidiary rights on Totoro alone soon reached a level where they could sustain the studio year in and year out.[5] In America fans began to wonder when the film would reach the States, since it was so obviously a perfect vehicle for the merchandise-obsessed U.S. market, but Studio Ghibli was in no mood to repeat the experience of Warriors of the Wind. It took until 1993 for rights to be licensed to 50th Street Films for American theatrical release—and Fox Lorber for video—and the deal was done by Tokuma, not Ghibli. Even then, there were no merchandise rights attached, though Suzuki told me that this was more owing to American concerns than Japanese. Apparently, U.S. companies wanted to edit out two sequences—the bathtub sequence and the early scene where the two girls amuse themselves by jumping around on the tatami mats in the old house—because they felt these sequences were unlikely to be understood by American audiences. Still smarting from what they and their Western audience perceived as the butchery of Nausicaä of the Valley of the Winds, Studio Ghibli insisted that no cuts be made. Obviously, no sensible company was going to put large amounts of money into merchandising a film it thought its audience would find culturally alienating.

As American video sales began their climb past the half-million mark and the promotional offer of a cuddly blue Totoro toy was massively oversubscribed, the mistake became just as obvious. Roger Ebert gave the film a rave review in the Siskel and Ebert at the Movies syndicated show; Gene Siskel took longer to be won over, finally capitulating after seeing the film in the company of children. In America as in Japan, the initial press wasn't uniformly ecstatic—some found the movie's pace too slow and its simplicity too boring—but a number of big guns like the New York Times came out in favor. The movie's potential to cross the line from cult favorite to Western children's hit was beyond question. By 1996, when the Disney-Tokuma deal was made public, the question on fans' lips was, How long before the Mouse finally teams up with Totoro? It's a question that still has to be answered.

The Fox dub of My Neighbor Totoro was not, in fact, commissioned specifically for the U.S. video market. Tokuma had previously commissioned a dub from Carl Macek of Streamline Pictures for showing on transPacific flights of Japan Airlines. The translated

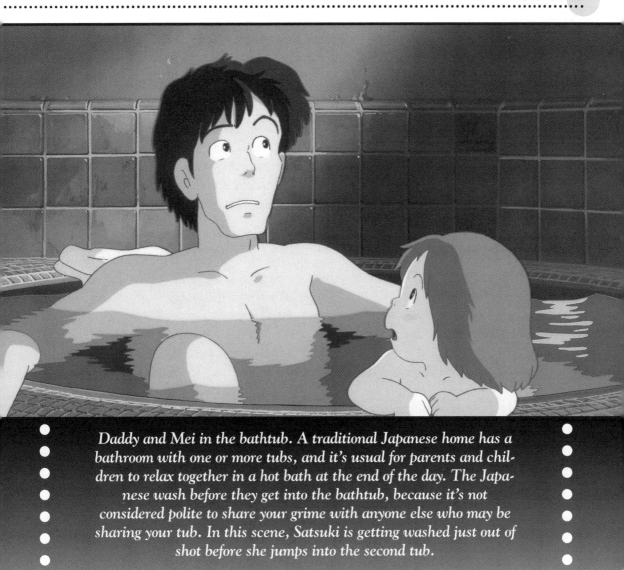

Daddy and Mei in the bathtub. A traditional Japanese home has a bathroom with one or more tubs, and it's usual for parents and children to relax together in a hot bath at the end of the day. The Japanese wash before they get into the bathtub, because it's not considered polite to share your grime with anyone else who may be sharing your tub. In this scene, Satsuki is getting washed just out of shot before she jumps into the second tub.

script had been submitted for Miyazaki's personal approval and amendment prior to recording, and it was this dub that was released by Fox.[6] The dub also had an airing in the U.K. prior to its U.S. release, when the movie was shown at the Barbican Cinema in London in the summer of 1991 as part of the Japan Festival, a nationwide program of events celebrating every aspect of Japanese culture.

It took exactly a year to complete *My Neighbor Totoro*, starting in April 1987. Miyazaki knew that he wanted to make a warm film, something that stood apart from the confrontational kids-against-adults stories of so many Japanese animated works, a film that would not fill a young audience's minds with conflict and struggle.[7] Yet, when he had to get the story down on paper, his mind went blank. A social visit to a colleague shortly before production was due to start saved the day. Miyazaki often mentions books or articles that he saw by chance that later proved to be potent sources of inspiration. It had happened on *Castle in the Sky*, and it happened again when he picked up his colleague's copy of the *Mainichi Graph* supplement entitled *Japan Forty Years Ago*.[8] He decided to return to the pastoral innocence of a country childhood before the advent of television and before the expansion of Tokyo had consumed so much of the rural landscape, sometime around the end of the 1950s. [9]

This, of course, was the time in which he grew up. A war baby, he entered his teens in the mid-1950s, lived in the area around Tokyo, and could clearly remember the kind of landscape he was describing. But there was an even more personal link between his life and his movie, since his mother had been hospitalized or bedridden with spinal tuberculosis for most of his childhood. We are never explicitly told the nature of Mother's illness in the movie version of *My Neighbor Totoro* (though in Miyazaki's novelization of the movie, the illness is explicitly named as tuberculosis), but the Shichikokuyama Hospital in which she is being treated was a real-life center of excellence for the treatment of tuberculosis at the time, and little Mei is around the same age as the young Hayao was when his mother first became ill. At the time, tuberculosis could and often did kill. For all its sunny optimism, the movie expresses the dread of loss that a very young child cannot articulate, from the heart of one who remembers its power.

The setting also had resonance for the grown-up Miyazaki, who lives in Tokorozawa City in Saitama Prefecture where the movie is set. It's now a bedroom suburb of Tokyo, but at the time the story took place it was a farming community set in the Sayama Hills. Parts of the region still have remnants of woodland, and Miyazaki has given and continues to give support to an organization dedicated to the preservation of the remaining ancient forests. They have raised funds to buy the forested land they call Totoro's Forest, and Miyazaki has donated artwork to be used for fundraising as well as a substantial cash gift to the cause of forest preservation. (Some visitors to the forest are said to be extremely disappointed that they don't see any Totoros, but all have an opportunity to appreciate the natural beauty around them.)

Once he started work, the ideas flowed fast. Early on in the writing process, the story revolved around one red-haired six-year-old girl, but as time went on Miyazaki changed the cast to feature two sisters ages four and ten. The small sister kept the auburn ponytails of her precursor, and Tokuma has since caused some confusion for fans by using early preproduction drawings of the first character to publicize the completed movie in which she does not appear. In June 1987, talking to Hong Kong magazine *A-Club*, Miyazaki said that the production was "already a quarter done" and described the Totoros and the Catbus in some detail. He referred to Totoros as "nature spirits" of the same kind as those familiar in Japanese religion, but despite the film's setting at a time when traditional values still held firm, and despite the elements of Japan's religious culture used on screen, he was adamant that "this movie has nothing to do with that or any other religion."[10] And although determined not to create conflict between children and adults in this work, he was equally determined that the movie should be set in a child's world. Only children can see Totoros and their fellow spirits, and children and spirits can understand each other without the need for words.

Miyazaki says he makes movies primarily for entertainment, and doesn't try to give his audience any particular message. Yet in *My Neighbor Totoro*, it seems to me that he is making a statement. The title tells us that humans and the rest of nature are neighbors; we should strive to be good ones, or the relationship between us will break down. Look, Miyazaki seems to say, at this beautiful country. This was ours not so long ago. Japan is very beautiful and the world is very beautiful, but we can't take it for granted. Be careful.

ART AND TECHNIQUE

The dominant image of the movie is the largest Totoro, called O-Totoro (King Totoro) in Japanese and Big Totoro in the existing U.S. release. There are elements of a number of creatures of nature and folklore in its makeup. It is related to the tanuki, the Japanese raccoon, with its playful spirit and magical powers. There are also links to the owl—its round eyes, its arrow-marked chest, and its hooting song, which was rescored by composer Jo Hisaishi onto the film soundtrack, played on the ocarina. The cat, long credited with shape-shifting ability in Japanese legend, lent some genes to the Totoros and their companion the Catbus. Lewis Carroll, creator of *Alice in Wonderland,* threw some elements into the mix for both—the ability to vanish at will and the huge, infectious grin. Many adult Totoro lovers also find that Big Totoro's comforting bulk and warm, uncritical nature bring back delightful memories of their favorite childhood teddy bear.

With *My Neighbor Totoro,* more than with any other of his works, Miyazaki is his own strongest influence. Reaching back into his youthful memories, he accessed both the most painful and the most joyous portions of childhood. He also paid homage to some of his favorite scenes from children's literature. Little Mei's fall down the tunnel in the camphor tree into Totoro's nest is another homage to Lewis Carroll. The two rides in the Catbus strongly reminded me of C. S. Lewis's description of Susan and Lucy's ride through Narnia on Aslan's back in *The Lion, the Witch and the Wardrobe.* I can never see the sisters swaying happily on the fur-covered seats with the rhythm of the Catbus's twelve-legged stride without thinking of Lewis's passionate evocation of rough fur and soft footfalls padding through the blossoming glory of summer woods. Yet the magic that suffuses Narnia is different, more a subversion of nature than a celebration of it. Mei and Satsuki are not a pair of princesses riding on the back of Christ in a neo-Dionysian post-sacrificial celebration; they are a pair of ordinary children on a bus ride to see their mother and go home again. Miyazaki's magic does not need to take us into a hidden kingdom to show us wonders.

Lewis placed religion at the heart of his created universe; *My Neighbor Totoro*'s plot deliberately sidelines religion in favor of nature.

Because it's set in Japan, the trappings of rural religious tradition are clearly visible, but as far as the plot is concerned, they're decorative, not functional. Miyazaki uses religious iconography to send one clear signal, which will be lost on most American audiences: when Mei is lost, she sits at the feet of a row of statues. They are dedicated to a traditional Japanese deity who protects children, and this sends a

The tiny Totoro thinks that being invisible will save him, but Mei is hot on his tail and isn't going to let a little trick like that put her off the scent. She chases him around the flowering garden and under the house before finally pursuing him into the woods and right up to his own doorstep.

subliminal message to the audience that she will be safe. Elsewhere in the movie are roadside shrines to which the characters pay the respect that good manners and tradition demand. There are statues of foxes and protective deities, Shinto shrine gates, and ritual cords of rice straw and paper streamers around the trunk of the camphor tree, but none of this affects Totoro and the Catbus or the daily life of the forest creatures. Religion is a human construct and has nothing to do with nature. Nature spirits live outside it, creatures of simple goodwill who mean no harm.

The forest in which the movie takes place is firmly set in the real world, even though its world has now vanished. But like the movie's story it also has other, less tangible roots. It is an allegory of pastoral perfection, the longing for which goes all the way back to classical Greece and Rome when sophisticated writers and poets yearned for the peace and simplicity of rural life, and praised the simple virtues though their practice had been abandoned by most wealthy urbanites. Chinese literati were saying much the same thing long before the birth of Christ. That yearning has echoed through the literary ages in both Eastern and Western traditions.

American scholar Harold Bloom described *As You Like It* as the sweetest-tempered of Shakespeare's plays and its heroines as fortunate in living in an idyllic forest world in which "no authentic harm" could come to them.[11] Totoro's forest is just such a place of peace and simplicity, and from that peace and simplicity the movie derives its sweetness of temper. The forest is perfectly poised at the point in history in which a small community

can live comfortably and safely amid its wonders but still marvel at them and show no desire to dominate them or wipe them out. One could describe it as the balance point between *Princess Mononoke* and *Nausicaä*, before population pressure causes domestic exploitation to tip into wholesale destruction.

Though nature and its spirits can express themselves in hurricanes and howling winds, the struggle and spite of human society are unknown to them, and the natural cycle of life and death is essentially a cycle of goodwill. No harm will come to our two heroines in the forest's sunlit glades and mysterious shadows. They may be afraid sometimes when they glimpse the power and majesty around them, but it is the scale of the power itself they fear. They know instinctively that nature has no malice.

Like Satsuki's and Mei's childhood, the delicate balance of forest and farmland cannot last. The adult in the audience knows that in a few more years Tokyo will swamp the small fields and quiet lanes, while the child in the adult is glad that Miyazaki has kept them alive and beautiful, giving us, whatever happens to our world, the key to the door into summer.

THE CHARACTERS

Totoro Totoro is the name of the whole race of creatures in the film, though people usually mean the Big Totoro when they use the term. The middle-sized blue Totoro, first seen carrying an acorn sack and running from Mei, is Chu-Totoro (middle-sized Totoro) in the Japanese original, and the little white one is Chibi-Totoro (little Totoro).

Totoros are forest spirits who live in huge camphor trees. They are entirely an invention of Miyazaki's, though they have elements of folklore that enable people from many countries to recognize them. The name is Mei's mispronunciation of "troll"; she sees a picture of a troll in a storybook and thinks the Big Totoro looks like him. Totoros are very sensitive to feelings and atmospheres and are benign spirits, though they can be angry or annoyed at times. They can become invisible, though it seems that the little ones can't keep this up for very long, at least not with children. They learn fast, love music, and have very good manners—they return gifts and are as helpful and kind as possible. They are very old; the biggest Totoro may be as old as the forest itself.

The Dustbunnies

Called Susuwatari, or Traveling Soot, by Nanny, the Dustbunnies are tiny creatures that are very delicate and easily crushed, as Mei proves when she catches one unfortunate specimen. They live in old houses, and the arrival of humans with their laughter and noise drives them away. They are not at all harmful, but they do make things rather dirty, and Nanny says that only the very young can see them clearly.

Satsuki Kusakabe

Satsuki Kusakabe is ten years old and has short dark hair. Although she has to take a lot of responsibility for her baby sister now that their mother is in the hospital, she's a cheerful girl who makes friends easily and enjoys life. Only occasionally do we see the shyness that tells us that she's growing up and beginning to experience all the uncertainties of the teenage years. She's also very worried about her mother, and sometimes secretly fears that she may die of her illness. She does her best to help her father with domestic tasks such as cooking and laundry, and takes the main responsibility for looking after Mei while he's at work. She knows that whatever happens to her mother, she must soon leave childhood behind, and is still not entirely sure she wants to.

Mei Kusakabe

Mei Kusakabe is the four-year-old sister of Satsuki. She is an inquisitive and boisterous little redhead who is often naughty but never means any harm. Like most very small children, she doesn't have much sense of direction or memory, and isn't really aware of danger yet, so she easily gets lost if left alone. She likes to follow her big sister and imitate her, to be the center of attention, and to have the people she loves close by her. She loves food, loud noises, and new experiences. She often mispronounces words, a characteristic that was lost in the Fox American video release but may be reinstated in any future releases.

Professor and Mrs. Kusakabe

Mr. Kusakabe, a professor at the university in Tokyo, buys a country house and moves out of town with his small daughters to be closer to the hospital where his wife is convalescing. He is rather strange and absent-minded, doesn't brush his hair often enough to keep it tidy, gets up late, and forgets to eat his lunch when he's working, but he is a loving and devoted father and his girls adore him. Mrs. Kusakabe, his wife, is a serene, elegant woman who is patiently waiting for the time when the doctors say she

Satsuki enjoys having her hair brushed and hopes it will one day be as long and beautiful as Mother's. The Shichikokuyama hospital where Mother stayed in My Neighbor Totoro really existed, and was renowned for the treatment of tuberculosis. Although most of the people in the film wear modern clothing of the postwar era, Mother is dressed in a lightweight kimono.

can leave the hospital and go home. The pleasure she takes in doing small things, such as brushing Satsuki's hair, helps to build a picture of the strong family bond between the Kusakabes. Satsuki looks a lot like her.

Nanny

Nanny is an old lady whose family owns a farm nearby. She helped look after the house while it was empty, and keeps an eye on the Kusakabe children while their father is at work in Tokyo. Although she's very old, Nanny is still strong and healthy, able to clean the house and work in the rice fields as well as grow the most wonderful vegetables in her garden. Satsuki loves and trusts her, and it's to Nanny that she confides her fear that her mother might die in hospital.

Kanta

Kanta, the ten-year-old son of neighboring farmers, has the same attitude toward girls as most boys his age—half fascination and half teasing. Although he tries to adopt a cool, don't-care attitude and is very embarrassed if anyone suspects he has a softer side, he has a caring nature. He lends his umbrella to Mei and Satsuki when they are caught in the rain, but won't tell his mother about it and lets her think he lost it. When Mei is lost at the end of the film, he does his best to help Satsuki and the men who search for her.

The Catbus

The Catbus is exactly what it says—a cat that's a bus, or a bus that's a cat. It has six pairs of legs, though for delicate situations like running along electri-

city cables it just uses the front and back pair. Its huge eyes are brighter than any headlights, but it's helped out by taillights in the form of mice with glowing pink eyes, and a similar pair of mouselights illuminate its destination board. Naturally, it has a fur-lined interior with luxurious upholstery that matches the ginger-stripe exterior. Its huge smile and ability to vanish echo that of the Cheshire Cat. Like Totoro, it can only be seen by those with innocent hearts. Even if it runs right across the tracks in front of a tram, or passes so close to people that its speed ruffles their hair, they don't see it.

THE STORY

The film opens with a wonderful sequence of broken bricks, old boards, and all the creepy-crawlies that can lurk in an old house, drawn in a simple, childish style, with little Mei walking across the screen as the titles roll. Right at the end of the titles, we see a dust-bunny and a small white Totoro making their first brief appearances. As the story starts, Mei and Satsuki are crammed into the back of the truck as they bring their furniture and belongings to their new house in the country. They're moving to be near the hospital where their mother is being treated for a long illness. It's a glorious, sunny day and as they drive through woodlands and past little farms they wave to their new neighbors.

The new house is actually a very old house—so old that the boisterous children almost pull the porch down as they swing on its half-rotted timbers! The garden is huge and wild, with an overgrown pool and stone lantern, and behind the house they can see a huge tree, which they later learn is a camphor tree. As their father and the driver unload the truck, the girls race around the empty house, jumping on the traditional rush mats and generally getting underfoot, when much to Mei's surprise an acorn falls from the ceiling and lands beside her. Before she can puzzle over it too much, Father asks Satsuki to open up the kitchen door and they race off, hoping to catch a glimpse of dustbunnies.

Looking for the steps to the attic so that they can open the windows, they see another acorn bouncing down toward them, but upstairs they're more interested in catching dustbunnies. As Satsuki races downstairs, Mei lingers, convinced she can catch them, and sure enough one unfortunate straggler tries to make it to safety and is emphatically caught between two fat little palms. She races downstairs to show Satsuki her prize, but runs into Nanny. Suddenly shy, she hides behind her sister, and when she tries to show her the dustbunny, all that's left is a coating of soot on her palms. The girls both have sooty feet, and Nanny laughingly tells them how when she was a little girl she used to see dustbunnies too, but that they leave houses behind if there is life and laughter there.

As the cleaning and unpacking go on, Satsuki meets a boy with a lunch basket at the kitchen door. He's one of the people she saw on the way in, but he won't speak, just pushes the basket at her and runs off, then stands at the end of the garden and makes a rude face at

her. It's Kanta, their neighbor's son. They finish unpacking, eat lunch, and finally the family is alone in their new home. Going out to the woodpile to get fuel for the boiler, Satsuki is momentarily scared by the wind as it tears powerfully across the grass, and by the strangeness of the unfamiliar landscape and its night noises. In the bath, the girls follow their father's example and laugh to scare away any evil spirits or lingering dustbunnies. As the family sleeps, we see a cloud of dustbunnies floating into the sky, heading for the peace and quiet of the camphor tree.

Next morning the girls help their father with the laundry; then they all set out on his bike to visit Mother. It's a long journey to Shichikokuyama Hospital, and on the way they pass Nanny and their other neighbors at work in the fields. Kanta is helping out too, and pulls another face at Satsuki. At the hospital, Father goes to speak to the doctor and Mei throws herself at Mother, but Satsuki hangs back a little until Mother compliments her on how well she's tied her sister's ponytails and offers to brush her hair for her. By the time Father comes in the three are laughing together, and as they head for home he tells the girls that Mother may be allowed home soon for a visit.

Next day, as Satsuki heads off to school and Father settles down to some research work, Mei plays in the garden. At first she just wanders around enjoying all the new sights and sounds, but it isn't long before she finds a whole trail of shiny golden acorns on the path. Following the trail, she reaches some long grass. Two white ears are showing over the top of it. A little creature who only reaches to

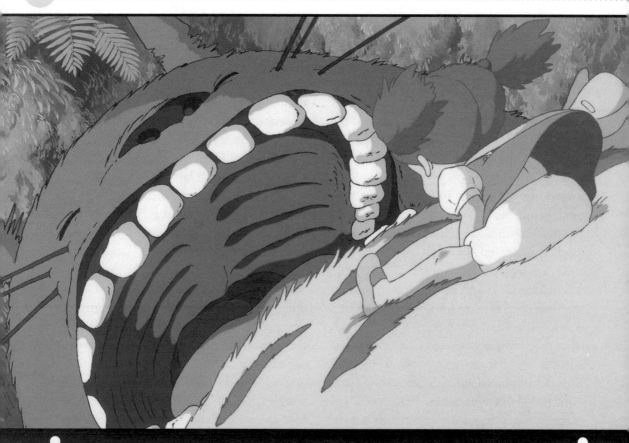

Bouncing on Totoro's furry chest, Mei looks gleefully down into a mouth that could swallow a small car as he yawns loudly. She is completely unafraid, and although the huge creature can shake trees with his roar, he's as gentle as a father with the little girl.

Mei's knees comes scurrying out. Once he realizes he's being followed he vanishes, but he can't shake her that easily, and can't seem to stay invisible either. A comical chase follows, with Mei trailing him under the old house and finally seeming to lose him. But as he sneaks out, with a slightly larger blue companion carrying a sack of acorns, the sound of acorns dropping from a hole in the sack alerts their relentless pursuer and the chase is on again. Mei follows them into the bushes, up a tunnel between the roots, and loses them again at the base of the giant camphor tree. Then, seeing the gleam of an acorn lodged in a crack in the tree trunk, she leans over to reach it and falls all the way down inside the tree, landing with a thump on the moss beside a huge, soft, furry form.

Inside the tree is a beautiful, enclosed world where flowers bloom and butterflies play. The big furry thing is asleep—but not for long. Mei climbs onto his belly, tickles his nose, is delighted when he opens a mouth the size of a garage, and roars right back at him. Sensing that she is a force of nature like himself, the giant settles back to sleep, and soon Mei is asleep on his massive chest. As peace descends once more, two rather nervous-looking little creatures, one white and one blue, emerge from their hiding place under a big leaf.

Satsuki and Father realize she is missing and search for her, finding her asleep in a little clearing amid the roots of the bushes. She tells them about her adventure, naming the creature she met Totoro, but, much to her despair, can't find the entrance to the tree trunk again. But Father assures her that they don't think she's lying, and tells her that although meeting the King of the Forest was a very great honor, she can't expect him to always be available. The family makes a formal visit to the camphor tree to say thank you to the forest spirit for looking after Mei, and that night Satsuki writes to her mother about her sister's adventure. At the very top of the great tree, we see the three Totoros playing their ocarinas under a silvery moon.

When Father has to go to work, Mei is left with Nanny while Satsuki goes to school, but after a while Nanny has to bring her to the school gates, saying she insists on being with her sister. Much to Satsuki's embarrassment, Mei sits beside her in class for the rest of the day. On the way home, the pair are caught in a sudden downpour. Kanta kindly, though gracelessly, lends them his old umbrella and they make it home safely. Realizing that Father has left his own umbrella at the house, Satsuki decides to meet him with it and return Kanta's on the way—much to his mother's surprise, since she was convinced he'd lost it. Then the girls go on to the bus stop in the forest.

The bus comes, but Father isn't on it. Satsuki decides to wait for the next one. It's very quiet—just the forest sounds—and Mei is bored and a little nervous at the strange sights and sounds, but too stubborn to go and wait in the safety of Nanny's house. As they wait, it grows darker, and the lamp above the bus stop comes on. A cyclist creaks by, a dim shape in the darkness under his raincoat. Mei is asleep on her feet, so Satsuki gives her a piggy-back so that she can doze and the umbrella can cover both of them. Then Satsuki hears light footsteps and the scritch-scritch sounds of claws. Peering under the rim of her umbrella, she sees furry, clawed feet under a huge body. It's Totoro, come to join them in the line for the bus.

Awed, she looks up, and they exchange the shy, brief greetings of polite strangers. He has a leaf hat on his head and the rain is hitting his nose, so Satsuki lends him Father's umbrella, as a polite stranger might. As Totoro listens to the noise of the rain dripping through the trees onto the stretched fabric, a wonderful possibility dawns on him, and we see his face split into a delighted grin as he leaps up. As he lands, the impact of his huge bulk shakes every drop of water off the trees. His roar of pleasure wakes Mei just as the lights of the bus appear out of the darkness.

But it isn't Father's bus. The girls stare in disbelief, a little scared but mostly stunned, as a huge, furry, multi-legged cat skids to a halt and opens a door in its side. Gravely, Totoro hands them a leaf-wrapped parcel and boards his bus. It roars off over the countryside, leaving the girls bemused—and then Satsuki realizes Totoro still has Father's umbrella. Luckily the rain has stopped, and when Father arrives on the next bus just moments later, they have an amazing tale to tell him as they walk home through the summer night.

Satsuki tells Mother all about it in her next letter, with news of the seeds in the package and how Mei is crouching over them waiting for them to grow. They're slower than she would like, but then most things are when you're four. One night as Father sits working, the girls are roused from sleep by the sound of a magical dance. All three Totoros are danc-

The Catbus sets off across the countryside with no regard for the rules of the road. Although it often passes close enough to send a breeze through people's hair, adults never seem to see it.

ing around the trench where the seeds were planted, borrowed umbrella and leaf stems wielded like totems, raising the seeds. The girls join them, and in a spellbinding sequence they raise a huge tree from the soil, its soaring crown sheltering and protecting the house.

The life-giving power of the earth has been unleashed, and Satsuki and Mei are part of it. Then Totoro, who has proved very light on his feet for such a huge creature, unleashes a spinning top and hops onto it as it hovers above the ground, balanced like a dancer on one foot. His two small brothers leap onto his chest, and Mei follows suit, clinging to the thick fur. Satsuki hangs back, but he encourages her with a beautiful smile and she joins them. They soar up above the great tree, roaring into the sky on a magical tour of the familiar woods and fields made strange by night. At last, under the light of the full moon, they sit in the branches of the tree they raised, playing on ocarinas with their neighbors the Totoros. Down below in the house, Father hears a strange music; it must be the hooting of owls. Next morning, the huge tree is gone but the seeds have sprouted. Totoro has let them see the future grow and has taught them that time is only perception.

Helping Nanny in her garden the next day, the girls are happily anticipating Mother's promised visit home and planning to feed her Nanny's fresh produce to make her strong again when a telegram arrives. It says they have to call Mother's doctor right away. In a panic, Satsuki rushes to Kanta's house to use the phone, and Mei insists on following, clutching an ear of Nanny's golden corn that she means to keep for Mother. In all the panic

she gets lost, and while Satsuki phones Father at the university she is wandering the lanes of the village, defending Mother's corn from a threatening goat and feeling anxious and afraid. When she finally catches up with Satsuki and Kanta they are walking back from his house. Father called the hospital and Mother can't come home this weekend. Mei can't accept this and she and Satsuki have a tearful argument that ends in Satsuki storming off alone, abandoning her baby sister and leaving a baffled Kanta to make sure she gets home. Nanny tries to comfort Satsuki when she expresses her fears, but Mei has had enough of waiting and wants action. Grabbing her corn, she sets off to find the hospital and give it to Mother. Maybe it will help her get better...

When Nanny and Satsuki realize she has gone, they hunt all over the garden, then Satsuki realizes that she might have tried to head for the hospital. Since it would take a grown man about three hours to walk there, Satsuki sets off to see if she can catch her on the road, while Nanny sends Kanta to tell his father and organize a search. Satsuki races through the beautiful countryside for hours, asking the few people she meets if they have seen a little girl alone, but no one can help her. Kanta catches up with her on a big old bike and sends her rushing back to the lake where a child's sandal has been found, while he heads on toward the hospital, just in case. When Satsuki arrives to find the men of the village dragging the lake with poles she is distraught, but the lost sandal is not one of Mei's. As the adults discuss the next step of the search all around her, she suddenly has an idea. So far, none of the neighbors has been able to help her, but she knows one who might.

Racing through the tunnel in the roots, she finds that the secret entrance to the tree is open and dives into Totoro's world. She is too scared and desperate to register its beauty, but as she blurts out the problem in a panic, one huge claw wraps around her and Totoro hugs her to his chest with a warm reassuring smile. Then they go flying again, up through the hollow trunk to the top of the tree, and with another mighty roar Totoro summons the Catbus. As it races across the fields and skids to a halt beside them on top of the tree, he grins again, almost smugly, delighted that he can help his little friends. He ushers her onto the bus, and as she sinks into the warm furry seats, the signboard changes to show their destination—Mei. The bus sets off, with Totoro waving and smiling, and Satsuki's anxiety gradually subsides as she begins to enjoy the fantastic journey. When they find Mei sitting forlornly by a line of old statues, the sisters fall into each other's arms, all differences forgotten, and the kindly Catbus, with a grin as warm as Totoro's, offers to help her complete her journey and leave her gift for Mother.

At the hospital, Father and Mother are talking by the open window. She had only caught a chill, and the hospital was being overly cautious; her homecoming has just been postponed a little. The children and the Catbus sit in a huge pine tree outside her window, and as they look on Father finds the corn on the window ledge, the words "To Mother" scratched on its husk. Just for an instant, Mother thinks she can see Satsuki and Mei smiling down at her from the trees.

Side by side, the sisters enjoy a wonderful journey home on the back seat of the Catbus, and the grinning cat perches on the roof of their house to watch them meeting Nanny and Kanta with hugs and kisses before he vanishes into the warm summer night. As they walk back to meet Father, the last frame of the film shows all three Totoros on the roof, watching benignly. The end credits roll over a series of still images showing us a happy future—Mother coming home for good, Satsuki and Mei enjoying life among their friends in the village. The Totoros are there too, playing in the forest, but Satsuki and Mei will not meet them again. Now that their mother is home and their world is safe once more, they no longer need the protection of the forest spirits.

COMMENTARY

My Neighbor Totoro possesses one of the strongest critical commendations in film history: It was among the relatively few Japanese films on director Akira Kurosawa's list of his hundred best movies of all time, along with such world classics as Gloria and My Darling Clementine.[12] Kurosawa said he was very moved by the film, and particularly loved the Catbus, but he also lamented that all the talents he wanted to see in the movie industry had gone into animation. There are, it is true, not enough fine directors of film, but there are even fewer fine directors of animation. Anyone who can make a movie as honest, beau-

FILMOGRAPHY AND PERSONNEL

My Neighbor Totoro

Tonari no Totoro

Theatrical release, 16 April 1988

RUNNING TIME: 1 hour, 27 minutes

Original story by Hayao Miyazaki

DIRECTOR, PRODUCER, SCREENPLAY: Hayao Miyazaki

ANIMATION DIRECTOR: Yoshiharu Sato

BACKGROUNDS: Kazuo Oga

MUSIC: Jo Hisaishi

EXECUTIVE PRODUCER: Yasuyoshi Tokuma

© Nibariki, Tokuma Shoten

Limited 1993 U.S. theatrical release on 50th Street Films/Troma, 1994 U.S. video release on Fox Video Family Feature. Possible U.S. release by the Disney organization is yet to be announced as this book goes to press.

U.K. theatrical screening of U.S. dubbed version 1991 at the Barbican Centre, London, as part of the Japan Festival.

Limited satellite TV release in the U.K., 1995–96.

tiful, and benign as *My Neighbor Totoro* must be cherished, because movies like this are very, very rare. In animation, though, they're even rarer. Miyazaki is one of the few contemporary makers of animation who truly respects his audience, his material, and his medium.

My Neighbor Totoro exhibits a level of attention to detail that is exceptional even in the Ghibli canon. I've watched the movie many times, and every time I find my attention caught by fleeting moments of perfection. Most recently, I was struck by a two-second shot in the opening sequence of the little family's arrival at their new home. We cut from a wide view of flooded rice paddies being tended and scenes of the day-to-day activity of a farming community to a close-up view of water gleaming as it runs quietly over a stone in a little stream. That tiny image shows a level of technical mastery that commands respect— the convincing naturalistic animation of water is a difficult task, and one at which Ghibli excels. More importantly, it sets up a link between the particular and the general, between the little natural stream and the ordered work of the farmers, between beauty and utility. And most important of all, it makes you catch your breath at its simple, perfect loveliness.

There are many such naturalistic images to marvel at. In the sequence in which the girls meet their neighbor Totoro at the bus stop, a golden brown toad is allowed to take its own time in progressing across the frame, and grounds that marvelous encounter with a huge final belch, its gaping mouth echoing Totoro's own smile. As a long afternoon fades, a snail crawls up a grass stem, perfect against the golden light. Mei bends over the garden pool and is enchanted, like us, by the irrepressible wriggle of tadpoles through the water. In Nanny's garden, a basket of vegetables put into the stream to cool is hauled out glistening, making our mouths water in anticipation of the ripe meat of the tomatoes and the crispness of the cucumbers. And which artist painstakingly practiced scratching a message on a corn husk, to be able to render it so perfectly in the last hospital scene? The everyday magic of life is depicted with a depth of love

and respect that cannot help but touch the most determined urbanite.

The other magic, the mystery of nature and its legendary manifestations, is linked with this through a series of images that, by accepting the presence of the supernatural as part of the natural, make us accept it on the level of a child. Seeing as the young protagonists see is a vital step toward entering Totoro's world, and Miyazaki uses the contrast between darkness and light effectively to blur the bound-

Seated by a line of statues, Mei wonders what to do now that she's well and truly lost. The statues represent a Buddhist deity who takes care of all children, so the Japanese audience knows she'll be okay. Help is on its way down the telephone lines that crisscross the Japanese landscape, forming a useful shortcut for the Catbus.

aries between the real and the mysterious, the predictable and the uncertain. When the light floods in to the darkened attic upstairs, we can see the little bits of darkness fleeing into the corners, and share the girls' fascination with the dustbunnies. Darkness under our control is fascinating, even charming. When Satsuki steps outside the back door at night to get some more fuel for the boiler that's heating the bathwater, the wind rushes wildly across the grass, and for a few moments the familiar landscape is transformed into something strange and menacing. Its shape shifts out of the natural and toward the formless, and its colors are subdued and changed by the darkness so that instead of grass and sky and solid ground we might be surrounded by deep water or the swirling nothingness of a nightmare. Darkness all around us, out of control, can be scary. Kazuo Oga's wonderful backgrounds are as effective at conveying abstraction as hyperrealism.

Jo Hisaishi's score is a work of magic. Taking elements as disparate as playground songs and orchestral chorales, he has created a perfect counterpoint to the film's visual splendors. There is much playfulness—the Catbus theme is an eight-bar boogie-woogie any jazzman could pick up on and relish, and the opening theme is infuriatingly infectious. I can testify to this: returning from a visit to Studio Ghibli, I was crossing a road in Shinjuku in the evening rush hour when a boy of about seven and his sister, perhaps a couple of years older, passed me going the other way. As we drew level, the boy sang out the first few lines of the *Totoro* opening theme loud and clear.

Hisaishi's score also demonstrates that he understands the power of silence, a much neglected element in contemporary Western cinema. The whole soundtrack is well planned in this regard. The relationship of natural background sounds, such as wind and the chirping of crickets, dialogue, and music, is perfectly balanced to enhance the imagery. Just as places and objects can be changed by darkness, so can sound. Is that an owl hooting, or a spirit playing its clay pipe in the treetops? Is that rustling in the attic a squirrel, or a ghost, or something really horrid—like a rat? The fun of making sound, the pleasure it gives to small children, is emphasized. When Totoro roars, the sound waves bend trees and shake rocks; no wonder Mei wants to roar too, to join in the fun of creating such an impressive noise. When Totoro leaps joyously into the air at the bus stop, his face split in a grin of anticipation, we are partly—but only partly—prepared for the wonderful shock of the cannonade of falling water onto his borrowed umbrella. We experience that glorious noise as gleefully as children, thanks to the careful balance of low-key night sounds and silence throughout the preceding scene.

The relationships within the movie work to emphasize the theme of goodwill and neighborliness. The family depicted in *My Neighbor Totoro* is one of the sanest and sunniest on film. Professor Kusakabe is a good husband and father: loving, supportive, perhaps a little absent-minded, but a wonderful companion and a rock-solid source of support in times of trouble. His wife is a woman of good sense and good temper, and although she is away from her family her influence is obvious. This was the first time that Miyazaki had portrayed an ordinary, happy family, and it is a charming portrait. The strength that sustains the girls' happy childhood is obvious, and the stress of their mother's illness, a threat that Satsuki recognizes with dread and Mei is only dimly aware of, is the one real shadow over the film's joyous world.

The two scenes that originally worried American distributors are integral to the film, though for a Western audience one may be problematic. In every culture in the world, children love to run around empty houses and make noise, so although Americans may not realize that jumping up and down on handmade, traditional tatami mats can seem shocking to the Japanese, they will understand the excitement and energy expressed in that scene. The bathtub sequence, in which father and his daughters share a traditional Japanese family bath, may raise worries for some but could provide a valuable point for discussion with children about appropriate and inappropriate actions and relationships, about setting their own limits with adults, and about deciding what is and is not right for them. I will only add that it is a sad culture that can see nothing in a father's loving relationship with his children but the potential for abuse.

Satsuki is a fascinating character. Miyazaki was to approach the problems of the transition into adult life in more detail in *Kiki's Delivery Service*; in Satsuki, he gives us a delightful portrait of a child not yet ready to start moving into the adult world, but with some of its responsibilities forced on her by circumstance. Unlike Sheeta in *Castle in the Sky*, she is not alone in the world or pressured into adult difficulties and decisions, but she has begun to

realize that such things do happen. When Satsuki hangs back a little as Mei leaps into her mother's arms, or hesitates before accepting Totoro's unspoken invitation to fly with him, she is expressing our own fears that leaving childhood behind means leaving spontaneity and unconditional delight as the province of the young. Her mother's love and Nanny's wisdom show her that there are pleasures ahead, as well as duties and responsibilities; but it is Totoro who tells her, and us, that flinging caution to the winds and flying off on a spinning top can be fun at any age.

Mei, on the other hand, is the natural child, almost a spirit herself in her blithe disregard for the world's tedious detail. She is still at the age when her own wants, needs, and reactions can legitimately form the center of her universe without turning her into a monster. In the same way that Mei imitates Satsuki, hoping for her sister's experience to rub off, the small Totoro imitates his giant brother, holding a leaf umbrella aloft, piping on a little ocarina. The cycle of life continues through young and old. Mei, Satsuki, Mother, and Nanny form a composite image of the development of female warmth, strength, and grace, adding a human rhythm to the natural cycle of growth and fertility around them.

All the sophistication and intelligence that Miyazaki and his team bring to *My Neighbor Totoro* is devoted to the most difficult task for any artist: to create a work that appears as simple and natural as breathing. A doctor or scientist understands the complex mechanisms of physical and chemical exchange that keep the human organism's lungs at work; a child only knows that it breathes in and out and can float dandelion seeds and feathers on its breath. To draw in their young audience, and to enable the rest of us to enter Totoro's rich and complex world in the spirit of childhood, the director and his staff have made a world that works—down to the smallest detail. We don't think of it as art; we accept it as life.

In comparison to the complexity of the visual world and the density of the relationships, the plot appears as slight as a dandelion seed, but this slightness is heroically deceptive. Mei and Satsuki are on a quest as compelling as any fantasy hero's journey; they are seeking the magic in their everyday world. The treasure they win will be the ability to find that magic, whatever circumstance or experience may hide it. The sequence of seemingly unconnected incidents subtly escalates the level of the quest—from Mei's accidental discovery of Totoro's world through his casually stepping into their world to catch a bus; his showing them the miracle of life; and Satsuki's fears of

In the trees outside the hospital, Satsuki and Mei watch with their friend the Catbus as Mother talks to Daddy about the delay in her home visit. Now that they can see she's well, the two girls are happy again.

life being taken away, first from her beloved mother and then from her little sister. At the moment of resolution, when Satsuki has found Mei and the two have seen for themselves that Mother is safe, the power of love pierces the blinds on adult eyes that keep us from seeing magic. Just for a moment, Mother thinks she can see her children smiling at her from the trees outside her hospital window. Few heroes achieve such triumph.

The pace that seems slow to those fixated on fast cuts and fast action is dictated both by nature and by childhood. Time is cunningly telescoped; days are elided through devices like Satsuki's writing to Mother at night, Mother reading the letter in the next cut, then back to Father putting up the mosquito nets to protect them from bites while they sleep. Time used to vanish like that when we were children. Events were mysterious—it seemed as if the seeds we buried would never sprout, then, suddenly, as if by magic, there were plants in the once-bare soil. Miyazaki has the supreme courage to let the movie grow at a pace that suits its purpose, and trusts his audience to walk with it.

My *Neighbor Totoro* is both my favorite Miyazaki work and my favorite film. Its apparent simplicity masks a depth of wisdom and grace found in few works for any medium. It is accessible to even the youngest child, yet it respects the intelligence of the most literate and cultivated adult.

If you don't believe me, take your children to see it. They'll convince you. It worked for Gene Siskel.

6

KIKI'S
DELIVERY
SERVICE

The Quest for
Confidence

In another world that looks much as ours did thirty years ago, a teenage girl sets out to make her way in life, full of hope and enthusiasm but with only one skill to offer. Kiki can fly—well, she's a witch, after all—but she's never been away from her loving parents and their quiet country home. Out there in the big city there are new people and new challenges to meet, but life can be scary as well as exciting, and when you're far away from everyone who knows and loves you, you have to make your own friends and find your own way. Using only "girl power," Kiki learns to make her own happiness and success.

ORIGINS

In 1989, after the modest success of My Neighbor Totoro and Grave of the Fireflies the previous summer and with little indication as yet of Totoro's merchandising potential, Studio Ghibli launched its new movie. Based on a successful Japanese children's book by Eiko Kadono, the film was written and directed by Miyazaki, who had originally planned to act solely as producer but found himself drawn further into the project when the script produced by a junior colleague didn't seem to him to capture the spirit of the hoped-for audience of preteen and teenage girls. The young director proposed for the project felt intimidated at the thought of working on Miyazaki's script, so Miyazaki had no option but to direct it himself.

Castle in the Sky had been a boy's adventure, My Neighbor Totoro a child's dream of summer. Kiki's Delivery Service was intended from the beginning as a film for young girls. In his English-language foreword to The Art of Kiki's Delivery Service, Miyazaki wrote of the difficulties facing young girls as they strive for independence and self-determination while they are still close to the dependency and safety of childhood. Interestingly, he also compared the heroine's situation explicitly with that of young people trying to break into the animation industry:

> This is like someone who wants to be a cartoonist coming alone to Tokyo. Today, there are said to be around 300,000 young men and women who are hoping to make it as cartoonists. Being a cartoonist is not that unusual

a job. It is comparatively easy to get started and to make some sort of living. But a characteristic of modern life is that once the needs of daily life are taken care of, the real problem of self-realization begins. . . . In Kiki's life we see reflected the lives of so many young Japanese girls today who are loved and supported economically by their parents, but who long for the bright lights of the city, and are about to go there and become independent. The weakness of her determination and shallowness of her understanding are also reflected in the world of today's young people.[1]

There is an unusual alarm call as Kiki realizes that her bed is actually someone else's breakfast! Having set off from home, she's been sheltering from the storm in a cattle truck, and now that cozy bed of hay is being munched from beneath by the truck's rightful occupants.

Kiki tries on the traditional witch's dress her mother has made for her, and wishes it were a little bit prettier. "Any color as long as it's black" is as true for witches as it was for Henry Ford. The detail of her country home is beautifully depicted in this scene.

A student of children's literature since his college days, Miyazaki considered Kadono's book "a fine work of children's literature warmly depicting the gulf that exists between independence and reliance in the hopes and spirit of contemporary Japanese girls."[2] However, he needed to transform it into a story that would support a feature-length film. The original novel is episodic and lighthearted. Kiki meets with no terrible challenges or traumas, she has no crisis of self-belief like the one in the movie, and the dramatic end sequence with the airship is missing altogether. In a movie for young people, the hero needs to grow through vivid, dramatic struggle and loneliness.

While a book can operate on a smaller, quieter scale and still win an audience, a movie heroine who has to attract teenage girls to the cinema needs some drama in her life. However, the original author was so unhappy with the proposed changes to her work that it took the combined persuasive powers of Miyazaki and Isao Takahata to prevent her from pulling the plug on the project before it got past the screenplay stage.

She wasn't the only one with an ax to grind. Her title had borrowed the trademark name of the Yamato Transport Company for their new door-to-door delivery service, and also alluded to their black cat logo. The company was not happy about this unauthorized borrowing. More diplomacy from Takahata smoothed out the problems and Yamato became one of the film's sponsors. In the end, both the author and the company gained from their association with the movie; a sequel to the novel followed with great success, and the company attracted much favorable publicity.

An English-language dub was commissioned by Tokuma from Carl Macek and shown on Japan Airlines' trans-Pacific flights. The proposed script translation was submitted to Tokuma for Miyazaki's personal approval and changes were made to his satisfaction before the dub was recorded.[3] However, when Disney decided to make the film their first World Animation Classics release in 1998, they commissioned a whole new dub for the Buena Vista Home Video version. Despite fan speculation that this was a plot by the Mighty Mouse and its minions to somehow diminish the work of a studio widely perceived as superior, Disney honored both letter and spirit of their contract with Tokuma, hiring a respected cast under the direction of overdub veteran Jack Fletcher. There were some additional lines of incidental dialogue, and some music changes, but nothing was done without ap-

proval from Studio Ghibli. The Disney press release for the movie quotes Michael O. Johnson, president of Buena Vista Home Entertainment Worldwide, Inc., a prime mover in the deal, as saying the Disney organization had "become a caretaker for this wonderful animation on a worldwide basis, but we don't want to alter it. You don't want to take the Mona Lisa and make her smile. It is our responsibility to deliver these products as they were meant to be delivered."

Just like the heroine's venture into the wide world outside her home, the movie's American release has met with success and helped build confidence in this kind of adventure on both sides. *Kiki's Delivery Service* has sold strongly, garnered critical acclaim, and appeared at or near the top of a number of video charts and awards listings.

The only truly negative aspect of Kiki's transoceanic adventure has been an attempt by an organization called the Concerned Women for America to have the film boycotted. Writing in *Variety* magazine, Ken Eisner describes them as "a right-wing group" that is "accusing Disney of promoting 'divination' and denigrating family values. . . . They cite *Fantasia* and *Peter Pan* as earlier evidence of Uncle Walt's 'darker agenda.'"[4] However, the vast majority of parents whose children have seen the film regard it as a positive influence.

Entertainment Weekly asked, "Are American audiences ready for films that, as the director once said in a rare interview, try to express the idea that 'the world is profound, manifold, and beautiful?'"[5] It would seem that the answer is yes.

ART AND TECHNIQUE

In preparation for filming, Miyazaki and his senior staff went to Sweden to take pictures. It was a return visit for the director, who had accompanied Mr. Fujioka of Tokyo Movie Shinsha there in the 1970s on his fruitless attempt to secure series rights to *Pippi Longstocking.* Sweden left a strong impression on Miyazaki, and on his return trip he and his team shot eighty rolls of film in Visby and Stockholm. The town of Koriko, where Kiki settles, has elements of many cities—Naples, Paris, Lisbon, Amsterdam, and even San Francisco have been put forward by those who feel they recognize a favorite street corner—but Stockholm is the primary inspiration. Miyazaki said that one side of the town looked as if it bordered the Baltic Sea and the other side the Mediterranean.[6] The influence of the seaside setting on the film's glowing summer light is evident, and the movie harks back to *Castle of Cagliostro,* and forward to *Porco Rosso,* in its evocation of perfect summers in romantic Europe. Koriko has expansive squares and parks, dignified public buildings, fascinating little side streets, quiet residential enclaves, and green suburbs on the outskirts of town. Once again, Miyazaki creates the dream of Europe as it never was but should have been.

The story's time frame and technology are also a mishmash. Miyazaki sets the story in a mythical version of the 1950s in which, he says, World War II did not take place.[7] Young people are losing respect for their elders in town—witness Madame's ungrateful granddaughter—but in the country communities still revolve around traditional relationships and ideas of mutual help. The buildings of Koriko include 1960s tower blocks, eighteenth-century villas with their old bread ovens still in place in the kitchen, and square town houses. Cars are reminiscent of the 1940s, television is black and white, and the shops have the kind of traditionally genteel air found in the better quarters of Europe's capitals. When Kiki gazes longingly at a pair of snappy red shoes, they are not in the window of a trendy boutique but an elegant shop with a discreetly uncluttered window display that today's young girls would pass by without a glance.

The technology sidelined when the Hindenberg crashed in our world is still around in Kiki's, with airships a major feature of the aviation scene. Kiki's new friend Tombo is building his own flying machine, and his ideas of technology don't seem to have advanced much from Pazu's 1890s version in *Castle in the Sky.* Tombo envies Kiki's ability to soar like a bird seemingly without effort, but he also likes her as herself—something she is at first too shy and self-conscious to appreciate. He is fascinated by the mechanics of what makes flight possible, whereas to Kiki it's simply an ability she possesses but has never questioned. As Miyazaki points out, there have been a number of Japanese cartoons about little witches, but their magical powers have given them the ability to fulfill all their dreams and become idols. Kiki's talent is not of that order—it's "really little more than that possessed by any real-life girl."[8] When her inherited magical talent fails her, she has to work at converting her limited innate ability into a viable, marketable skill.

All spruced up in his best suit, Tombo shelters under the bakery awning as he waits for Kiki to get back from work so he can take her to a party. She misses her very first date because she's been held up making her delivery, and catches a bad cold when she gets drenched in the rain on her way home. Notice the delicious display of bread in the window behind him—good enough to eat!

She also has to learn that she is more than just a witch. If she defines herself only by her ability to fly, she may miss all the other experiences the adult world has to offer—going to parties, making friends, helping people in other ways, and using other skills like her knack with an old-fashioned oven. Her ability to fly gives her freedom to go wherever she will and see the world from a unique viewpoint, but it's a lonely viewpoint. It cuts her off from most of her fellow humans and isolates her high in the sky with her cat as her only companion—an icon, not a girl. She must learn to create her own independence, not simply rely on her heritage or her family but carve out her own relationships and survival strategies. Kiki has to choose and earn her wings if they are to be part of her new, independent life.

Jo Hisaishi provides another beautiful and varied score, though it was altered somewhat for the U.S. release. The Japanese opening and ending songs, *Rouge no Dengon* ("Message in Rouge") and *Yasashisa ni Tsutsumareta Nara* ("If I've Been Enveloped by Tenderness") are 1970s golden oldies written and sung by Yumi Arai. Affectionately known as Yuming, she was one of the most popular Japanese singer/songwriters of the time. In the Disney dub, the opening and ending songs *Soaring* and *I'm Gonna Fly* were written and performed by Sydney Forest. Those who want to hear the originals might be in luck: at the time of this writing it is planned that Buena Vista's English-subtitled video release will retain Yumi Arai's work.

THE CHARACTERS

Kiki

Kiki is just thirteen, a cheerful girl who loves clothes (she even asks her mother to shorten the skirt of her traditional witch's dress!), laughing with her friends, and listening to her radio. She is friendly and outgoing but when she leaves the security of her home she finds that her confidence is less solid than she believed. Her kind heart and good manners help her make new friends, and thanks to them she broadens her horizons and discovers new depths of determination and courage she never knew she possessed. She also realizes that people like her for herself, not just for what she can do, and that she can enrich her life if she opens her heart to people and experiences.

Jiji

Jiji has been raised with Kiki, as is the custom for a witch's cat, and at the beginning of the film they can understand each other's speech. They remain deeply attached to each other, but as time passes and they each grow more independent and form new relationships, this instinctive understanding vanishes and they both have to work at their partnership. Jiji is a cat with a practical streak and a strong sense of irony, and his help and companionship is invaluable to Kiki as she takes her first steps in her new life. He's also ready for new experiences himself, and in the course of the film he changes from a wisecracking cat-about-town to a responsible father.

Mother and Father

Mother and Father are a happy couple who are devoted to each other and their young daughter. Father is an ordinary human; Mother is a witch who came to their town to earn her wings, just as her daughter does. Mother's skill is in making pills and potions and in healing, and the townspeople trust her to cure their aches and pains. The pair do their best to prepare their daughter for the adventure of living independently, but not even the assurance of their enduring love can spare Kiki the pains and anxieties involved in growing toward independence.

Ursula's artistic hand catches Kiki's spirit of adventure as the two sit in Ursula's forest cabin. The drawing becomes a painting, which in reality was designed for the movie Kiki's Delivery Service by a special group of children from a school for challenged youngsters.

Osono

Osono is a warm and kind-hearted woman who is expecting her first baby, and her strong maternal instincts extend to helping Kiki find a start in her new life. She runs a bakery shop. Her husband, the baker, is as kind-hearted as she is but very quiet and reserved. The couple are won over by Kiki's kindness and determination, and encourage her to try and overcome her difficulties.

Ursula

Ursula is a young artist a few years older than Kiki who lives alone in a cabin in the woods some distance from the city. She befriends Kiki when she is trying to find and repair the lost toy cat. When Kiki loses her confidence, a visit to Ursula's cabin in the woods helps her find her focus again. As she sits for Ursula's painting, Kiki starts to think again about her own skills and how she uses them. Ursula's greater con-

Kiki goes above and beyond the call of duty when she arrives to collect a package for delivery and ends up baking the contents herself! Her customer, a sweet old lady, wants to send a pie to her granddaughter's birthday party but the modern oven has broken down. Country girl Kiki knows how to use the old-fashioned baking oven set into the kitchen wall, and her kindness saves the day and makes her a new friend.

fidence and experience of life provide inspiration and support for her young friend.

Tombo

Tombo is a real plane freak and wants to build his own flying machines. He's also a warm, caring boy who is concerned about Kiki and her feelings not just because she can fly but because he likes her.

He's persistent, ingenious, and determined— how many guys would go to such lengths to get a date with their chosen girl?

Madame

Madame is a lovely, gracious lady who lives with her devoted maid in an old house in town. She's very kind and considerate and is impressed by

Kiki's ingenuity with the old bread oven and her willingness to go to a lot of trouble in order to help someone out while still staying cheerful.

THE STORY

Kiki is just thirteen. She lives with her mother and father in a lovely, rambling old house on the outskirts of a friendly little town, and she wants to be a witch, just like her mother before her. This is perfectly usual—witchcraft is an inherited skill in this world that is very like ours, but not exactly the same. Girls born into a witch family don't win their wings—or their broomsticks—easily. Instead, they have to leave home at the age of thirteen and live for a whole year in another town, one that doesn't have its own magical practitioner, supporting themselves by their witch's powers. Kiki's mother has healing powers and makes wonderful potions on which all the people of the district rely—but Kiki's only magical talent is an ability to fly. And she isn't always too steady on takeoffs... but at least she has her black cat. Kiki and Jiji have been raised together from infancy and they can understand each other perfectly. As long as Kiki has Jiji at her side, she'll always have a friend.

Kiki puts her radio and her savings into a small bundle, dons the new black witch's dress her mother made for this great occasion, and sets off with Jiji on Mother's old broom. Her family and friends all gather to wave her off, and she's full of enthusiasm as she flies high

over the countryside. Even an encounter with a snooty older apprentice witch doesn't put her off, but when rain hits she is glad to find shelter in a freight train full of friendly cows who don't begrudge her a warm bed of hay. Next morning, the rain is gone and she spots Koriko, a beautiful city gleaming like a jewel on the edge of the sea. A friendly local workman, winding the clock in the great tower, tells her there's no witch in town. Kiki has found her new home.

At first the city looks very exciting, but wandering around the streets in search of a room, Kiki finds herself ignored, jostled, and even getting into trouble with the police! One boy seems friendly but she's too shy to ask him for help and ignores his overtures. She's beginning to despair of finding a place to stay before nightfall when she stops on the terrace of a baker's shop and sees a chance to help the pregnant owner, Osono, return a lost item to a customer who's already way down the hill. Chatting to the friendly and sympathetic Osono, she gets the offer of a room over the bakery. It takes quite a bit of cleaning out, but Kiki is energetic and determined, and she soon has the place looking cozier. As she and Jiji shop for household necessities she worries that paying high city prices means her savings won't last long, but Osono's wonderful idea that she should run a delivery service from the bakery, using the phone to take messages and orders so that she doesn't have any setup expenses, is a lifesaver.

Kiki's a little nervous around Osono's silent giant of a husband, but she's beginning to settle into her new life when a pleasant lady comes to the bakery to order a delivery to a house out of town. It's a birthday gift for her nephew—a toy cat in a pretty cage. The cat looks amazingly like Jiji, and the delivery address is some way out of town. Kiki sets off eagerly, enjoying the flight, and Tombo, the red-haired boy she met on her first day, sees her soaring over the bakery and asks Osono about her. As she swoops over the forest on the outskirts of town, she's attacked by some very territorial birds who think she's coming to disturb their nests. After a few very tense minutes, she and Jiji get safely away, but then they find they have a big problem. In the scuffle with the birds, the toy cat has somehow fallen out of the cage. There's only one thing to do if they are to make the delivery on time—Jiji has to stand in for the stuffed cat until Kiki can find the original.

A very nervous Jiji is delivered to the right address, sitting stiffly in the cage as he's presented to the birthday boy. His new owner is not exactly careful with his toys, but luckily he soon loses interest and leaves Jiji on the floor while he watches his favorite TV show. Unfortunately for Jiji, the family dog is watching too, so he has to lie without moving a muscle, unable to do anything except sweat. Meanwhile Kiki is frantically scouring the forest for the lost toy, and eventually spots it in the window of a cabin where Ursula, a young artist, is staying. She and Ursula hit it off and the older girl offers to mend the slightly damaged toy if Kiki will help her clean the place up. Promising to call again so Ursula can sketch her, Kiki takes off with the stuffed cat, who looks almost as good as new, to rescue her old friend. The wise old hound who worried Jiji so much is really a kind-hearted soul. When he picks

Jiji up in his mouth and carries him out of the house, he's really being helpful—but Jiji doesn't know that and gets even more panicky, until Kiki drops off the stuffed cat and whisks him into the air on her broomstick.

Back at the bakery, business is slow when Tombo comes in and hands her an envelope addressed to Miss Witch. Kiki is very standoffish and brushes him off when a customer arrives with a parcel for delivery. Later, when she opens the envelope with Osono, she finds it's a party invitation! At first she's not sure about going, but Osono tells her she really should accept.

On the day of the party itself, she is asked to call at a house in town and collect an item for delivery. But when she arrives, she finds an elderly lady and her maid with a real problem. Madame bakes a pie for her granddaughter's birthday party every year, but today the oven has failed and the pie isn't cooked. Kiki spots a solution to the problem—the kitchen still has its old-fashioned bread oven, and she knows how to use it. She sets to work and manages to fire up the oven and finish the pie, but by the time it's baked the afternoon is over and the sky is darkening. As Kiki flies off the rain comes down, and by the time she makes her delivery she's very wet—and very late. To make matters worse, the birthday girl is bad-tempered, contemptuous, and not the least bit grateful for her grandmother's thoughtfulness or Kiki's determination to make the delivery despite getting soaked. A sad Kiki flies home to find that Tombo waited for her a long while and then left. She goes to bed feeling completely miserable, and before long she has a very severe cold. Osono comes to see her the next morning and convinces her that nothing but complete bed rest will do.

But even bad colds get better, and even the most miserable times end. Kiki wakes up feeling much better and is able to make breakfast for herself and Jiji. As she calls him in to eat, he catches sight of the neighbor's cat, Lily—a beautiful white creature with a fluffy tail. She's an ordinary pet, not a witch's cat like Jiji, but Jiji thinks she's so beautiful that he scoots in-

side in a state of total confusion. Meanwhile Osono calls Kiki down to take a delivery. A customer has asked to have some bread delivered. It's a strange address but it's in town, so Kiki won't even have to fly. When she reaches the terrace overlooking the harbor, it turns out that her customer is Tombo, who's determined to get a date with her somehow! Disarmed by his friendliness, she finds she really likes him as they talk. He's always loved flying

With the streets of Koriko City spread out below her, Kiki takes off on her broom on a beautiful summer's day. The city is based on field drawings and photographs of a number of cities from Stockholm to San Francisco!

machines and plans to build his own. The latest model is really just a bike with a propeller, but he persuades her to try it out with him and they have a wonderful afternoon. Then some other friends of his arrive and invite him to go and see the new airship on its launch pad nearby. He asks Kiki to go too, but she feels shy and left out among this group of old friends, and rushes off, leaving him puzzled.

Miserable, confused, and missing the security of her home and her old friends, Kiki finds the grown-up world can be a bleak place. Suddenly she can't even talk to Jiji—he is spending more and more time away from her and she can't understand his speech any more. And worst of all, she has lost her ability to fly. The one talent that made her able to function as a witch has gone. When she breaks her mother's old broom in her desperate efforts to revive her skill, it seems her world has come to an end. Not even a call from Tombo asking her to come and see the airship can cheer her up.

When Ursula arrives the next day, asking her to come and visit, Osono urges her to go—a rest and change of scene might be just what Kiki needs. After a long journey by bus, hitchhiking, and on foot, they reach the cabin Kiki last saw from the air and she sits for Ursula as she promised. The friends talk far into the night, and Kiki is comforted by the older girl's optimism and intrigued by the painting in which she is to appear, which sits half-finished on an easel in the cabin. The next day, feeling more cheerful, Kiki calls Osono from a nearby phone booth and hears that Madame wants her to call at the house that afternoon, so she heads back to find Madame and her

maid watching the latest news of the airship launch on TV. Madame wants to thank her for being so helpful over the delivery to her ungrateful granddaughter, and has baked her a special cake. Kiki is so moved by the kindness of the two ladies that she finds herself telling Madame some of her troubles, but already they seem a little less terrible than before. Then they go out of her mind altogether as she sees the scenes on the TV screen. The airship has slipped its moorings and is floating free, and Tombo is hanging onto the end of the rope.

Kiki races into town, determined to help her friend—but how? The only thing that can save him now would be someone flying up to grab him. Borrowing a street sweeper's old yard broom, Kiki summons all her courage and skill and makes a dangerous but effective takeoff. Her directional skills have become a little rusty through lack of use but she manages to get to Tombo and save him in the nick of time, just as he loses his grip and plummets down. The two of them land on the fire crew's safety net amid a cheering crowd, and Jiji pushes his way through to Kiki's side. Maybe they no longer speak exactly the same language, but they are still good friends, and good friends always understand one another. As the TV crews and reporters crowd in, all the excitement has another effect—back at the bakery, Osono's baby decides it's time mother stopped watching TV and got on with giving birth.

As the film closes, we see Osono isn't the only new mother. Jiji and Lily have kittens, and Kiki finds that Jiji's son is also great company. She and Tombo become even closer

FILMOGRAPHY AND PERSONNEL

Kiki's Delivery Service

Majo no Takkyubin
(literally, Witch's Special Express Delivery)

Theatrical release, 29 July 1989

RUNNING TIME: 2 hours

Based on a novel by Eiko Kadono

DIRECTOR AND WRITER: Hayao Miyazaki

CHARACTER DESIGNER: Katsuya Kondo

PRODUCTION DESIGNER: Hiroshi Ono

CAMERA (COLOR): Shigeo Sugimura

PRODUCER: Hayao Miyazaki

EXECUTIVE PRODUCERS: Yasuyoshi Tokuma, Mikihiko Tsuzuki, Morihisa Takagi

ASSOCIATE PRODUCER: Toshio Suzuki

EDITOR: Takeshi Seyama

MUSIC: Jo Hisaishi

SPECIAL EFFECTS: Kaoru Tanifuji

© Kadono, Nibariki, Tokuma Shoten, NTV

American Video Release

A Buena Vista Home Entertainment presentation of a Studio Ghibli production, in association with Eiko Kadono, Tokuma Shoten, and Nippon TV Network.

Produced by Hayao Miyazaki. Executive producers: Yasuyoshi Tokuma, Mikihiko Tsuzuki, Morihisa Takagi. Executive producer: Jane Schonberger.

Directed and written by Hayao Miyazaki, based on a book by Eiko Kadono. Adapted by John Semper and Jack Fletcher, with voices cast and directed by Fletcher. Camera (color), Shigeo Sugimura; editor, Takeshi Seyama; music, Joe Hisaishi, Paul Chihara, and Sydney Forest; production designer, Hiroshi Ono; character designer, Katsuya Kondo; sound (Dolby), Shuji Inoue, Ernie Sheesley; special effects, Kaoru Tanifuji; associate producer, Toshio Suzuki; assistant director, Sinao Katabuchi.

VOICE ARTISTS

Kiki: Kirsten Dunst
Jiji: Phil Hartman
Ursula: Janeane Garofolo
Tombo: Matthew Lawrence
Madame: Debbie Reynolds
Osono: Tress MacNeille
Barsa: Edie McClurg
Mom: Kath Soucie

WITH: Jeff Bennett, Pamela Segall, Debi Derryberry, June Angela, Corey Burton, Lewis Arquette, Fay Dewitt, Susan Hickman, Sherry Lynn, Matt Miller, Scott Menville, Eddie Frierson, John and Julia Demita.

friends and she gets to know the rest of his crowd, making more friends socially as well as through her now-thriving business. When she writes to her family, her parents are delighted to hear that she's settling in well and really likes her new home. Kiki has found her own place in life, and she's done it through her own efforts.

COMMENTARY

Kiki's Delivery Service is a film almost entirely without external conflict. Those who believe that cinema must be built around conflict will write it off immediately, yet its gentle and understated plotting is one of its great strengths. It's a stealth movie; given half a chance, it sneaks under the best-prepared defenses and wins over the sternest and most action-addicted critics, including ten-year-old male Nintendo freaks. The film was screened at the Institute of Contemporary Arts in London as part of its festival of Japanese animation in October 1992, and won over audiences originally attracted by such more obvious fare as *Akira* and *Urotsukudoji*.

This is not to say there is no action in the story. Kiki's first, somewhat erratic takeoff sequence, her flight through a flock of hostile birds, and above all the rescue sequence at the end of the movie are all masterfully plotted and paced and fraught with real excitement. But the central thesis of the film is that action and excitement are only part of independent life. How many films for young people also show the weight of long, slow afternoons when no one comes by and nothing moves, and admit that this can happen at work as well as at school, that sometimes things are just plain dull for everyone, even people with magical powers? Most teenagers will recognize that feeling of hanging around, waiting for time to pass until the bell rings or the shop closes and you can go home. Most, too, will understand the sudden panic that can hit the new girl in town who wonders if the crowd

will really accept her and whether she can make new friends as good as the old ones. Delicately and gently, the film reminds adults and reassures children about the minor embarrassments of staying in someone else's house, the panics when plans don't proceed on schedule, the worry of being seen liking a boy, and the awful sense of failure when a problem seemingly can't be solved or a technique mastered.

For the first time as both director and writer, Miyazaki depicts a completely stable family unit facing no challenge to its integrity. In *My Neighbor Totoro*, the family is happy but stressed by the uncertainty of the mother's long illness; in *Nausicaä* and *Castle in the Sky*, parents die and children are left to cope alone with both emotional and practical difficulty. Presenting a "typical" Japanese father and mother, loving and concerned for their child's well-being, yet able to let her go to find her own place in the world, Miyazaki gives us a picture of normality and its positive results. The child of these two contented and loving people is a happy, well-adjusted, helpful girl ready to make the transition to young womanhood with all the usual fears and questions but with every chance of a good outcome. There are no wars, invasions, or evil forces waiting to strike, not even the shadow of illness—simply the worries every teenager knows: can I cope with looking after myself? How do I find a place of my own? What will I do if I can't get a job? What if nobody likes me? Kiki makes it through the transition to young adulthood; her childhood has a happy ending and her grown-up life a hopeful beginning. Young girls watching her succeed can

Kiki's father swings her over his head as his little girl prepares to fly away into the grown-up world outside her childhood home to make a new life. Notice the tiny background details of decor and furnishings.

hope that they too will be able to make it on their own in the world.

Writing in *Village Voice*, Elisabeth Vincentelli described Miyazaki as "a humanist concerned with rites of passage and periods of transition."[9] This is a perceptive reading, but it doesn't touch on his ability to seduce an audience with the sheer physicality of his vision. *Kiki's Delivery Service* is a movie about transition and emotional growth, but it's also a movie about the intensity of physical experi-

ence. In the opening scene, Kiki is lying on a hillside in the country. The movement of the grass in the wind is so beautifully depicted that we can almost feel the cool, silky strands and the soft breeze brushing our own skin as she listens to her radio. When her father sweeps his little girl up into his arms and swings her around before gathering her close to his heart, everyone who has ever held a beloved child can feel that weight against their own heart. As Kiki swoops over Koriko on a day of

In the streets of the big city, arms full of household necessities, Kiki looks longingly at a beautiful pair of shiny red shoes in the window of an elegant dress shop. But when you're just starting out in the world and you have a black cat to feed, frying pans and groceries take precedence over new shoes!

sparkling sea and sunshine, we know how it feels to fly through clear, crisp air. When she winces as the city girls giggle at her old-fashioned witch's dress, we can feel her shrinking inside the dull black fabric. The detail is presented with a light hand, but its accumulation and precision lend the massive weight of reality to every frame. In the Japanese original, such tiny elements as the voice on the radio—

Japanese in the first sequence, placing Kiki safely at home; English in the city, indicating that she's moved away from all she knew—enrich the subliminal soundscape as powerfully as the visuals. The difference in tone between Jiji's human voice and his cat's mew is powerfully handled in both language versions, reinforcing Kiki's sense of isolation from everything she knew and loved at home.

The color palette of the film is predominantly summery, with greens and blues the most powerful hues. Where darker tones creep in—the velvet blue of the night sky for Kiki's departure, the ominous depth of the pine forest around Ursula's cabin, and the rain-slashed skies of Kiki's worst flights—they fulfill a very specific story function, literally darkening the mood to one of foreboding, which can be the delicious foreboding of the unknown or the awful anticipation of fear and failure. Yet green isn't the only color. Despite Miyazaki's reputation as a passionate advocate of ecological harmony, he loves cities and renders them beautifully in his works. The city of Koriko is as sparkling and gorgeous as the blue seas and blue skies around it, its buildings reflecting the richness of brick, stone, and terra cotta, giving the city a sense of continuity, strength, and potential. It's a place with a secure sense of itself, its old heart as vibrant and powerful as the white towers and modern buildings on the outskirts, a city where a young girl can feel safe and secure as she embarks on the excitement of independent life. The contrast between Koriko and the countryside is also metaphoric; as Kiki's world widens with her new experiences, so her new surroundings offer more diversion,

more challenge, and more potential than the peaceful country home she has left behind.

Flight is a metaphor with a triple purpose here—for independence, for the loneliness of being different, and also for talent of any kind. Kiki's friend Ursula is a painter, and the picture she produces, which plays a central role in Kiki's recovery of self-confidence, was painted by pupils at a special school for challenged children. A senior Ghibli staff artist touched it up and Miyazaki added Kiki's face. It's entitled "The Ship Flying over the Rainbow." Its presence on film and its central role in the story affirm that even those whose independence is circumscribed at the most basic level can still spread their wings in their own fashion, given opportunity and encouragement.

Kiki's Delivery Service is Miyazaki's affirmation of the value of ordinary humanity and everyday life. Like everyday life, it could be described as a movie in which very little happens—but only if you're not paying attention. It's a warm, gentle, and very beautiful film, and should be in every family's collection, as well as that of every animation buff. There are so few films that say that ordinary, untrendy girls can fly, and even fewer that say flying isn't the most important thing.

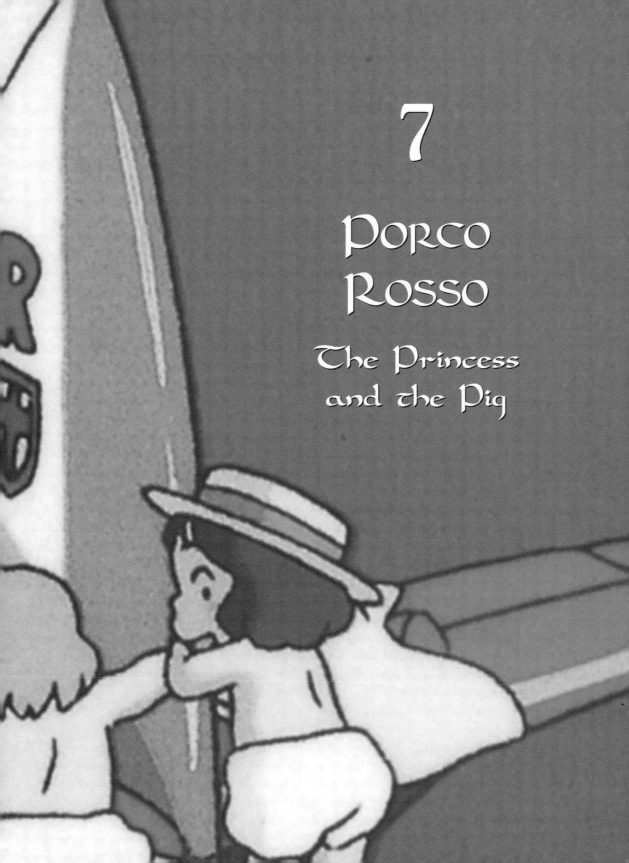

7

PORCO
ROSSO

The Princess
and the Pig

In the years between the two world wars, the Adriatic Sea and the Balkans were places of mystery and intrigue, where adventure still beckoned and the sky-pilots in their flying ships ruled both air and water. In such a place, Marco Porcello, an air ace with the head of a pig and the heart of a hero, searches for a life with meaning and integrity. Two women love him. Gina is strong and beautiful, and like him has suffered and lost much; Fio is an innocent child with a boundless faith in mankind as strong as her passion for planes. Can they show a man who is tired of fighting that it's worth becoming human again, even in a world that is losing its way?

ORIGINS

• •

The introduction to *The Art of Porco Rosso*, written in 1992, confirms that Miyazaki sees it as a "personal film . . . made for [his] own pleasure." Asked about his inspiration for the film in an interview that took place early in 1999, his reply was: "Bottom line, I like that style of aircraft. Although I make films for children, that particular film is really because I wanted to express my love for all those ships. Until finishing *Mononoke Hime*, I felt a little—not really guilty, but that I'd indulged myself in *Porco Rosso*." [1]

His passion for old planes and for Italy was well known to his colleagues, but he'd also wanted to make a film about a pig for many years. Miyazaki likes pigs. He's often sketched them in various guises. His new studio is affectionately known as Buta-ya (Pig's Place) and a jolly Victorian pig adorns the nameplate on the porch, while a whole flight of blocky, potato-print-style pigs is painted around the upper story of the house. But there's more to his use of the term "pig" in the movie.

In *Porco Rosso* "pig" is a metaphor for a man who has lost faith in mankind and has chosen to reject his own humanity. He's not bad, hard, or mean—he simply does not see himself as having any stake in human society. In the English dub commissioned by Tokuma for screening on Japan Airlines flights,[2] hero Marco Pagott is an ace pilot who has been transformed into a pig by a mysterious spell. Yet according to Japanese press releases and *The Art of Porco Rosso*, Marco somehow transforms himself into a pig on purpose, in response to his disillusion with war and politics and the despair of losing touch with his dreams. In a number of Japanese interviews and commentaries on the film, the word "pig" is specifically linked to tired, middle-aged men who have lost touch with the golden optimism of their youth and can no longer imag-

ine themselves ideal heroes who will always win the race and get the girl. And talking about the film in a 1993 interview, Miyazaki said, "I'm disgusted by the notion that man is the ultimate being, chosen by God. But I believe that there are things in this world that are beautiful, that are important, that are

Against a glorious Adriatic sunset, Marco accompanies his damaged aircraft to Milan, where his old friend the master mechanic Piccolo has a factory that can breathe new life into the broken machine. At the time of the movie, it was still possible for individual mercenary pilots to operate as guns for hire in the troubled skies over Italy and the Balkans, but the rise of fascism was rapidly ending such rampant individualism.

In an inner room at the hotel, Gina keeps an old photograph. It shows her with four childhood friends. Three are dead, and one, whose face is crossed out, is now a disillusioned man who no longer thinks being human is worthwhile.

worth striving for. I made the hero a pig because that was what best suited these feelings of mine."[3]

Miyazaki's original lighthearted idea for a film about a pig nearly made it to video with another director at the helm. In 1988, in a talk given at the Nagoya Film Festival, Miyazaki recounted the story of a project he'd dreamed up with a pig as hero.[4] A former mil-

itary officer, the pig resigns his command, builds a huge tank, and sets off with a legion of nephews in a quixotic quest for fun and glory. (The tank commander idea resurfaced in Miyazaki's 1998 manga *Tiger in the Mire*, but that story was serious.) He kidnaps a girl, falls in love, and attempts to woo her with a tissue paper flower—an echo of Lupin's "magic tricks" scene with Clarisse in *Castle of*

Cagliostro. As Miyazaki recounted at Nagoya, the tale moved closer to the final form of *Porco Rosso*: "As I kept fiddling with the story . . . it finished up with a happy ending in which the pig's love won the girl over. At first, she was supposed to be an ordinary girl who was working at a station restaurant, but she began to change as well, and she became a bar singer like Marilyn Monroe in *River of No Return*, in which [Monroe] was really lovely, only this girl was a little younger and purer."

There was interest in making the production for release on video, but Miyazaki was just about to start work on *Castle in the Sky*, and not even he had yet worked out a way of directing two titles at once. A young director was assigned to the project, but director and writer couldn't agree over the outcome of the story. The younger man felt that an older man who'd stoop to kidnap a girl could not have a genuine love, one that would inspire him to wait for her and win her heart; Miyazaki insisted that he could. The director quit, and the project was scrapped.

He was still thinking about it in 1989, when he told *Comic Box* magazine that he'd like to make "something like *Buta no Sensha* [Pig's Tank], a silly movie which will show my embarrassing side. . . . The truth is that I am happiest when I am writing about stupid airplanes and tanks in magazines like *Model Graphix*. . . . I could write the story all by myself, but animation requires an enormous amount of manpower. It has to be done by an organization, and it's difficult to make frivolous movies for a company. Therefore, sometimes I dream of making a silly movie with my own money, a videotape (OAV) that can't even recover the costs. I'd love to do a film that is frowned upon by the PTA."[5]

That idea resurfaced, somewhat reworked, in his manga *Zasso Note, Hikotei Jidai* (Miscellaneous Notes: The Age of Seaplanes) serialized in *Model Graphix* magazine in 1989 and later published in English in *Mangazine* and *Animerica* magazines. Now the story had moved to the Adriatic in the summer of 1929. The hero, a pig aviator and former war hero, lived on an island off the coast of Croatia, and the action took place in Dovrok City and in the air.

Then came a proposal to make a short in-flight movie for Japan Airlines' domestic flights, a forty-five-minute distraction for tired business people in a stuffy airplane cabin. As Miyazaki's imagination took flight with his hero, the idea gradually expanded and costs mounted. Producer Toshio Suzuki intervened and announced that the film would become a full-fledged feature-length movie.[6]

But while the film was in production, civil war broke out in former Yugoslavia and Miyazaki, perhaps feeling that art should not imitate life too closely in such terrible situations, changed the setting. What had been intended as a fun movie for middle-aged business people whose brains were turning to tofu from overwork became rather more serious. In a long interview in *Yom* magazine, given in 1994 to mark the completion of the *Nausicaä* manga, Miyazaki commented that he originally intended to make *Porco Rosso* a lighthearted film that would make people laugh. The advent of war, his own thoughts about middle age and manhood, and his tendency to create complex sto-

PORCO ROSSO

ries and characters seem to have changed the evolution of the movie.

ART AND TECHNIQUE

All the planes in *Porco Rosso* but one were created from Miyazaki's imagination, but they're all based on the technology of the period. The only authentic 1930s plane featured in the movie was American pilot Donald Curtis's plane, the Curtiss Model R3C-0, a close copy of the Curtiss R3C-2 except for the modifications added by Miyazaki to turn it into a fighter. The R3C-2 was a racing aircraft; Jimmy Doolittle of *30 Seconds over Tokyo* fame won the real-world 1925 Schneider Cup in it, beating the Italian Macchi M33, a close cousin of Porco's Savoia S.21. The movie attributes the British Flight Lieutenant S. N. Webster's real-life 1927 Schneider victory in his Supermarine S-5 to the Curtiss R3C.

There is a real Italian Savoia S.21, but it looks nothing like Porco's plane. In fact, Miyazaki had never seen it when he designed the lyrical curves of the bright red seaplane for his hero. He was looking back to a boyhood memory of the Macchi M3. His uncle's company had made parts for the aviation industry before and during the war and, as noted in chapter 1, he had grown up drawing planes and ships. In the same way, the MC72 flown by Feralin is somewhat like the Curtiss, and the Italian Air Force's S/M S.55s are similar to, but not the same as, the real-world equivalents. The planes in the World War I flash-

back sequence are also lovingly rendered versions of planes in keeping with the technology of their time. Miyazaki harks back to his earlier work with a reference to the TV series *Three Thousand Miles in Search of Mother*. The ship that carries young hero Marco (born in Genoa, like the older Marco of *Porco Rosso*) in search of his mother is the *Folgore*. It means "lightning" in Italian and is the name of the engine Piccolo puts into his rebuilt plane.[7] The heroine of that series, by the way, is called Fiolina.

In a neat in-joke for fans, the name Ghibli is stamped on the engine's cylinder head. Italian plane-maker Capronini, which folded in 1937, produced some of Miyazaki's favorite aircraft (Studio Ghibli was named for one of their planes). In Miyazaki's view, form follows technology in matters of design, and the Italians were masters of aircraft elegance.

As long as a plane is flying slower than 300km per hour, there's room for inventiveness and originality in the design. The Italians were the best plane makers at that time because they were real design geniuses—they used their unique sense of style to create really beautiful, elegant planes, which is what I really admire about their work. Once you go to speeds over 300km per hour, then you have to pay more attention to materials and engineering, and you can't make such beautiful designs any more. Even the Italians forgot that their early planes were so appealing and so attractive—when fascism really started

8t
164

up, they stopped making such beautiful designs. The thing about technology is that, generally, more and more technology requires larger and larger infrastructure. When it comes to individual expression, that gets lost. There isn't room any more for such individuality; it moves into the realm of the hobbyist or disappears under the pressure of a complex infrastructure. The Italians were masters of that kind of individuality, but once the technology became more and more advanced and needed more and more infrastructure, that individual expression disappeared.[8]

The way in which the aircraft functioned is

Marco's beloved plane has lines as elegant as one of Gina's dresses, and its brilliant color is what has won him the nickname "The Crimson Pig." The aerodynamically inventive and beautiful designs of the Italian plane-makers Capronini were one of Miyazaki's prime inspirations for Porco Rosso.

just as knowingly rendered. Stalling engines, jamming machine guns, and wooden frames and hulls, capable of superb aerodynamic performance but fragile as eggshells, were all well known to flyers of the 1920s and 1930s. The technology of the Piccolo factory is accurate and the working practices would be familiar to anyone who made planes in the early years of the century. The nail-biting dogfights and the long, serene sequence in which Marco sails through sunbeam and cloud shadow before his first fight with Curtis are among the most beautiful and truthful renditions of flight during this period ever put onto film. Mark Schilling, in his review for the *Japan Times*, describes the film's flight sequences as possessing "a beauty beyond mere realism. This is the way flying ought to look and feel."[9]

The settings and backgrounds are given the same fine-art treatment used to such superb effect on *Kiki's Delivery Service* three years earlier. Every color in the flight and island sequences is bleached or brightened by the Adriatic sunlight, heightening the grayness of the scenes in drab industrial Milan and the workshop where Marco buys his equipment. The contrast between the fantasy playground of the adventurers and scoundrels who live on the edge of society and the harsh reality of everyday life elsewhere is stark. Gina's Hotel

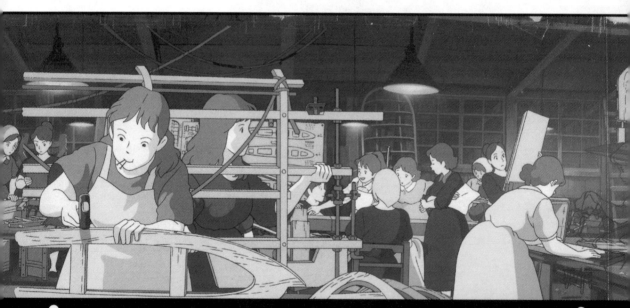

Many hands make light work, and in the Piccolo factory all the hands except Papa's are female. Recession in the 1920s meant that many of the young men of Europe went abroad to look for work, some of them to America, and the women and old people who were left behind kept economic life as well as family life going as best they could.

Adriano, with its elegant lounges and sophisticated, slightly louche bar, glows like a jewel in the perfect blue of the sea, and her private garden at the far end of the island is a dream setting for a fairy-tale love affair, reflecting her grace and beauty while rendering her resolve to wait for Marco even more poignant. Against its backdrop of ancient walls and fragile blossoms, the American Curtis appears brash and noisy, meriting the schoolboy dismissal Gina gives him. Marco's private island is perfectly rendered, a dream of golden sand and blue water shut away from the outside world of politics and passions inside the high, protective walls of an extinct volcanic crater. Water is almost as vital to this story as sky, surrounding all the central confrontations between the various adversaries, and the animation of water is superbly done. As much skill and love is expended on a single brief shot of tiny fishes skittering away from the S.21's keel when Marco and Fio come aground on the island's beach as on the vast, glorious skies of the aforementioned long flight sequence.

The opening credits of the film introduce us to the story with teleprinter-rapped lines in Japanese, Italian, Korean, English, Chinese, Spanish, Arabic, Russian, French, and German. In theory this may have been to provide a quick introduction for the Japan Airlines inflight screenings that were the movie's first raison d'être, but in practice the machine-gun rattle of old news technology puts the audience into the perfect frame of mind for the opening scenes. The closing credits repay close attention, being a wonderful montage of sketches showing pigs in flight and around airplanes in all sorts of 1920s and 1930s settings. The main theme was originally a haunting rendition of the French Communard anthem "Les Temps des Cerises" from Gina's Japanese voice actress Tokiko Kato, who also wrote and sang the original ending theme. At the moment it is not known who will render the songs on the Disney release, but it seems likely that "Les Temps des Cerises" will remain an important feature of the soundtrack. It sums up perfectly the nostalgic yearning for summers past, for the joys of young love and the simple pleasure of living. The brief sequence in the cinema in which Marco talks to his old friend Feralin is Miyazaki's homage to the Fleischer Brothers and Windsor McKay, whose work had such a powerful influence on Japanese animation in the years around World War II.

There have already been two foreign-language dubs of Porco Rosso. The Japan Airlines English-language dub has also been shown on cable and satellite television in England, but it was barely mentioned in listings and attracted fairly limited audiences. The French dub met with more success; it was shown in cinemas in major cities. The dub had the commitment of a superb voice cast, headed by international star Jean Reno of Leon and Godzilla fame. When asked if there was any chance of Reno reprising his role in the forthcoming Disney/Buena Vista dub, Miyazaki said, "I hope so. The French cast were superb, in fact I thought they gave an even better performance than the original Japanese actors. Those characters really need French voices. There's a quality in the French voice that you really need for those roles. The

French Gina was even better than the Japanese—there's something wonderful in her voice. That's a woman who could stand on her own two feet, by herself, and yet she's a very feminine woman."[10] No details of the Disney dub cast are available as this book goes to press, but the story and characters will certainly offer a challenge worth taking to both writer and actors. While fantasy epics like *Princess Mononoke* can use wild talents such as that of Neil Gaiman, *Porco Rosso* demands a writer who understands the colloquial speech of this century, the history of interwar Europe, and the proper expression of full-blown, grown-up romance.

THE CHARACTERS

Marco Pagott, a.k.a. Marco Porcellino, a.k.a. Porco Rosso

Marco, the boy who would become the Crimson Pig, was born in Genoa in 1893 and was passionate about flying from an early age. There's a photograph on a wall in the Hotel Adriano dated 1912 that shows the young Marco standing proudly behind the pilot's seat of a small aircraft, Gina and three friends by his side, and he tells Piccolo that he's been flying since he was seventeen. At the time of the film, around the end of the 1920s, all three of those young men are dead and Marco and Gina alone remain. His love for Gina is deep and sincere but he keeps it locked inside himself and is reluctant to express his feelings.

Joining the Italian Air Force at the start of World War I, Marco quickly rose to the rank of Captain and became a hero. During the fighting, however, he lost many friends—including his boyhood flying companion Berlini, who had just married Gina—and began to question the validity of his own actions and the purpose of flying and dying for any nation. Unable to resolve the conflicts in his mind regarding the meaning of loyalty, humanity, and love, he became a pig. With fascism gaining ground in Italy he quit the Air Force and became a bounty hunter.

He lives on a small island in the Adriatic, where a ruined building, a small tent, and a radio constitute his "home comforts." The beauty of the setting and the complete peace and privacy are very important to him, and when the Mamma Aiuto gang and the American Curtis find his hideout he is furious. However, he isn't reclusive by nature, as is shown by the beautiful women who ask him to join them in the bar of the Hotel Adriano and by his holiday plans. He's loyal to old friends like Piccolo, is very brave, and despite his cynicism he has a deeply romantic nature and an old-fashioned, chivalrous view of women—which Fio and Gina both find infuriating.

Asked how he came to create such a very different hero from his earlier films, Miyazaki said, "Marco wasn't intended to be the kind of character children would appreciate. I wasn't really making the film for children, but in fact when it came out children went to see it, so there wasn't much I could do. When I make a film for children, I want to show the kind of heroes children can relate to. They have great optimism and believe nothing is impossible—the future is full of possibilities. With *Porco* *Rosso*, I was making a film for adults and so the hero is a character who can't go back to the past and try things again. He can't revisit his past, he has to live with what he's done."[11]

Gina

Gina is the owner of the Hotel Adriano. This beautiful and intelligent woman has had more than her share of tragedy and,

As Marco arrives at the Hotel Adriano after his successful sortie, Gina is singing for her guests in the bar. The song, "Les Temps Des Cerises," is an old French ballad with political connotations. The simple elegance of her dress and jewelry are notable.

Zap! Pow! Ker-unch! The planes are grounded and now it all comes down to who can stay on his feet the longest, as Marco and Curtis lay into each other like cartoon villains of old. But the thing that bowls Marco over isn't the American's fist—it's the news that Gina is in love with him.

like Marco, she is at the age when she can't go back and relive her past. She married three childhood friends only to see each of them killed. Marco is her last surviving link with the happy past, and even though she would like their romance to go further, she cherishes the deep friendship they share. Gina is a wonderful singer as well as a shrewd businesswoman,

and is more than capable of operating high-tech equipment—like her Morse receiver—as well as organizing and running a complex business operation.

Gina is depicted as a strong woman, but some fans have expressed the view that her ongoing dream of romantic fulfillment with Marco makes her a bad role model for a post-feminist world. In an interview in *Manga Max* magazine, Miyazaki remarked, "If I met a woman like Gina and a very 'politically correct' feminist, I think I'd rather talk to Gina. That's because she is trying to be herself; even in a man-dominated society, she tries to express her own feelings and wishes. Even under difficult circumstances, a woman can express herself if she's strong, and I think Gina is like that."[12]

Fio Piccolo and Her Family

Fio Piccolo is the granddaughter of the owner of Marco's chosen aircraft company, Fio is just seventeen and determined to prove that she's every bit as good as any man in her chosen field—aircraft design. Despite Marco's initial reluctance to trust her with his precious plane, she soon shows him that her work is first-class, and his respect is a sure sign that she knows what she's doing. Despite being a brave and intelligent young woman, she's still a child in matters of the heart, and finds herself falling a little in love with Marco as well as being confused and sometimes startled by the events unfolding in the world outside her family home in Milan. Fio grows up to inherit the Piccolo aviation company, and the friendship she develops with Gina at the end of the film is enduring.

Father Piccolo runs the Milan aviation company with the help of his mother, aunts, sisters, cousins, daughters, and daughters-in-law because all the young men have gone abroad to try and find work as the recession bites deeper into Europe. Like Marco, he is passionate about aviation and particularly engines—he is acknowledged as one of the best engineers around. His mother, Fio's great-grandmother, is an old friend of Marco's and the whole family treats Marco as an old and trusted friend, even to the extent of letting him take Fio on his rebuilt plane's maiden flight.

Since many of the principal staff (such as supervising animator, art director, and color design) on Porco Rosso were female, some fans theorized that the scenes in the Piccolo factory were really set in Miyazaki's Studio Ghibli. In the *Porco Rosso Roman Album*, several female Ghibli staff members discussed this scene. Some viewed it as a positive statement of their director's respect for his female workers, but some didn't take such an affirmative view, thinking that Piccolo's status as boss and his praise for women's work ethic implied that women workers are easy to exploit, and may put across the message that since women are less assertive they make for a more easily controllable mass workforce. However, it should be noted that it is Fio, not one of her uncles or brothers, who inherits the Piccolo corporation, and that while the men of the story are rootless adventurers living on the fringes of society, she and Gina are shown as independent and capable businesswomen.

Donald Curtis

Donald Curtis is an ace pilot who is hired by the Aero Viking Association to fight Porco Rosso and to avenge the defeats he's inflicted on them. He is a true innocent abroad in sophisticated Europe, the stereotypical wide-eyed American boy who really believes he'll be a movie star one day—and then president—and who thinks he is invulnerable. He's impulsive and romantic, given to falling in love at first sight—which he does first with Gina and then with Fio, setting himself once again in conflict with Marco. Despite his naïveté and his being a bit of a mama's boy, he has some good qualities—he's brave and determined, he keeps his word, and even when he fulfills his ambition to become a big Hollywood movie star, he never forgets his old friends.

Boss and the Mamma Aiuto Gang

Boss and the Mamma Aiuto Gang are mercenaries who will attack anyone for profit, have their own vague code of honor, and turn out to be complete softies at heart. In the early scenes of the film they are soon overrun and bullied by their little girl hostages, and when Fio gives them a good telling-off they fall meekly and adoringly into line and take her to their hearts like a band of dim-witted but loving siblings. Their name translates as "Mamma, help!" which has two possible origins—it could be that's what their victims cry out as they see the pirates approaching, or it could be that's what they themselves yell when they see a pig in a crimson plane on the horizon! They are really just a collection of overgrown schoolboys—*The Art of Porco Rosso* records that they hate baths and never brush their teeth.

Aero Viking Association, a.k.a. The Sky Pilots

Aero Viking Association is a loose grouping of mercenaries and bandits working the Adriatic coasts. These independent fliers band together when Porco Rosso and other fliers working for the steamship and transit companies foil their raids on shipping in the area. Like Marco, they are all men for whom there is no place in the rising fascist states and the more restricted society that is developing as Europe moves deeper into recession and closer to war.

Feralin

Feralin is an old comrade of Marco's from the war days. He is still with the Italian Air Force, having decided to carry on fighting for his country despite the political situation. He is still determined to do all he can to protect Marco and Gina from the state's attempt to capture the Crimson Pig, and his warnings save Marco's bacon on more than one occasion.

THE STORY

It's a long, hot summer afternoon in the late 1920s on a tiny islet somewhere in the Adriatic Ocean. Marco Pagott is dozing in a deck chair, magazine over his pig's face, radio on, when his peace is interrupted by the news that

Marco finds Fio still at her drawing board after working through the night. Despite her youth, she is a gifted aviation designer, and he is persuaded to entrust the rebuilding of his beloved plane to her despite his early misgivings.

the notorious Mamma Aiuto gang has attacked a ship and gotten away with a large sum of money and a whole class of elementary schoolgirls as hostages. Grumbling as he guns the under-serviced engine of his beloved Savoia S.21 seaplane into life, Porco Rosso, the hero of the skies, takes off to the rescue.

The members of the Mamma Aiuto gang are really the ones who need rescuing. They had underestimated the disruption that a group of wholly under-terrified, overconfident little girls can cause on an aircraft, and by the time our hero catches up with the gang they are unable to control their hostages. As Marco attacks, the girls make Mamma Aiuto's job impossible; the outcome of the fight is never in doubt. The gang's ship is devastated, but at least, as the pig makes off with his rescued hostages and half the money, it's their own again.

That evening, after making what running repairs he can to his plane, Marco docks at the Hotel Adriano and strolls into the bar. The owner, his childhood friend Gina, is singing to her customers. The clientele includes some of the scum of the Adriatic, and many old adversaries of Marco, but none of them would dream of making trouble near Gina's place. Despite this, they don't hesitate to plot against Marco there, and are so determined to best the pig that they are even contemplating the indignity of hiring outside help—Donald Curtis, an American (though his agent claims his grandmother was a quarter Italian) and an ace pilot. The barman tells Marco he beat the Italians in the renowned Schneider Cup air-race two years in a row, but now, smitten with Gina's beauty, Curtis is more concerned with shutting up those unwise enough to talk while she's singing.

Marco is asked to join their party by a pair of beautiful women, but goes instead to a quiet corner to eat his supper, where Gina joins him. She has just heard that her third hus-

A photo opportunity not to be missed, and Boss doesn't miss it. The rest of the Mamma Aiuto gang are left flat on their faces as Boss makes sure he's the one next to Fio in the commemorative snapshot for the big race.

band's death has been confirmed—the wreck of his plane has been found in India. On the wall is a faded photograph more than fifteen years old—the two of them and three young men, all now dead. Marco's face is scratched out, but it's the only picture Gina has of him while he was still human. He spends the night at the hotel, and the next day the Adriano's launch takes him to the mainland, where he has business to conduct and weapons to buy. As a military parade goes on outside, he picks up his machine gun and is offered some new, high-tech, state-of-the-art ammunition by an excited young assistant. After pointing out that fighting is no game, he buys his usual bullets and leaves.

Back on his island, as he works on his engine and finally concludes that it's beyond his skill and he'll have to go back to the mechanics at Piccolo, he receives another urgent plea for help—Curtis and the Aero Vikings are attacking the steamship *Mediterranean Queen*. We see the attack, their ships a mad carnival of inventive, colorful design, but Marco is unmoved. He is, he says firmly, going on vacation, and nursing his sputtering engine into the skies, he promises himself "soft beds, good food, beautiful women" if he can only keep her going until they reach Milan.

The skies are serene, despite a scattering of gray storm clouds here and there, but then Curtis, on his way back from the robbery of the *Mediterranean Queen*, attacks out of nowhere. Marco does his best to avoid him and offers no resistance, saying he doesn't want a fight, but the American shoots him down anyway, seeing the death of the pig as a fast way to fame and fortune. The red plane

plummets toward the ocean, and Curtis scans sky and water, looking for proof of his victory. He spots a fragment of crimson fuselage and flies off triumphantly. Meanwhile, hidden with the battered S.21 under thick foliage on a tiny islet, Marco watches him go.

Two days later, Gina is called back from her boat as it pulls away from the hotel jetty to take a phone call from Marco. He had managed to flag down a passing boat to get to the mainland; she had been about to go in search of any news that might indicate he wasn't dead. Loading the plane onto a flatbed trolley, he sets off for Milan against lavender-and-gold skies. He reaches the Piccolo workshop by truck, under cover of night, and is welcomed by the master mechanic and his seventeen-year-old granddaughter Fio. Over the next few hours, he finds himself agreeing to let Fio have a crack at designing the modifications to his beloved plane, despite his misgivings, and then learns that, with all the men of the family away looking for jobs elsewhere, the work will be carried out by the Piccolo womenfolk. Yet he can't help but admire their skill and the dedication with which they work, and as the work progresses he even finds himself rocking a baby's cradle while the mother joins her cousins and sisters on the production line. Meanwhile Piccolo senior has a treat for him—a superb Folgore engine. It's the one that lost the Schneider Cup against Curtis in 1925, but the mechanic who worked on it then wasn't in Piccolo's class and the fuselage on which it was mounted wasn't as sleek and aerodynamically balanced as Fio's new design.

To get away from the hive of feminine in-

FILMOGRAPHY AND PERSONNEL

Porco Rosso

Kurenai no Buta, a.k.a. *The Crimson Pig*

Theatrical release, 18 July 1992

RUNNING TIME: 1 hour, 33 minutes

Original story by Hayao Miyazaki

DIRECTOR AND SCREENPLAY: Hayao Miyazaki

KEY ANIMATION: Masashi Ando

ORIGINAL ART: Yoshifumi Kondo

© Nibariki, Tokuma Shoten

U.K. screenings on satellite/cable TV in 1997/1998. French video and theatrical release in 1997. U.S. release dates and casting not yet announced.

dustry around him, Marco goes to the movies, and his old friend and former Air Force comrade Feralin comes to warn him that the secret police are on his tail. With the political climate changing, mavericks who sell their skills to the highest bidder are not considered patriotic, and there are certain people who think it would be a good idea to get the pig out of the way. As Fio picks Marco up on the way home, they are followed by an ominous black car and have to fling their truck around some very tight corners to escape their pursuers. It's obvious that not only is Marco in serious trouble but the whole family may be in bad straits with the government for helping him. But the resourceful Piccolo womenfolk have a plan to deal with this—Marco will take Fio with him, and they will tell the authorities that Fio was his hostage and they were all forced to work on his plane to keep her safe. Marco protests, but he can't think of a better idea, and in any event if they don't move fast the government agents will storm the Piccolo factory and no one will get away. The snag is that the new airframe and retuned engine are still com-

pletely untested, but there's no time to worry about that. Marco and Fio take off down the canals of Milan in the gray dawn light, and after a hair-raising escape from the bullets of the government agent and a near miss with a slow-moving barge, they are away. Feralin warns them of a trap set by the Italian Air Force, and before long they're over the ocean again and heading for home.

Marco makes a detour via the Hotel Adriano before going back to his island. But he isn't Gina's first visitor that day. While she is sitting in her secluded garden at the far end of the hotel grounds, Curtis scales the wall to offer a bouquet and a proposal of marriage. Gina laughingly turns him down, telling him the story of a bet she made with herself long ago. She's waiting for the man she loves; her bet is that one day he'll finally come and visit her in her garden. As she thinks back to the days when a boy called Marco first took her flying, a crimson plane loops overhead in salute, but it doesn't stop. She's lost her bet again, and Curtis must leave without his hoped-for romantic triumph.

After refueling in a tiny hamlet where all the young men have left to look for work and only old-timers and boys remain, Marco and Fio reach his island—only to find the Aero Vikings lying in wait. They overpower Marco and threaten to destroy his plane, but Fio explodes in rage and gives them such a tongue-lashing that they fall meekly into line. Curtis makes a swashbuckling entrance and is immediately smitten by Fio. (He rebounds very quickly, it seems.) Nervous and overexcited, she suggests a race between Curtis and Marco to settle the Vikings' grievances. If Marco wins, Curtis settles all the bills for work on his plane. If Curtis wins, he proposes that Fio should marry him. Despite Marco's fury, the whole thing is agreed and the Aero Vikings leave.

Marco and Fio argue about her rashness, but he admires her courage and realizes that she is not yet quite old enough to give up hero worship. She has convinced herself that he'll win. They resolve their differences and settle down to pass the night before the big race. For one sleepy moment she thinks she sees his human face. To distract her, he tells her the story of how he came to be a pig after a terrible dogfight in the last war when his friend Berlini was killed just a short while after he'd married Gina. The absolute silence of the night and the moonlight reflected in the surf at the water's edge form a perfect backdrop to the strange tale. For a while Marco and Fio are in world of their own, but news of the planned contest is already spreading, and by the time they turn up at the starting point for the race the whole thing has been turned into a carnival, with vast crowds of spectators, gamblers,

hucksters, thieves—the scum of the Adriatic. The Mamma Aiuto gang is doing well on the bookies' stand; Boss has donned his best suit for the occasion and Fio is showered with bouquets as she takes up her place of honor on the stakeholders' platform.

Marco won't shake hands with Curtis, but once the two are in the air he doesn't fire, even when he has the advantage, until Curtis taunts him. As the two weave and circle overhead, old sky pirates remark to each other that a dogfight like this comes once in a lifetime. The crowd is awed and astounded by the skill and daring of the pilots. They can't see the comic moments as the two hurl insults and implements at each other when their guns jam.

Meanwhile Gina is on the radio, picking up a Morse signal from a source that can only be Feralin. The Air Force is on the way to the race site, and if they get there before the crowd breaks up a lot of people will be in a lot of trouble. Undaunted, she sets off to warn them. Meanwhile Marco and Curtis, unable to fire a shot, have landed and are continuing their titanic battle hand-to-hand. The toughness of Marco's skull is a revelation to Curtis, who hurts his hand landing an uppercut, but he has an even bigger revelation for Marco—that Gina keeps waiting for him in her secret garden. The shock almost knocks out the pig, but he resurfaces just in time to win the fight, Fio's freedom, and the money to pay for his beautiful plane.

As he sinks back under the water, Gina arrives. She claps her hands as firmly as a teacher calling the class to order and tells the crowd to get out of the way, then offers everyone a drink at the Adriano on the house. Marco surfaces and asks her to get Fio safely back to her family; she asks if he's going to make another girl unhappy, but bundles a protesting Fio into her plane anyway. As they leave, Marco asks the still-dazed Curtis if he'll help draw the approaching Air Force planes away to give everyone else a better chance of escape. But Curtis can only gape and mumble, "Your face…."

Has a young girl's innocent faith in humanity and a lovely woman's enduring love healed Marco's self-hatred and disillusionment? Fio's voice-over as the film ends leaves us room to make our own judgment. But as the grown-up Fio's state-of-the-art light aircraft swoops down over the Adriano for a visit to Gina, years afterwards, we glimpse a crimson plane docked at the jetty at the far end of the island, the one that leads to the secret garden.

COMMENTARY

The introduction to *The Art of Porco Rosso* mentions the rise of "girl power" and the consequent belittling of men's role in the world. All men can be viewed as untrustworthy, and older men in particular don't seem to be natural choices for the heroic role in any story. However, for the lead in his story, Miyazaki chose a man who was no longer in the first flush of youth, as far from conventional good looks as could be imagined, and with nothing to offer to a woman—except a brave heart, a

good nature, and a dream of freedom and joy that not even the cynicism of age could entirely overcome. What prince could give his princess more than that?

Its romanticism excites strong and even contradictory reaction from critics. Mark Schilling commented that, "Like that other master of the medium, Walt Disney, Miyazaki is something of a genius and something of a flake—and sometimes it is hard to tell which is which. . . . Stripped of its wonderfully realized animation, *Kurenai no Buta* is mock-Hemingway pretentious, with Porco as a mucho macho Papa figure, and '30s B-picture schlocky." Schilling went on to praise Miyazaki's knack for "bringing a scene to fresh, vibrant life, and for humanizing his cartoon heroes."[13]

Made as the director entered his fifties, *Porco Rosso* recognizes that inside every older guy who will never again get the girl or win the fight (if, indeed, he ever did), there may be a dreamer's heart fighting to survive the indignity of the years. Like many films inspired by the young fliers of Europe's two world wars, it is suffused with an elegiac sense of beauty and transience. In Marco's mystical near-death experience, which is the turning point on which his decision to reject humanity hangs, Miyazaki is referring back to a Roald Dahl story, *They Shall Not Grow Old*. Those who only know Dahl's works for children might be surprised by the realism and maturity of the former World War II pilot's work *Over to You: Ten Stories of Flyers and Flying*, published in 1946. Like Dahl, Miyazaki is better known for his works for children, but the power and resonance of his vision in *Porco Rosso* is the mark of a director at the height of his powers. His firm statements that this is not a film aimed at children are borne out by the fact that *Porco Rosso* is the only Miyazaki film not to top the *Animage* magazine reader poll for best animation of its year. The largely teenage readership of the magazine understood neither the pity of war nor the poignancy of middle age; its choice for the year was *Sailor Moon*. The film did, however, top Japan's box office list for 1992 and was the biggest money-maker of Miyazaki's films until *Princess Mononoke*.

Years after the big fight between the pig and the American, Fio, now president of the Piccolo Corporation, pilots her own plane into the jetty at the Hotel Adriano to spend the summer with her good friend Gina. Can you just make out the little plane at right moored by the private garden at the end of the island?

Porco Rosso is made with a technician's exactness of expression, an artist's power to create beauty, and a humane sense of frustration and compassion. In the depiction of its male characters it invites us to understand weakness, greed, arrogance, lack of faith, and loss of hope without passing judgment on those who fall into despair. In the beautiful portraits of its central female characters it gives us two roles any actress would kill for, two women separated by a span of years but united in understanding and able to build a deep and sincere friendship independently of the men they continue to love and value. Gina in particular is worthy to stand among the great romantic heroines of live-action cinema. Some have argued that she is a poor feminist role model, but that argument requires a view of feminism too narrow for me to accept. Gina and Fio's every action and thought might not match those of girls and women today, but both characters are capable and respected in their own world.

Alongside the intensely romantic love story and the powerful allegory of loss of personal and political innocence, there's another film—the action-adventure-comedy that Miyazaki sketched out in *Castle of Cagliostro* and realized here in full good-humored measure. From our first encounter with the Mamma Aiuto gang we know that their ham-fisted attempts to be the feared masters of the Adriatic skies are doomed to failure. Throughout the film, undercurrents of humor and levity surface like bubbles along the keel of a flying boat, culminating in the comic slugfest of the final confrontation between Marco and Curtis.

This is a film with a cheerful face and a serious heart. It addresses grown-up issues—women's place in the world, the relationship between the sexes, the different devastations of war and depression, the importance of political and moral leadership—alongside the age-old dreams of childhood that linger in all our hearts, the yearning for heroes and great deeds and a life less ordinary. As long as people can still dream, whatever their age, this movie will find, and deserve, an appreciative audience.

8

PRINCESS
MONONOKE

The Nature
of Love

Far in the past, when what would become Japan was still a collection of warring tribes fighting for control of land and resources, a young man called Ashitaka sets out to find the cure to a strange curse that afflicts him when he kills a boar god. Leaving his people far behind in the north, he travels to new lands and encounters a wild girl who lives in the forest, running with wolf-gods and fighting with them against the humans who are trying to build a life on their territory. An epic struggle between gods and men is building, and the world will be changed forever. Whatever happens, whoever wins, there is no going back once the gods have been killed.

ORIGINS

Miyazaki had made sketches in the late seventies for a movie about a beautiful princess living in the woods with a savage beast. The story was rooted in Japanese history and folklore, but it also had echoes of the Western fairy tale *Beauty and the Beast*. In Miyazaki's version, the third daughter of a nobleman was forced to marry a *mononoke*, a beast-spirit who strongly resembled the Catbus in My *Neighbor Totoro*. But her father was possessed by a demon, and the princess and her unlikely spouse saved him. In a departure from the Western version, the monster did not turn into a handsome prince at the end. Miyazaki was not worried about comparisons with the Disney cartoon version of *Beauty and the Beast*, since his story was quite different.

The project was turned down, but the image boards and story were published and are available in book form in Japan. Miyazaki returned to the idea almost fifteen years later, when the success of *Porco Rosso* meant he had more freedom to choose his scenario. Early in the production process, however, the simple fairy tale began to evolve into something different from anything Disney—or any other animation studio—had ever done. The main character became a young man, Ashitaka, an outsider on a quest for freedom from a curse, and the title proposed was now either *Princess Mononoke* or *Ashitaka's Journey*. The princess who married a mononoke became a mononoke herself.

The story moved from the mists of fairy tale and took up residence in the mists of Japan's history. Miyazaki returned again to the themes that had inspired him in earlier works—the strength of nature, the struggle of lesser peoples against greater oppressors, the search for utopia, and the eternal importance of love. And once more, as in *Porco Rosso*, he created a hero with echoes of himself.

In a round table discussion for Kyoto Seika University's 1998 *Kino Review*, he mentions folklore as a vital source. He was particularly drawn to the tale of "a princess with a birthmark" and says, "for the longest time I wanted to make her the heroine of a movie," but over the years the idea developed until the birthmark became a burn on the arm of a young man, and finally developed into Ashitaka's curse."

These themes had been present in all his works to various extents, depending on the context, though they were never allowed to

Ashitaka and San talk over their future at the end of the film. Neither insists that the other change their whole way of life for love; instead, they reach an agreement to carry on living their own lives but to see each other as often as they can.

Here is the Shishigami, the deer form of the great forest god, glimpsed through the trees in a glowing circle of light. The eerie beauty of this sequence is almost dreamlike, and the many different kinds of flowers and creepers growing on the bark of the trees add to the sense of a rich and ancient forest habitat.

impede the audience's enjoyment of the story. In 1989, *Comic Box* magazine reported him as saying, "The most important thing that Japanese animation should *not* do is to categorize the fans as a certain type of people and then make movies only for that type. How can we make films which will gain the acceptance of those people who've never seen animation before?"[1]

So, in *Princess Mononoke*, he sought to make something completely different from anything he'd done before but that still expressed those ideas he regarded as important. In an *Animage* interview with Mamoru Oshii in 1993, he remarked that he wanted to make a straightforward love story because "whether the world loses dogma or does whatever, love remains."[2] In the same year he told *Animerica*,

"I don't like a society that parades its right-eousness. The righteousness of the U.S., the righteousness of Islam, the righteousness of China, the righteousness of this or that ethnic group, the righteousness of Greenpeace, the righteousness of the entrepreneur. . . . They all claim to be righteous but they all try to coerce others into complying with their own stan-dards."[3] When asked if he was optimistic about the future on a BBC documentary in 1994, he talked about the hole in the ozone layer, AIDS, the international refugee crisis, and the pollution of air and oceans, and said, "We can see the twenty-first century clearly, and I wonder how we ourselves and our audi-ence and our children can live in this chaos. We're in a period when we can't avoid asking ourselves questions. We're making films in this situation. We can't make films in the same way as in the past."[4] Yet it was to the past he returned when looking for a starting point to rewrite his Japanese fairy story for production.

The Muromachi period lasted around two hundred years, from 1336 to 1573. It appealed greatly to Miyazaki, who saw it as the point at which the Japanese people began to feel they could control nature, rather than having to placate or worship it. They cleared large tracts of primeval woodland and produced iron ore in greater quantities than ever before. This de-parture defined their relationship to their ecology. As he said in 1997, finishing work on the film, "I've come to the point where I just can't make a movie without addressing the problem of humanity as part of an ecosys-tem."[5] Two years earlier, his movie proposal spoke of depicting the "unchanging basis of humanity, by overlapping the current era of change as we move toward the twenty-first century with the confusion of the Muromachi era," when the medieval system began to col-lapse and Japan started its movement toward modern times.[6] A girl who hated her own kind and a boy under curse of death would meet in a world of change. The usual samurai and courtly nobles would not appear, or would be kept to the margins; instead, the common people of early industrial Japan, the traders and ironworkers and subsistence farmers, would fill the stage.

Miyazaki began to write the detailed treat-ment for the movie in August 1994. Hitting writer's block in December, he took a break to make a music video, *On Your Mark* (see chap-ter 9). In April 1995 he completed the formal proposal, and the next month he started work on the storyboards. Animation began in July 1995 and was finally completed in mid-June 1997, less than a month before the premiere. For a Miyazaki film, *Princess Mononoke* (the final title choice) had an unusually long schedule, and was by far the most expensive Studio Ghibli production to date.

Toshio Suzuki, the film's producer, believes that all movies should recover their cost through the box office. *Mononoke Hime* cost just over two and a half billion yen (around twenty million dollars) to make. Adding on distribution and marketing costs probably raised the break-even point to around thirty million dollars. Between July 1997, when it opened opposite *The Lost World: Jurassic Park*, and November of the same year, the movie was seen by twelve million people—or to put it another way, in the five months following its release one tenth of the total population

[handwritten: cultural significance + effect on pop culture]

of Japan went to the movies to see *Princess Mononoke*.[7] Ticket sales raised over one hundred and sixty million dollars in that period. Before a single videocassette or merchandise license was sold, *Princess Mononoke* paid back her sponsors with a handsome chunk of interest and became Japan's highest-grossing movie ever. The movie out-earned *E.T.*, the previous Japan box office record holder, in around a quarter of the time it took the Spielberg movie to attain the record it had held for fifteen years. *Princess Mononoke* held the supreme championship only briefly, losing it to James Cameron's costlier and more expensively promoted *Titanic*, but it remains Japan's highest-grossing homemade box office earner.

In its first three weeks on domestic video release, *Princess Mononoke* sold two million copies. According to the *Screen Digest* report that gave that figure, 20 percent of sales were to people who said they had never bought a retail videocassette before.[8] The sales were made in the context of a market that is, in general, slow; the same report states that very few titles apart from children's animation sell more than two hundred thousand copies. By the end of 1998 sales had climbed past four million. In January 1999, when the film was screened on Japanese TV at peak time on a Friday evening and you might have thought that everyone who wanted to see it had done so, it achieved an audience share of 35.1 percent.

Miyazaki is unimpressed. "I want my films to be seen in a theater. I don't care if you watch the video fifty times; it's nothing more than background music."[9]

ART AND TECHNIQUE

Japan's history and landscape is one of Miyazaki's main influences for this movie. Japan is a country that values its ancient culture, and civic and religious festivals dating back centuries are still observed in many parts of the country. In the middle of November, for instance, Hiroshima City and the surrounding region celebrates the Inoshishi Matsuri—the Festival of the Boar. There is no direct link with the boar god of *Princess Mononoke*, but the way his culture and history have influenced Miyazaki's storytelling is obvious.

Miyazaki and his staff went into the field to research locations, taking many pictures and making sketches. Art director Kazuo Oga, who was responsible for many of the exquisite background paintings in the earlier films, went to the Shirakami Mountains, a UNESCO World Natural Heritage Property on the tip of northern Honshu, for the location of Ashitaka's village. The other four art directors went with Miyazaki to Yakushima, another UNESCO World Heritage site off the coast of the southeastern island of Kyushu, to find inspiration for the Shishigami's home among the island's ancient rain forests. These rain forests with their unique old trees, including cedars thousands of years old with trunks up to five meters in diameter, had already provided inspiration for the Sea of Corruption in *Nausicaä of the Valley of the Winds*. Miyazaki said that one of the biggest problems he and his staff face is that when they go on sketching sessions and try to envisage how this field or that road might have looked in the past, they

Ashitaka takes aim, a look of intense concentration on his face. The archery sequences move so fast that it is not until we look at still frames that we can see how accurately the weaponry, equipment, and movements are rendered.

have to edit out all the overhead power lines and modern features.[10] In the wilderness of the Yakushima forests there are few such problems. The change of light and the seasons bring out nuances which even the best photographs often fail to catch, and the team's onsite drawings and observations were essential in giving the forest of the movie its sense of reality.

Using a wide range of historical research based on the work of archaeologists like Ei-ichi Fujimori, Miyazaki created a world in which his "Emishi boy," Ashitaka could meet a girl who "resembled a Jomon pottery figure" from even further back in Japan's history, in a world in which there was no clear distinction between farmer and samurai. (Emishi are the aboriginal inhabitants of Japan, who may possibly be related to the Ainu who now live on the northern island of Hokkaido.) In the prehistoric Jomon period (10,000 B.C. to ca. 300 B.C.), Miyazaki felt women had more freedom and society was more fluid. Rather than focusing on lords or courts, he went to the fringes of society, to the ordinary man and woman struggling to survive in a world of change. He commented, "Recent studies in history, anthropology, and archaeology show that this country has had a far richer, more diverse history than the generally accepted images." [11]

Using such a period and such a social group as his starting point allowed Miyazaki to create characters more freely, challenging and breaking down the stereotypes of existing pe-

riod dramas. The movie also uses the simple language common in later primitive societies, where people and things are named simply for their appearance or attributes. Eboshi's name is just the word for her distinctive hat, and guns are called "flint-fire-arrows" because Japanese had no word for "gun" until the Portuguese arrived in the sixteenth century. The Tatarigami, or cursed god, has a name very close to that of the ironworkers' village, Tataraba, the place of the bellows. It shows

The Kodama are tiny forest spirits whose eerie appearance scares some humans, but they are entirely harmless. Here in the trees of their forest home, they watch the strangers passing through their world.

very clearly the destructive connection between the two curses of industrialization and outraged nature.

The color palette of the film is overwhelmingly green, with bareness and barrenness, absence of leaf cover, used to indicate the disruptive impact of man. Although *Princess Mononoke* uses more computer graphics (CG) effects than any previous Ghibli film, the richness of the visual effects is largely produced in the old-fashioned way, by hand drawing and painting onto cel. It's interesting to observe the way computer animation was integrated into the animation process. This helps to reveal the nature of Miyazaki's creative thinking just as powerfully as his storytelling or characterization. Each frame is drawn by hand. The computer is used for color, to enhance some areas in ways only it can, and to speed up the process and reduce the physical load on the creative team. The process was partly pre-planned and partly a response to changing circumstances, just as the processes of change in the story are partly willed by the characters and partly reactive to changes around them. (For more on CG, see chapter 1.)

Miyazaki himself retouched and corrected about eighty thousand of the film's one hundred and forty-four thousand cels. The huge physical strain of this level of involvement in the animation process was obviously on his mind in his interview in *Asia Pulse* magazine in May 1997, just before the film was released. Asked about rumors that *Princess Mononoke* would be his last film, he responded, "A pictorial animator has to make pictures move. Even if I have others do it, I end up having to fix a majority of it anyway. This is the most ex-hausting aspect of my day-to-day work. Physically, I just can't go on. I suffer from everything from poor eyesight to shoulder tension and hip and thigh pain."[12]

The music of *Princess Mononoke* is a wonderful backdrop to the film, although to my mind it stands up less well on its own (for listening without pictures) than any of Hisaishi's other works. The pentatonic scale is used to interesting effect alongside the more familiar Western scale; one of the best examples of use of the pentatonic is in the scene in which the Kodama lead Ashitaka through the forest. The main theme, as sung in the Japanese release by countertenor Yoshikazu Mera, has an eldritch quality that raises the hairs on the back of the neck. Hisaishi found himself working in a whole new way with Miyazaki; in the past, he had finished his work and then invited the director to the orchestral recording session, but on *Princess Mononoke* they collaborated far more closely from the beginning, with Hisaishi first writing several pieces which were released as an "image album" of music inspired by the movie story, then going on to adapt, rework, and rewrite, with Miyazaki and Suzuki frequent visitors to his recording studio. The composer sees himself as a contributor to the process of creating the movie's world, rather than an outside contractor hired in to do one specific job, and he tried throughout to express the subtle atmospheres and feelings of the story and characters.

Once again, the sound mix is marvelous, using silence and natural sound as a counterpoint to the score and dialogue in a manner that enhances the movement of the story and highlights points of tension. Many American animators have said they study Studio Ghibli's works; if American sound directors could be persuaded to do likewise, we might be spared the incessant noise that assaults the ears in contemporary films. *Princess Mononoke*'s use of sound demonstrates the validity of the old movie tradition of having sound and music support the story, instead of forcing the audience to listen to the film above the constant thumping of the latest MTV hits.

Aside from Japanese history and folklore, the film also echoes Bunyan's *Pilgrim's Progress* and the *Gilgamesh* epic. The hero must journey far from everything he knows, into strange worlds where he will be confronted by new dangers and challenges. Yet the second main influence, as with *My Neighbor Totoro*, is Miyazaki's own experience. There is a sense in the film of summing up, of taking stock, as if he were looking back over his years as a writer, artist, and director and pulling together the strands of thought that have evolved over that time. He had hinted on many occasions that this would be his last film as a director, and its elegiac beauty and reflective nature seem perfectly suited to serve as a swan song.

In *Castle of Cagliostro* he made a film packed with action and adventure, but one that still upheld the idea that true love was something precious, wherever it might be found. In *Nausicaä of the Valley of the Winds* he spread a glittering tapestry of adventure across the story of a girl's growth through exploration and understanding to the ultimate sacrifice, and brought out themes relevant to the growing ecological awareness of the time. There was also a very strong awareness of the impact of a dominant power on a weaker one. In *Cas-*

tle in the Sky he recognized the importance of community and brotherhood, and once again put love and understanding at the core of an epic adventure story. *My Neighbor Totoro* celebrated Japan's natural riches and looked back to the beauty and simplicity of a country childhood, while *Kiki's Delivery Service* focused with sympathy on the anxieties of the young and the terrors of independence. Both of the latter two films subtly emphasized the importance of the community in helping to keep children safe and enabling them to grow up into happy, healthy adults. *Porco Rosso* reminded us that appearances aren't everything, and that even a middle-aged pig can dream of beauty, romance, and heroism; once again we saw Miyazaki's awareness of how political forces impact the lives of individuals.

Throughout his career, a breadth of cultural, historical, and literary understanding has enriched his work and emphasized its relevance to movie-lovers throughout the world. Yet he is adamant that he makes movies for a Japanese audience. Interviewed for CNN, he said, "I'm only worried about how my film would be viewed in Japan. Frankly, I don't worry too much about how it plays elsewhere."[13] When I asked him how he viewed Western fans' concerns about possible changes to the translation and dub script of his works, he replied that he's not at all worried about translation or mistranslating. "After all, for years now people in Japan have been seeing things and reading things about England, probably by people who have never been to England and don't even speak English, but they've still enjoyed what's been written and have taken something out of it to a certain extent. As far as I'm concerned, if it's translated properly and done well, that's great; but what I really hope is that at least as a minimum people will see it and say, '…there's something other than the place where I live, things that I'm familiar with, there is something else out there that has value to it.'" His view was that, like all directors, he has no control over how an audience will receive or interpret his work in any language. As long as the viewer leaves the cinema entertained, and perhaps with his or her horizons expanded a little, Miyazaki the director will be happy. [14]

THE CHARACTERS

Ashitaka

Ashitaka is a young prince of the Emishi, the northern

San has entered the town of Tataraba to avenge the assault on her adoptive mother, the wolf god Moro. She faces Eboshi in hand-to-hand combat and finds that the town-dweller's ferocity and determination are a match for her own.

tribes who may have been the aboriginal people of Japan.[15] In the theater program for the movie, Miyazaki describes him thus: "Ashitaka is not a cheerful, carefree boy. He is a melancholy guy who has a destiny. I feel that I am that way myself, but until now, I haven't made a film about this kind of character." Living a happy and useful life in his own community, among people who love him, Ashitaka acts to help save his friends from danger and as a result is cursed. It's completely unfair, but it changes his whole life. Miyazaki draws a parallel with twentieth-century life, in which people can be "cursed" through no fault of their own. He views Ashitaka's scar, the evidence of his curse, not just as a symbol but as a real, physical problem that gives him pain and may kill him.

When I interviewed Miyazaki at length in 1999 he made a direct comparison between the scar and physical curses such as AIDS that modern children have to bear, and he said that this is what makes Ashitaka a contemporary person.

Slightly naive and unused to the outside world, Ashitaka is obviously a very skilled warrior—his shooting skills are amazing—but he's also a courageous and tenderhearted person with an open, trusting nature. It is his acceptance of her as she is that eventually wins San's love.

Yakkle is Ashitaka's faithful, intelligent steed. He's a fanciful creature partly resembling a large mountain goat or antelope. Miyazaki's main reason for not giving Ashitaka just another horse was to distance him from the usual image of the samurai in period dramas. (He also commented that he thought it might be easier to draw an imaginary animal!)[16] A similar animal appeared in his early manga, *The Journey of Shuna.*

Oracle is the wise woman of Ashitaka's village. She is instrumental in the decision that he has to leave and advises him on how he might shake off his curse. In the Japanese film she's called Lady Hii.

San was abandoned by her parents as a child and raised in the woods by the wolf god Moro with Moro's own children. She thinks of Moro as her mother and the other children as her siblings, and she will fight to defend them. She's dressed in a more primitive style than any other human in the film, partly to emphasize that she's living apart from humans with only what she can find or make to wear, and partly to show that her ancient way of life, with its gods and beliefs, is dying as new peoples and ideas move into the forests. At the beginning of the movie, San is as fierce and wild as the wolves, but she is also as wise and brave as these ancient gods. By the end she has learned and grown enormously as a person—from hating all humans, she has developed far enough to admit her love for Ashitaka. I asked if Miyazaki had observed this kind of learning process in children and young people, and he said it was more the result of how he wanted a character to develop; he wanted to show "the kind of development that makes them a good person in their heart."[17]

Moro

Moro is a huge wolf god who has roamed the ancient forests for longer than anyone knows. She is a noble and tragic figure. She is noble because she was able to love an unwanted child of the humans and raise her as her own. She is tragic because she knows that her world is coming to an end because of these same humans. She and the other beast gods see their children growing up smaller than they themselves are, literally diminishing in stature as their powers diminish.

Overlord

Overlord is a boar god who is injured, like the Tatarigami that attacked Ashitaka's village, by iron made by man. He too is a noble creature but his injury maddens him and in the end he is unable to resist the madness.

Shishi/ Didaribotchi

Shishi/Didaribotchi is the great god of the forest, the embodiment of the powers of nature. Like the landscape, he changes form when night falls. By day he is a deer-like creature with huge antlers above a wise, gentle face, surrounded by a golden light. At night he becomes a huge, evanescent shape of light and color, towering above the forest into the starry sky. His healing powers are great enough to bring a creature back from the dead and regenerate a denuded forest in moments, but if angered he can also be a force of destruction. It is said that the head of his deer form can grant immortality.

Jiku

Jiku is a priest and an agent of the emperor, but at heart is also a trader who would sell anything. Like Eboshi, he's one of the Yamato people who conquered central Japan and drove Ashitaka's tribe north long ago. He acts as middleman to persuade Eboshi to kill Shishi for money, while selling her and her people down the river to the nobles who want to combine a chance at immortality with a strike at a peasant movement that is challenging their power. One of the strengths of the movie is that he's not shown as a really bad, black-hearted villain—he's just another ordinary person trying to make a little profit and get through the day.

Lady Eboshi

Lady Eboshi is a tough, resourceful woman who dresses in a manner reminiscent of a medieval Japanese prostitute, though her distinctive black hat is a piece of nobleman's attire. Miyazaki says in the theater program that she has had a very tough life and has endured considerable hardships to get where she is. She wouldn't hesitate to kill or do anything else necessary to fulfill her dream of security for her people. "What Eboshi is trying to do is to build her idea of paradise. That makes her a twentieth-century person."

She is practical as well as compassionate—she encourages and harbors the lepers who are developing their skills as gun-makers, because in a world where lepers are rejected and driven out this guarantees her a skilled workforce, and she makes sure the women who work the machinery get good food and good treatment at a time when elsewhere they are treated badly. She admires San's courage and skill but will not hesitate to kill her and her gods if it furthers her aims. She relies on no man, god, or demon, and does not care that her efforts to develop the iron industry devastate the landscape and kill animals and plants. She's a complex character whose motivations and drives can't be understood in terms of "good" versus "evil."

Koroku and Toki

Koroku and Toki are a couple who live and work in Eboshi's community of Tataraba. Koroku is a cowherd, an average working man who is good-natured and not too bright and just wants to do his work, eat, and sleep. Toki is a bright, vivacious woman who expresses her affection for her spouse in joking abuse.

Gonza

Gonza is Eboshi's second in command, a cautious and reserved man with a serious nature. He's no match for the feisty women around him.

THE STORY

Ashitaka is out riding his faithful steed, Yakkle, when a group of girls from his village is attacked by a terrible creature. It is a huge mass of writhing bloodworms, and anything it touches is scarred. Ashitaka manages to kill it with his arrow but is badly injured and left with a terrible infected mark on his arm. As the creature dies its true nature is revealed—it was one of the boar gods of the forest, and it had been wounded with a ball of stone embedded in its flesh. It became a *tatari*, a curse. How did a god become infected with such evil? How could anyone drive a ball of stone into a god's body? And is Ashitaka now cursed, his scarred arm a reminder of its power and a threat to the village? The local elders think he is, and after receiving advice from the wise woman of the village they conclude that Ashitaka must leave and travel south, looking with "unclouded sight" for the source of the evil that is corrupting the gods and making them attack men, against all reason and custom. Only so can the curse be lifted.

Ashitaka cuts off his topknot of hair and leaves. He has been cast out of the only world he knows, and cutting his hair is a symbol of leaving his old life behind. All he takes with him as a memento is a little jeweled knife given to him by his sister. As he and Yakkle travel south, they meet bloodthirsty samurai and have to fight for their lives. He finds that the curse, which re-activates sometimes as spirit worms writhing around his scarred arm, gives him huge strength—he can shoot the head clean off a man's shoulders with one arrow. Reaching a small town, where he feels very much alone, he meets up with Jiku, a priest who invites him to share his camp for the night. Jiku is interested in his curse and tells him that the forest far to the west is the god Shishi's forest, where many strange things are found. He also learns that the local lord is at war with the ironworkers who have built a village upstream. The pollution generated when iron ore is washed out of sand destroys rice crops as the muddy water washes downstream to farmland, and anyway Lord Asano wants a share of the iron for himself. None of this interests Ashitaka as much as the news of the god Shishi's forest, and he leaves early next morning.

Eboshi and her men have been to buy rice for their people, but as they return home they are attacked by the wolf god Moro's children, one of whom is the "spirit princess" San. When Moro herself joins the fray she is wounded by one of Eboshi's guns, which fire

balls of stone into flesh, but the caravan too takes casualties, and in the struggle to escape and get the rice home some have to be left behind. Ashitaka, passing through the same place later, finds two of them still alive. One, Koroku, is able to tell his rescuer what happened and he's able to travel if he sits on Yakkle's back, but the other is near death and Ashitaka has to carry him on his back. It's a long journey. At one point Ashitaka meets San, but she runs before he can speak to her. Part of the way they are guided by *kodama*,

The head that was carried off by Jiku-Bo is rescued by Ashitaka and San. Lifting it out of its container, they raise it up to offer it to the enraged god in the hope that this will stop its rampage of destruction.

FILMOGRAPHY AND PERSONNEL

Princess Mononoke

Mononoke Hime

Theatrical release, 12 July 1997

RUNNING TIME: 2 hours, 13 minutes

Original story by Hayao Miyazaki

DIRECTOR, SCREENPLAY: Hayao Miyazaki

ANIMATION DIRECTORS: Masashi Ando, Kitaro Kosaka, Yoshifumi Kondo

ART DIRECTORS: Kazuo Oga, Nizo Yamamoto, Naoya Tanaka, Satoshi Kuroda, Yoji Takeshige

MUSIC: Jo Hisaishi

PRODUCER: Toshio Suzuki

EXECUTIVE PRODUCER: Yasuyoshi Tokuma

© Tokuma, NTV, Dentsu, Studio Ghibli

Partial U.S. Credits

(Full credits were not available as this book was completed.)

A Miramax Films (U.S.) release of a Tokuma Shoten Co.-Nippon Television Network-Dentsu-Studio Ghibli production. Produced by Toshio Suzuki. Executive producer, Yasuyoshi Tokuma. Directed, written by Hayao Miyazaki. Animation direction, Masashi Ando, Kitaro Kosaka, Yoshifumi Kondo. Camera (Fujicolor, Panavision widescreen), Atsushi Okui; editor, Takeshi Seyama; music, Joe Hisaishi; sound (Dolby Digital), Kazuhiro Wakabayashi. English-language script by Neil Gaiman. English voice direction by Jack Fletcher. With the vocal talents of Billy Crudup (Ashitaka), Claire Danes (San), Minnie Driver (Eboshi), Gillian Anderson (Moro), Billy Bob Thornton, Jada Pinckett (Toki).

Although the movie is still being discussed and described by Miramax as *Princess Mononoke*, there has not yet been final confirmation of the movie's release title. "Princess" is a word with specific links to young audiences for Disney, and *Princess Mononoke* doesn't fit the classic "Disney Princess" mold. It remains to be seen whether Miramax will revert to one of Miyazaki's suggested titles from the proposal, such as *The Legend of Ashitaka*, or will stay with *Princess Mononoke*.

tiny, doll-like forest spirits whom Ashitaka recognizes from his own homeland. They spot San's tracks again, but don't see her. At one point, just before they leave the forest, they glimpse the god Shishi himself, and Ashitaka feels his curse activate once more, but he also feels the man he carries grow lighter for a while, and Koroku's arm doesn't hurt so much.

When they reach Tataraba, the ironworkers' village named for the huge bellows they use to keep their fire going, Ashitaka is not at first welcomed with open arms—the cautious Gonza wants to know who this stranger is. But Koroku's wife Toki chides him into welcoming the man who saved her husband, and Eboshi also welcomes him. He finds a community where lepers are looked after and taught skills, where everyone works and everyone eats, and where there is plenty of good-humored teasing and laughter. He doesn't like it when he learns that Eboshi is having the lepers make more and lighter guns, and that it was she who shot the boar god that attacked his village and ended his carefree life. His curse activates again and moves his arm to try and kill her, but one of the lepers pleads for her life. When he joins the women working at the great bellows, he sees even more clearly that although he may not agree with all Eboshi's methods, she is doing her best to create a better life for her people. He plans to leave the next day to continue his quest but is happy to spend the night and work in return for food and a bed.

But San and the wolves are coming to attack the town in revenge for Moro's injury. Eboshi has been hoping to meet San—she wants to fight the wolves and push them deep into the forest so that the people of Tataraba can live without being attacked and so she can strip the forest and wash the soil for iron-making. After an exciting chase across the rooftops and alleys of the town, San and Eboshi meet. Ashitaka intervenes to try and stop their fight—he shows everyone his arm, the curse activated, spirit-worms writhing, and tells them this is what happens when you let hatred and wrath into your being. Since no one is in the mood to listen to reason, he is forced to knock both women out, and picks up San to take her back to her own people. The guards try to stop him and he is shot in the back, but the huge strength of the curse enables him to push the heavy doors of the settlement aside and he walks into the forest with her and Yakkle.

When San comes to, she is angry and puzzled. She has no idea why he saved her and risked his own life to do it, but she feels she

owes him. She fends off her wolf god brothers with the warning that he is her prey, talks down the orangutans who want to eat him in the hope that they will absorb human skill with human blood and be able to stop the humans from cutting down the forest, and decides to take him to Shishi. Once again, Ashitaka journeys through the forest and glimpses the god. His life is saved, but the curse is not lifted and his scar remains. However, he knows that his feelings for San are deeper than any curse.

The boar gods are arriving to confer with the wolf gods on what to do about the intrusion of humans into their territory and the attacks on them. The Overlord of the boars has been injured by a human weapon. His brothers accuse San of favoring her own kind in having a living human at their meeting, but Moro insists that her daughter will do as she thinks best. They are even more angry when they hear that it was Ashitaka who killed their brother in the north, but when Ashitaka tells them that he had become cursed and then turned into a mindless mass of rage, Moro reveals that the same thing has happened to her and she too is dying. She has been shot by one of Eboshi's fire-arrows, and she does not know whether Shishi will save her or suck out her life. The boars are adamant that this human threat must be fought. San and Ashitaka spend the night together in a cave high above the forest, and he gives her the dagger that was his memento of home. Whatever happens in the great battle between humans and gods, he wants her to know that he does not blame her.

Jiku and imperial agents have been hiding

in the forest, watching the boars gathering. They plan to infiltrate the animals' ranks for reasons of their own. When Asano's samurai attack another of Eboshi's supply trains, he approaches Eboshi with a proposal. The Emperor himself has signed Shishi's death warrant, a god authorizing the killing of a god; there are rumors of Shishi's blood bestowing immortality. Jiku wants Eboshi to use her guns to carry out the warrant. The relationship between the two of them goes back further than is apparent and it seems she owes him a debt. Now, after the boars and wolves have been weakened by battle, is a good time for the attempt. The people of Tataraba are neither impressed by an imperial warrant or worried about killing a god, if the price is right, and as for danger, they'll follow their leader just about anywhere. They don't know that there is a double cross going on; while they attack the god, samurai will attack their home.

The epic battle between beast gods and men has been fought with huge losses, thanks to the imperial agents who hid under boar's hides and killed many of the animal gods by stealth. Moro is half dead, and San, who was the Overlord's scout during the fight, is almost entirely hidden inside the seething mass of bloodworms that cover him as the curse takes over. The wise and brave old god is a mindless, speechless thing, but Ashitaka's only concern is saving San. Moro does her best to help, but she is fading fast. When he finally gets her out of the mass of worms, she can only watch as Shishi arrives. Instead of saving Moro and the Overlord, restoring the ancient animals to health and strength, he sucks out the last of their lives before beginning his nightly trans-

formation into the Didaribotchi, the night spirit.

As he begins to transform, Eboshi fires at him and hits his elongating neck. The hole in his neck widens and the head flies off, to be grabbed by Jiku and shut inside a wooden pail. But gods don't die so easily. The transformation goes on but not in its usual peaceful fashion. A glowing mass of some strange fluid, part of his life force, comes from Shishi's severed neck, killing everything it touches as it flows. Kodama fall like dead birds from the trees. The glowing slime takes off Moro's head and as it flies through the air it bites off Eboshi's right arm. Ashitaka moves quickly to stop the blood and bind up the wound as best he can.

San, beside herself with rage and grief, wants to kills Eboshi with the dagger Ashitaka gave her and reject all things human. Ashitaka stops her and says he promised Toki that he would get Eboshi safely home. The god is raging above them, threatening to destroy everything and everyone in its blind path. Ashitaka asks San to help stop him. She says she will not help humans, but he reminds her that she is human; torn between both her people, she hesitates, but finally she agrees. Jiku and his men have tried to escape with the head, but in vain; returning it is the only thing that will placate the god.

Despite the danger, Ashitaka and San succeed in returning the head. The god is whole again and his renewal renews much of the devastation of the battle, but he withdraws into the depths of the forest, far from the threats of man.

The struggle is not yet over. Back at Tatara-

San leaps into battle, her face hidden behind a primitive mask, knife at the ready. She has been raised by the wolf-god Moro as her own daughter after her human family abandoned her.

ba, the women have fought off a samurai attack and have barely survived it. When Ashitaka and Eboshi struggle back to the village with their few rescuers, the devastation there is terrible too, and the gods are unlikely to step in and repair it. But despite their losses, some of the community have survived, and they will rebuild and thrive in the future under Eboshi's guidance.

Ashitaka and San meet again in the grasslands at the edge of the forest. He will never be able to go back to the innocent boy he was before the curse, but he has kept innocence and gentleness alive in his heart through all the deceit and disappointment he has faced. San will never trust humans and does not want to live in a human community, but she has learned that she loves Ashitaka and wants to be with him as much as possible. They have time to work things out.

The end credits roll on the two lovers and the glorious, reborn landscape around them. In a world of change and complexity, love can survive.

COMMENTARY

All nations are born in legend, and the legend is usually manufactured by those who come afterward, on the most tenuous of bases, to suit the prevailing circumstances. Miyazaki's darkest and most daring film turns its back on dreams of Europe and looks into Japan's misty, half-imagined past. Yet, looking to the future, it also uses computer graphic imagery to a greater extent than any of Studio Ghibli's previous works.[18] The film is a series of dazzling contradictions, reflecting its central theme of the tensions and strivings of different creatures with different aspirations forced to fight for their share of scarce resources in a world that is growing more complex and more dangerous every day.

Miyazaki once tried to make an animation set during the Heian period (794–1185), in a ruined mansion within a walled enclosure. Outside, plague and famine raged, but inside it was completely peaceful until, one day, the wall was broken down. "Like we have earthquakes and the appearance of the AUM cult, reality comes rushing in through the cracks in the wall. When the wall breaks, there are people who don't know what to do."[19] In a sense, Princess Mononoke is that story. Everyone in the movie except Ashitaka is trying to build their own little enclave, but reality keeps breaking down the walls. The old gods want only to roam their ancient domains undisturbed. The rich, powerful humans want only to use the gods as bolsters for their own influence. The poor humans want only to cut down the virgin forest and make a space

where they can live and work in freedom. The visionaries and technologists want only to develop their ideas. Some are aware of the price they or others will pay for their choices, some are ignorant and some are reckless. But nature has an overriding power, overriding even that of the gods. All life is change, and what does not change dies. Humans are part of the process of change, but those who think they are controlling its course are self-deluding.

Academic and critic Julia Sertori sees Princess Mononoke as a summary of Miyazaki's and Ghibli's achievement, citing its likeness to Nausicaä of the Valley of the Winds in the presentation of civilization as a "poisonous, unstoppable juggernaut" and to My Neighbor Totoro in its evocation of a lost pastoral idyll, pointing out Ashitaka's links with Marco in Porco Rosso and San's with Nausicaä, "a princess from a different world, whose people are fated to die."[20]

Princess Mononoke also reprises and reworks many of the human relationships shown in the earlier movies. San's relationship with Eboshi gives a new angle on the younger/older woman pairing of Castle of Cagliostro, Nausicaä, and Porco Rosso. Eboshi's leadership is an interesting comparison with Dola's or with Kushana's. Like Kushana, Eboshi will lose an arm in battle with a force she does not understand. In her world, technology hasn't yet reached a level where she can simply replace it and physical deficiency can mean death. Eboshi has built a community that will sustain her, but it's never easy for a warrior to deal with the lessening of physical prowess. Ashitaka must win San's confidence and trust just as Pazu must win Sheeta's. In a beautiful echo of Castle in the

Sky, Ashitaka and San fight to retrieve the severed head of the enraged forest god and return it to stop the god's devastating rampage. When the bloodstained, battered pair haul the head out of its wooden bucket and hold it up so that the god can see it, they are risking themselves to save the world for others.

The community of Tataraba is part of a chain of development that links the mining community of *Castle in the Sky*, the country village in *My Neighbor Totoro,* and Koriko City in *Kiki's Delivery Service*. Our religious impulses also come under scrutiny, and more harshly than in *My Neighbor Totoro*. In the earlier film, religious observances were part of the backdrop of everyday life but were purely human constructs and had no influence over nature. In *Princess Mononoke*, the gods are real and tangible—but the growing greed and cynicism of humans is literally diminishing them, making them physically smaller, and their own rage and incomprehension is focusing on every injury offered to them and turning them into seething masses of pain and suffering that can be passed on to man.

Perhaps the most interesting relationship in the film is that of man with nature. Sertori reads the film as a plea for human warmth and kindness. "*Princess Mononoke* is not about ecology. It is about the fact that nothing lasts forever . . . a gentle reminder that in a thousand years, no-one will care who we were or what we did, and that we should concentrate on making a difference where we can, with each other." This is a good reading, very much in the spirit of the film, but I think it misses part of the picture. Miyazaki is making a film about love, the extent to which love involves

loss of many kinds, and how that loss can be borne. San and Ashitaka, the human embodiments of love and loss, come to an agreement that is ideal for neither but respects both. She will continue to live in the forest, in the world she loves, with the few survivors of her doomed family of gods, and the lovers will meet each other from time to time, halfway between her world and his. There are no guarantees as to whether the relationship will last, but they have just seen how promises can be broken, gods die, and forests wither and grow again; they are no longer so naïve as to ask for guarantees. If we could find a way to allow nature its own space and relate to it in love and respect rather than seek to bend it to our will and our need, perhaps man and nature could get along. There are no guarantees, but there is hope. The violated Didaribotchi withdraws into the deep forest, yet heals the scars of man's attack on the woods.

The problems of modern life are presented as timeless; pain, loss, fear, change, and complexity are not twentieth-century constructs. Miyazaki grounds the metaphysical question of man's relationship with the numinous in the physical struggle between men and gods, and shows us that this too is a twentieth-century issue. We have limited resources—of time, of energy, of faith. How much of that will we devote to serving a remote idea, and how much of it to making improvements in our own lives and the lives of those we care for? Nature is not endless and its regenerative powers, while seemingly miraculous, are not guaranteed. How far can we trade on those powers and exploit them for our own purposes, and how far do we need to consider the future

*San faces the onlooker with bloodstains around her mouth
and a knife in her hand, a picture of savagery. Yet she has merely
been trying to suck a bullet out of the flesh of her wolf-god
companion. This contrast between appearance and truth
is one of the underlying themes of the film.*

our descendants will inherit? Technological progress can make life easier, but it also brings loss. And we may not be the only factors to be considered in the equation. Ashitaka acts for a good reason but is still cursed, and the curse that iron brings spreads through men and gods, changing all it touches. Modern agro-chemical companies are promoting genetically modified foods for what they tell us are good reasons, but will future generations, both plant and animal, be cursed with change we can neither predict nor control? Like any great work of art, nature is not as simple as it seems.

The beauty of nature and the beauty of love are both magically framed. Ashitaka's love for San is born in adventure, when she makes her daring, swashbuckling attack on the town, and grows in settings of awesome beauty in the forest. His fellow-feeling and affection for the people of Tataraba grow in the homelier, messier setting of the town itself, which to a rural boy from a tiny northern village is as amazing as the forests. Yet love, the transforming force of life, is neither soft nor sentimental. When we see San with a knife in her hand and blood all over her face, it is because she has been trying to get a bullet out of her mother's body, an act of love.

At the end of the film, everything is changed, yet most things have survived. The forest is diminished and will go on being diminished by the impact of man. Its old gods have chosen retreat, and are still retreating today. San is not going to leave the woods for civilization, Tarzan-like; Ashitaka is not going to join her and abandon the world of noise and muddle and compromise that is humanity. Miyazaki said in his proposal that there can be no happy ending to the war between gods and mortals; yet, in the midst of loss and pain, beauty can exist and wonderful things can happen. San and Ashitaka love each other.

Tataraba has survived and will rebuild. Out of the ugliness of the ironworks lepers will eat, children will be born, their parents will grow old. *Princess Mononoke* is a beautiful evocation of the dogged, determined, and wholly unconquerable persistence of life and love, an epic movie about ordinary people adrift in confusing times, with a core of power and passion rarely seen in modern works of art.

From the Utopian idealism of *Nausicaä of the Valley of the Winds*, Miyazaki's vision has developed to encompass the mature and kindly humanism of *Princess Mononoke*. He has always sought to entertain and excite his audience, but he has never accepted that this should preclude making them think and feel. If *Princess Mononoke* had been Miyazaki's last film, it would have been a finale of almost unparalleled splendor, fit to stand alongside Kurosawa's *Ran* as the capstone of a great artist's career. I wait with delighted anticipation for what comes next.

9

The Miyazaki Machine

More Than Just Movies

Aside from his movies, Miyazaki has been active in a number of other fields, including illustration, comic art, and writing. Many of the characters he has created have acquired a life of their own in the form of stuffed toys, stationery, and a host of other items of merchandise sought after by fans throughout Asia and, increasingly, in the West. Now that his work is moving into a new arena, his fans wonder what comes next.

MERCHANDISE

Miyazaki's breadth of interest has led him into many areas as an artist and illustrator. His admiration for the works of favorite authors such as C. W. Nichol and Antoine de Saint-Exupéry is demonstrated in a range of book covers and illustrations. His love affair with the world of comics did not stop at the mammoth task of completing *Nausicaä* in manga form; there are several other manga by Miyazaki, all naturally shorter than *Nausicaä* but each with its own charm, including an eight-page history of in-flight catering for Japan Airlines' in-flight magazine. In 1997 he even contributed to an issue of New York art-house magazine *Visionaire*, a hugely expensive limited-run publication that stretches the magazine genre into areas most creative teams would never even consider.[1] Reflecting this diversity of activity, the team at Studio Ghibli has become involved in a wide range of other activities related to the movie-making that is their central purpose.

In January 1999, sitting in a small meeting room at Studio Ghibli, waiting to talk to studio head and producer Toshio Suzuki, I was surrounded by beautiful things. A cuckoo clock carved with Totoros and oak leaves ticked softly on one wall above an array of stuffed toys and figurines. An elegant red seaplane model recalled *Porco Rosso*. A replica of Ashitaka's sword from *Princess Mononoke* was propped in a corner among a mass of intriguing objects. In a library area where I chatted to a cameraman filming an interview for Japanese TV, a stuffed Totoro as tall as the average six-year-old sat atop a pile of chairs in one corner, next to a big toy dog from *My Neighbors The Yamadas*. Elsewhere in the studio building, a small but energetic team worked to coordinate the Ghibli merchandising operation in an office full of yet more beautiful things. These are items that can be seen in shops all over Japan, and increasingly around the world. Merchandise is a major contributor to the financial success of the studio's creations.

Yet later in our discussion, Suzuki told me that he would really like to make a film with no merchandising, not even a video release—just a film that went onto the theatrical circuit and recovered its costs through people coming to the theaters to see it. It is his passionate belief that movies ought not to depend on merchandising, that the film should come first and should make money on its own merits. He has even turned down a movie deal with an internationally renowned Japanese corporation because their executives were more concerned with the merchandise than the movie.[2]

Princess Mononoke has, of course, done just that. It is the most successful and highest-earning film in Japanese cinema history apart from James Cameron's *Titanic*. It has its raft of merchandising, the posters and art books and handkerchiefs and stationery and CDs, but they're an adjunct to its massive success at the box office, a success confirmed when a screening on Japanese TV in January 1999 attracted a 35.1 percent audience share.[3] That level of viewer involvement is of the order expected only for major international sporting events or huge political and social news stories—certainly not for a movie that had already been seen by a vast slice of the Japanese population at the movies, and bought by many on video.

There are many misconceptions about the scale and importance of the local animation industry in Japan, but it cannot be denied that it ranks higher in the mass-entertainment media league than its English-language equivalent. On a rough-and-ready analysis, carried

More then a decade after he was first brought to life onscreen, Totoro is the beloved companion of millions of children in Japan. Stuffed toys ranging from pocket-sized to giant are available in almost every major toy store.

out via counts from Japanese program schedules and industry release announcements in the latter part of 1998, around 3 to 6 percent of weekly Japanese-made TV programming was animation, approximately 25 to 30 percent of Japanese-made videos released commercially were animation, and about 5 percent of Japanese-made theatrical releases were animation. In addition, Japanese viewers show a strong interest in foreign animation from studios such as Disney, and there is a well-established market for erotic animation, almost all of which is locally made. Considering its small scale, Studio Ghibli picks up a strikingly large share of cinema and video market sales, and of audiences whenever its

A picture frame for treasured memories from Princess Mononoke.

works are screened on TV. *Princess Mononoke* is an exceptional performer by any standards, but *Porco Rosso* is also among the top-ten Japanese movies in terms of box office gross, coming in just above Kurosawa's classic *Kagemusha*. Studio Ghibli is therefore one of the most successful Japanese production houses in box office terms. Suzuki's wish to make a movie that would succeed at the box office, with no need for merchandise, is no vague pipe dream.

Nevertheless, Miyazaki's movies have always been merchandised to some extent, even before Studio Ghibli was set up. His first feature, *Castle of Cagliostro*, triggered a wonderful range of toys and goods that are still sought after by collectors today. The most glorious item, and the one that most closely reflects Miyazaki's own working method on the film, is a three-foot-high, immensely detailed toy castle model kit, complete with furnished interior, turrets, dungeons, and a whole cast of tiny figures that can be used to recreate the film in the lucky owner's home. *Nausicaä of the Valley of the Winds* was also marketed through

stationery, CDs, and model kits of the heroine on her glider, the mehve, or with the baby Ohmu. Of course, both these films were made through other studios, since Studio Ghibli didn't exist at the time, but for *Castle in the Sky* and *My Neighbor Totoro* merchandising started out on a small scale. The first stuffed toy Totoro didn't appear on the market until 1990, two years after the film had its theatrical release. By this time, Studio Ghibli had taken control of the merchandising process. (There are two Totoro stuffed toys listed in the *Totoro ga Ippai* catalogue as produced in 1988, but they do not seem to have been widely released, perhaps because they are not much like the Totoro fans know and love.)

It's a difficult process to control, and the studio handles it chiefly by limiting the number of product licenses issued, working with manufacturers they know and trust. Ghibli receives large numbers of proposals for new merchandise, but of more than a hundred companies who have approached them only around thirty have succeeded in getting a license. The current *Studio Ghibli Character Goods Catalogue* lists just twenty-four makers for a range of goods from soft toys to furnishings and porcelain to neckties. (This excludes videos and books, published through parent company Tokuma.) Suzuki also has strong views on what constitutes good merchandise. "Basically, I don't want to manufacture any product that's already there and all they have to do is just put the image of the character on it."[4] The variety and artistry of the Ghibli merchandise, which includes many styles of artwork and design that differ from the original images rather than just following the movies in slavish imitation, reflects those views.

My *Neighbor Totoro* remains Ghibli's biggest earner as far as character merchandise is concerned. Suzuki says in his essay *Ten Years of Studio Ghibli* that *Totoro* merchandise keeps the studio out of deficit year in, year out.[5] On my bookshelf is a large-format Japanese paperback with more than two hundred full-color pages, which clearly demonstrates how this was achieved. *Totoro ga Ippai* is a catalogue of every item of *Totoro* licensed merchandise produced between 1987 and 1995, and an essential reference guide for collectors. The sheer size of the range is astounding, especially when you take into account the relatively small number of licensees; each licensee has made a major commitment to the continuing success and quality of Ghibli productions. Yet other Ghibli characters also make increasingly important contributions to the studio's balance sheet. The whole Ghibli range is surviving and thriving in the crowded Japanese market. Walking around a downtown shopping mall in Tokyo I saw Jiji, Kiki's talking cat, in backpack form alongside a whole range of Disney and other character backpacks in a mainstream luggage store. In Harajuku's giant Kiddyland toy store, *Princess Mononoke* photo frames, ornamental boxes, and face towels were selling strongly. Most CD outlets rack all the Ghibli soundtracks and spin-offs. Almost every stationery store can offer you a *Nausicaä* notebook.

Anyone might reasonably assume that this would be a major attraction for the Disney organization, and a major component of the deal between Disney and Tokuma to release Ghib-

Japanese video cover for Castle in the Sky, *depicting the moment in the film when Sheeta falls out of the sky into Pazu's arms. Notice the detail of the nineteenth-century technology.*

li movies worldwide. After all, Disney is one of the world's greatest marketing and distribution engines. Their level of expertise in moving character-based products is immense, and their worldwide chain of outlets and licensed dealers is sustained and reinforced via the movies and TV shows. The U.S. video success of *Kiki's Delivery Service* and the forthcoming theatrical and video launches of *Princess Mononoke* and *Castle in the Sky* would all seem to offer perfect opportunities for Disney to launch massive amounts of Miyazaki merchandise across the world. Yet Disney's contract with Tokuma for the distribution of Studio Ghibli films does not include any merchandising rights!

This is largely because Suzuki and his colleagues want to keep control of the production standards of merchandise relating to their titles in their own hands. Stephen Alpert, President of Tokuma International, told me that if an arrangement to export the existing Japanese merchandise could be made, that would probably be acceptable to Studio Ghibli because the quality of those goods is under their direct control. The idea of any other company, even a trusted partner, having control over the quality of products carrying their name was not one they were currently prepared to consider.[6] When I asked Alpert if Disney was also trying to pick up the rights to *My Neighbor Totoro* when Fox Lorber's rights lapsed, he confirmed that this was the case, but again, merchandising rights are not part and parcel of the distribution deal.

So at present, the world's master merchandisers have the right to distribute some of the world's most merchandisable high-quality movies but not the right to merchandise the immensely lovable characters from those movies, whose success has already been tested in a critical and well-supplied market. It remains to be seen if this situation will change over time. Meanwhile, Western Miyazaki fans must seek out specialist importers or venture onto Internet auction sites, where charming little resin figurines from *My Neighbor Totoro*

Listen to the soothing ticking of a cuckoo clock that looks just as beautiful as it sounds, enhanced by carvings of Totoro. The hours are marked by everyone's favorite woodland spirit in place of the traditional cuckoo.

and porcelain teacups bearing the cuddly creature's image in delicate watercolor sell for outrageous multiples of their Japanese price to a host of eager bidders. Many go to the eBay auction site, where searches on the names Totoro, Miyazaki, or Nausicaä invariably bring up some new and tempting item of merchandise. Other sites are also worth investigating, but prices can go high. Fans might well hope that Disney will turn importer of Ghibli goods, bringing prices down and ensuring a steady supply.

Miyazaki doesn't see what all the fuss around the Disney deal is about, viewing it as just another business venture for the American giant. He told the Japanese newspaper *Daily Yomiuri*, "[Disney] will pull out of the deal if it doesn't pay off. Just like the deception of Japanimation as a global phenomenon, this is something that's been blown out of all proportion. I never understood why people made so much fuss about the deal."[7] As far as he's concerned, overseas distribution is not a major concern and merchandising and video are completely unimportant. To him, the movies themselves, seen full-size in the cinema, are the only things that count.

ON YOUR MARK

Television, the area in which Miyazaki gained much of his early experience, is one area that Studio Ghibli hasn't ignored. They brought in an outside director, Tomomichi Mochizuki, to make *I Can Hear the Ocean*, a TV special that

was well received on screening in 1993, and has gone to video with reasonable success. However, senior staff at the studio take the view that the usual level of TV budgets is far too low for the kind of work they produce. And if the project can't match their internally defined standards, it simply won't be made. In the same way, they have dipped a toe into the waters of TV advertising, but only for a very special reason—the fortieth anniversary of the NTV network in 1992 led to their producing two short station identification slots, *Nandaro* and *Sorairo no Tane*.

The studio has had one venture into music video. *On Your Mark* was produced in 1995 for the soft rock duo Chage and Aska and was screened at a number of their concerts. It also accompanied *Whisper of the Heart* on its cinema release. It came about for one very simple reason: Miyazaki had hit writer's block on *Princess Mononoke*. And, as usual when he hits a major development problem, he looked for another project to distract him. The last time that happened, in the early stages of work on *Porco Rosso*, he designed and built a new studio. This time, he agreed to direct and write a music video. The videotape available in stores all over Japan has the original music video and the Leica reel (storyboards and working drawings shot in sequence to sketch out the story), as well as another video showing Chage and Aska in performance. The tape sheds fascinating light on the concerns and preoccupations of an artist with his mind on a movie set in Japan in early medieval times, in the midst of everyday life in Japan in the last years of the twentieth century.

The *On Your Mark* animation opens with a

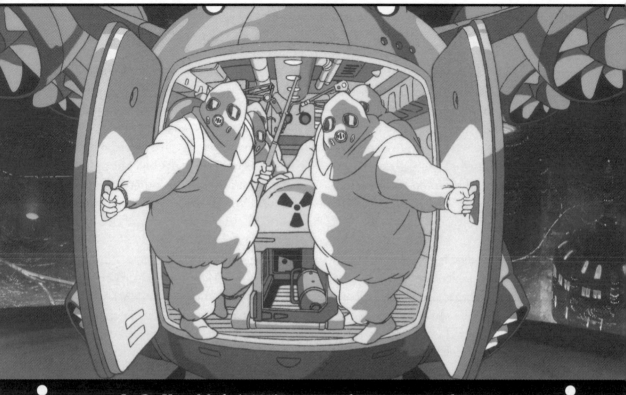

In On Your Mark (1995), *a group of scientists suited up in decontamination gear and looking remarkably like the hero of Porco Rosso, take the winged girl held prisoner by the cult in their headquarters into police custody.*

city sequence that could easily be taken for homage to *Akira* or *Blade Runner*, a classic science fiction metropolis of looming towers and glittering lights, threaded by flying vehicles like swarms of bright insects. A dazzling shot focuses the viewer on the particular swarm in question as police vehicles swoop through the interior of a floating apartment block built like a tube, with the rooms around a hollow central space, and both ends open so you can fly straight through. Neon signs signal the search for God, some kind of still center in a world of continual change. The police are attacking a building belonging to a cult, perhaps a reflection of the impact the AUM Shinrikyo movement made on Japan in the mid-1990s, when well-educated middle-class young people flocked to join the cult and participated in or supported a range of activities culminating in a nerve gas attack on a Tokyo subway. At first the officers are seen as the brutal invaders, masked figures gunning down cult members who seem to offer no resistance. Then one officer finds a still, chained figure in a dark corner; perhaps the holy are not all they seem. The prisoner is a slender young girl with great white wings springing from her shoulder blades. Why would people of God want to imprison an angel? The officer pushes back his mask, revealing a young, handsome, concerned face.

The girl is rushed into an isolation unit by the authorities, just as much a prisoner as she was before, and with perhaps a worse end in store. The young cop who rescued her and his partner are left to ponder what she was. (The pair are, of course, intended to represent the rock duo providing the soundtrack, suitably glamorized.) They decide to rescue her from what may be a fate worse than death at the hands of religious fanatics, and break into the scientific facility in a sequence that raises a glorious cacophony of echoes, from *Porco Rosso* (retro-styled isolation suits that make the wearer look oddly like the Crimson Pig, especially when inflated) and *Splash* to the rescue of Princess Leia in *Star Wars*. They get the girl, steal a vehicle, and break out of the facility—and then the track down which this classic hero-tale is leading us divides. Our heroes get the girl out of prison, but is that the same as rescuing her? Not unless they get away.

Miyazaki gives us two possible endings, one nihilistic and one romantic. The nihilistic version sees the brave cops plummeting to their deaths as the truck spins off a collapsing road bridge into the depths of the huge city, far, far below. Right up until the last minute, they are desperately urging the girl to open her

wings and save herself, but she doesn't—perhaps she can't. We don't see the gory details, but we know the truck hits the ground. Then, as the impact fades out, we loop straight back into the tunnels as our heroes race to get their rescued princess into a truck. This time the truck sprouts wings of its own, and instead of plunging to their deaths the trio head out of the city altogether. Signs warn of danger if they go ahead, and we see that the city is contained in a great dome, its atmosphere artificial, its life quite separate from that of the world outside. At first the world outside looks

If tea for two isn't to your taste, what about a Totoro gratin dish, a chopping board or a complete dinner service? Respected porcelain maker Noritake produces a range of fine dinnerware showing the cuddly character in delicate watercolors.

Cute and cuddly incarnations of Kiki's companion Jiji sell strongly in the Japanese toy market. Although Totoro is the company's flagship character as far as merchandising is concerned, merchandise featuring all the Ghibli stars sells strongly in Asian markets.

and she soars high above the road, into the pure blue sky, until she is only a tiny speck against the sun. The two young men speed along the road beneath, following her with their eyes. Whatever music is to be faced, back in the city, they'll deal with it later. For now, there's only the truck, the road, the sun, and the girl. Fade out on a happy ending.

Dr. Patrick Collins, guest researcher at the Japanese National Space Development Agency, a leading figure in the field of commercial space activity, and a discerning science writer, described *On Your Mark* to me as "the most perfect short science fantasy film I've ever seen, with more than enough ideas to sustain a ninety-minute movie." The Studio Ghibli team might not agree; Toshio Suzuki told me that they felt they hadn't really given the project "100 percent."[8] Nevertheless, its visual richness and density of context will continue to give viewers pleasure and may bestow more longevity than is entirely deserved on the song that forms its backing track.

gentle, tranquil, part of a more peaceful era, the road like any country road leading past little farms and houses. Then we see the huge, dark bulk of some terrible relic of industrial idiocy, dominating the quiet countryside, and we remember the poisoned farms and houses in the countryside around Chernobyl.

But perhaps that terror has passed, as eventually all manmade terrors will pass. Our heroes and the girl are unafraid. As the truck spins along the open road, the girl glides above it, holding the hands of one of our heroes, her wings spread wide. The wind lifts her, he drops one gentle kiss onto her fingertips,

OTHER PROJECTS

Many companies and creators in the anime field have become involved in computer games. Gainax was saved from financial ruin by their games division, and Masamune Shirow has lent his name, though not his unique and off-the-wall sense of plotting, to a number of console projects. Computer games, however, are not an option Studio Ghibli plans to explore in the future. Some of the studio staff worked on a computer game released in 1998, *Jade Cocoon,* providing assistance with designs and animation sequences. This arose out of a long-standing relationship. Katsuya Kondo, who worked on *Kiki's Delivery Service* and knows many of the Ghibli staff, was working on the game over a year earlier and needed help with the animation. So he called on his old friend Toshio Suzuki. It just so happened that at that time Studio Ghibli was in the throes of working out the computer graphics for *Princess Mononoke,* and Suzuki saw an opportunity to help his staff gain some valuable experience on CG equipment, as well as help out a former colleague. However, Suzuki is adamant that this is not something the studio will take further, saying that if they have spare time they'd rather use it for other projects. When I asked him if he would allow Miyazaki and Takahata's films to be turned into computer games, he said crisply, "Never!"[9]

But one project that is definitely proceeding is a museum devoted to the work of Studio Ghibli. Designed by Miyazaki, it's scheduled to be built over the next two years and will feature exhibits of the studio's work as well as displays of animation technique and short films by young directors. [10] The proposed site is Inokashira Park in Tokyo, and it is hoped that the museum will open in 2000 The only dedicated museum on a similar subject in Japan to date is the Osamu Tezuka Manga Museum in Takarazuka near Osaka. Tezuka's influence on the whole manga and animation field was such that even today, more than a decade after his death, he is still known as the "manga god." It seems fitting that Miyazaki, the modern master of animation, should be honored in the same way, and entirely typical that he should want the museum to focus on the work of the Studio Ghibli team and not simply on himself.

Meanwhile, work is going ahead on the next Miyazaki film. After the huge success of the sometimes dark and difficult *Princess Mononoke,* aimed at an older market, he is turning his sights once more toward the audience he regards as most important of all—children.[11] The new film will star a ten-year-old girl, based on a real child he and his staff know well. When I met him in January 1999 he couldn't say much about the story—in fact, he told me he had "just three pieces of a huge jigsaw" so he didn't know yet how the whole picture would turn out. [12] But based on his body of work to date, we can assume that it will be a warm and humane film that will encourage its young audience to grow, to dare, and to wonder at the world around them—a film that, above all else, will affirm the importance of kindness, the struggle for harmony, and the enduring value of life.

• • • • • • •

I'd like to end this introduction to the world and work of Hayao Miyazaki with the story of an incident that occurred during my visit to his private office, Buta-ya. While we talked, a song thrush cannoned into the rear window of the room at high speed. Almost immediately Miyazaki was on the phone to the local bird sanctuary, and within a couple of minutes one of the staff arrived. She picked up the bird and brought it into the main room, while Miyazaki went to find a large cardboard box and lined it with cloths he first warmed in front of the stove. Carefully placing it on the corner of the wide hearth, the sanctuary worker popped the bird inside to recover, gave a few instructions and left, and we resumed our interview. About half an hour later a loud chirp from inside the box indicated that the patient was well on the road to recovery. Smiling broadly, Miyazaki excused himself, got up from the table, opened the side door and placed the box carefully on the porch, lid open so the thrush could make its own way out, then came back to complete our interview.

There are quotes from the interview scattered throughout this book, but actions speak louder than words.

Filmography with Selected Manga

1963
Watchdog Woof-Woof
Wan Wan Chushingura
Theatrical feature
1 hour, 21 minutes
© Toei Doga
- Miyazaki worked as an inbetweener on the film.

SYNOPSIS
This is an adventure tale of a band of doggy friends based on the legend of the forty-seven Ronin, loyal retainers who avenged their dead master in medieval Japan. Their refusal to abandon his memory until his killers had been brought to justice has spawned a large number of adaptations and inspired many gentler and less violent stories showing the virtues of loyalty and devotion.

1963
Wolf Boy Ken
Okami Shonen Ken
TV series
Eighty-six episodes, each approximately 25 minutes, screened November 1963 to August 1965
Series director: Sadao Tsukioka
© Toei Doga
- Miyazaki worked as an inbetweener on the series.

SYNOPSIS
Lost boy Ken is found by a wolf pack, who take him in and raise him as one of their own. As he grows up, he vows to become a defender of the peace and freedom of life in the forests. The series follows his woodland adventures.

1964
Gulliver's Space Travels
Gulliver no Uchu Ryoko
Short film
20 minutes
Based on the novel *Gulliver's Travels* by Jonathan Swift.
© Toei Doga
- Miyazaki worked as an inbetweener. He returned to Swift's book more than two decades later as one of the inspirations for *Castle in the Sky*.

SYNOPSIS
Take Jonathan Swift's famous character Gulliver back to his boyhood and send him on a journey into space where he'll meet various fantastical people and adventures, just as he did in the original book set on Earth. That's what Toei Doga did for this short film, a longer version of which appeared in the cinemas the following year.

1964
Wind Ninja Boy Fujimaru
Shonen Ninja Kaze no Fujimaru
TV series

Sixty-five episodes, each approximately 25 minutes, screened from June 1964 to August 1965
Based on the manga by Sanpei Shirato
© Toei Doga

- Miyazaki started as an inbetweener and moved on to key animation.

1965
Hustle Punch
TV series
Twenty-six episodes each approximately 25 minutes, screened from November 1965 to April 1966
Opening sequence director: Isao Takahata
© Toei Doga

- Miyazaki did key animation.

SYNOPSIS
Hustle is a brave bear who is forced to fight to defend his animal friends from the attacks of Garigari, a ferocious wolf.

1966
Rainbow Warrior Robin
Rainbow Sentai Robin
TV series
Forty-eight episodes each approximately 25 minutes, screened from April 1966 to March 1967
Based on the manga by Shotaro Ishinomori
© Toei Doga

- Miyazaki did key animation.

SYNOPSIS
Robin and his brave band of friends are fighting to defend Earth from invasion by the people of the star Parta.

1968
The Little Norse Prince
Taiyo no Oji Hols no Daiboken

(literally, The Great Adventure of Hols, Prince of the Sun; a.k.a. *The Great Adventure of Little Prince Valiant* in Italy; Toei's own English-language title is *Little Norse Prince Valiant*)
Theatrical feature
1 hour 22 minutes
Despite the seeming connection with the *Prince Valiant* comic imposed on it by the Italian release title, the story is original and unconnected to the comic in any way. There was a U.S. release on American-International Pictures in 1969, and this was frequently screened on TV in the U.S. during the 1970s and 1980s.
Director: Isao Takahata
Animation director: Yasuo Otsuka
Scene designer: Hayao Miyazaki
© Toei Doga

- Miyazaki also did key animation.

SYNOPSIS
A Nordic village is terrorized by the evil Grunwald, and Hols and his friends band together to protect their homes and families from his malevolent magical powers.

1968
Little Witch Sally (episodes 77 and 80)
Mahotsukai Sally
TV series
Ninety-two episodes, each approximately 25 minutes, screened from December 1966 to December 1968
Based on the manga by Mitsuteru Yokoyama
Director: Yoshiyuki Hane
© Toei Doga

- Miyazaki did key animation on episodes 77 and 80.

SYNOPSIS
One of Toei's most popular series and the first of the "magical girl" genre, this was the story of a ju-

venile witch, Sally, sent to Earth to study humans and human life, and her adventures as she tries to help her new human friends.

1969
Puss in Boots
Nagagutsu o Haita Neko
Theatrical feature
1 hour, 20 minutes
Based on the fable by Charles Perrault
© Toei Doga

- The film had some screenings on U.S. children's television but I am unable to give details.
- Miyazaki did key animation.

SYNOPSIS

This humorous version of the fairy tale starring a cunning cat with the power of speech was so successful that the cat character, named Pero after his originator, became Toei Animation's official mascot.

1969
The Flying Ghost Ship
Soratobu Yureisen
Theatrical feature
1 hour
Based on the manga by Shotaro Ishinomori
© Toei Doga

- Miyazaki did key animation.

SYNOPSIS

Two children, a boy and a girl, encounter the mysterious robot Golem and a ghostly flying ship.

1969
Akko-chan's Secret (episodes 44 and 61)
Himitsu no Akko-chan
TV series

Ninety-four episodes, screened from January 1969 to October 1970
Based on the manga by Fujio Akatsuka
© Toei Doga, Fuji Production

- Miyazaki did key animation on episodes 44 and 61.

SYNOPSIS

In this second "magical girl" series, the heroine is not a witch but an ordinary schoolgirl until a spirit gives her a special gift—a magic mirror that enables her to transform into any human or animal she chooses. She uses her new power to help solve problems for her friends and family.

1969
People of the Desert
Sabaku no Tami
Manga written and drawn by Hayao Miyazaki for *Shonen Shojo Shinbun* (Boys and Girls Newspaper) under the pseudonym Saburo Akitsu.

1971
Animal Treasure Island
Dobutsu Takarajima
Theatrical feature
1 hour 18 minutes
Based on the novel *Treasure Island* by Robert Louis Stevenson
Director: Hiroshi Ikeda
Design, idea construction: Hayao Miyazaki
© Toei Doga

- The film had some screenings on U.S. children's television, but I am unable to give details.
- Miyazaki also did key animation. There are indications of the fondness for pigs as characters that would culminate in *Porco Rosso*.

SYNOPSIS

A boy, a girl, and a group of anthropomorphic animal pirates seek treasure and adventure on the high seas.

1971
Ali Baba and the 40 Thieves
Ali Baba to Yonjuppiki no Tozoku

Theatrical feature

55 minutes

Based on the fable from *Thousand and One Nights*

Director: Hiroshi Shidara

© Toei Doga

• Miyazaki is credited as organizer and key animator.

SYNOPSIS

A descendant of Ali Baba has become a rich tyrant thanks to the treasure left him by the efforts of the forty thieves his ancestor encountered. A boy descended from the chief of the band decides to try and steal the magic lamp and use it to free the people from poverty and tyranny. His band consists of thirty-eight cats and one mouse. Scope for humor in plenty.

1971
Sarutobi Etchan (episode 6)

(a.k.a. *Hela Supergirl* in Italy)

TV series

Twenty-six episodes screened from October 1971 to March 1972

Based on the manga by Shotaro Ishinomori

Director: Yugo Serikawa

Screenplay: Shotaro Ishinomori

© Toei Doga

• Miyazaki did key animation for episode 6.

SYNOPSIS

Etchan is a girl with true superpowers, despite her cute, harmless appearance. The series chronicles her humorous escapades in contemporary Japan.

1971
Pippi Longstocking
Nagakutsushita no Pippi

TV series, abandoned at preproduction stage

Based on the book by Astrid Lindgren

• Miyazaki and Takahata did preliminary work, and Miyazaki went to Sweden with the president of Tokyo Movie Shinsha, who hoped to produce the series. Rights for the book could not be secured and the project was abandoned.

1971
Lupin III (some episodes)
Lupin Sansei

TV series

Twenty-three episodes, each approximately 25 minutes, screened from October 1971 to March 1972

Based on the manga by Monkey Punch

Director: both Miyazaki and Takahata directed on the series, and seventeen of the twenty-three episodes are directed by them working together, with another director, or alone

Design: Yasuo Otsuka

© Monkey Punch, Tokyo Movie Shinsha

SYNOPSIS

Lovable thief Lupin III and his gang are involved in a variety of exciting capers. They are pursued constantly by Inspector Zenigata, who is determined to bring Lupin to justice.

1972
Yuki's Sun

The project was never completed for release.

1972
Panda & Child
Panda Kopanda
Short film
33 minutes
Original concept by Hayao Miyazaki
Director: Isao Takahata
Screenplay, design: Hayao Miyazaki
© Tokyo Movie Shinsha
• Miyazaki also did layouts and key animation.

SYNOPSIS
The everyday adventures of a panda, his cub, and their young human friend, aimed at younger children and with a gentle outlook on life. The panda's resemblance to Miyazaki's later creation, Totoro, is marked, and this film and its sequel are seminal in the evolution of what is perhaps his most beloved character.

1971
The Impudent Frog
Dokonjo Gaeru
TV series
One hundred and three episodes screened from October 1972 to September 1974
© Tokyo Movie Shinsha
• Miyazaki drew storyboards for the first episode, but they were not used.

1972
Akado Suzunosuke
TV series
Fifty-two episodes screened from April 1972 to March 1973
Based on the 1950s radio drama by Tsunayoshi Takeuchi
© Tokyo Movie Shinsha
• Miyazaki did key animation, and also storyboards on episodes 26 and 27.

SYNOPSIS
A young samurai fights evildoers who want to invade his homeland.

1973
Panda & Child: Rainy Day Circus
Panda Kopanda Amefuri Circus no Maki
Short film
38 minutes
Original concept by Hayao Miyazaki
Director: Isao Takahata
 Screenplay, art design: Hayao Miyazaki
© Tokyo Movie Shinsha
• Miyazaki also did layouts and key animation.

SYNOPSIS
Charming, everyday adventures of little Mimiko and her panda friend. Once again, note the influence on the later creation of Totoro and his peaceful, simple world.

1973
Wilderness Boy Isamu (episode 15)
Koya no Shonen Isamu
TV series
Fifty-two episodes, screened from April 1973 to March 1974
Original story by Noboru Kawasaki and Koji Yamakawa
Series director: Shigenori Yoshida
Director, episode 15: Isao Takahata
© Tokyo Movie Shinsha
• Miyazaki did key animation on episode 15.

SYNOPSIS
Isamu is the son of a Japanese man and a Native American woman. He is a crack shot; he needs to be, since during his search for his father he encounters all the dangers and adventures of the old West, including racism.

1973
Samurai Giants
TV series
Forty-six episodes, screened from October 1973 to September 1974
© Eiken
• Miyazaki did key animation on episode 1.

SYNOPSIS
A sports series set in the world of baseball.

1974
Alpine Girl Heidi
Alps no Shojo Heidi
TV series, first in the *World Masterpiece Theater* series
Fifty-two episodes, screened from January to December 1974
Based on the novel by Johanna Spyri
Director: Isao Takahata
Scene design and layout: Hayao Miyazaki
© Zuiyo

SYNOPSIS
Orphan Heidi goes to live with her grandfather in the Alps, and although at first the relationship is difficult the two grow to love each other deeply. Then Heidi gets a job as companion to an invalid girl, Clara, in Frankfurt, and has to leave her beloved Alps and her friends, including the shepherd boy Peter. But she and Clara soon become friends, and she helps Clara grow strong and well so that she too can come to visit the mountains Heidi loves so much.

1975
A Dog of Flanders
Flanders no Inu
(a.k.a. My *Patraasche*)

TV series, part of the *World Masterpiece Theater* series
Twenty-six episodes screened from January to December 1975
Based on the novel by Ouida
Director, episode 15: Kenji Kodama, Isao Takahata
© Zuiyo, Nippon Animation, Tokyo Movie Shinsha
• Miyazaki assisted with key animation of episode 15.

SYNOPSIS
Nello lives in poverty with his grandfather, but has dreams of being a painter. He takes in a maltreated dog and is rewarded with his complete devotion. The story is a tragic melodrama of the highest order and ends in death for the young hero.

1976
Three Thousand Miles in Search of Mother
Haha o Tazunete Sanzen-Ri
TV series, part of the *World Masterpiece Theater* series
Fifty-one episodes, screened from January to December 1976
Based on a novel by Edmondo de Amicis
Director: Isao Takahata
Scene design and layout: Hayao Miyazaki
© Nippon Animation (formerly Zuiyo)

SYNOPSIS
Europe is in the grip of a depression, and Marco's mother leaves Genoa to work as a domestic in Argentina so she can send money home. Then she writes that she is sick, and no more letters arrive. Marco goes in search of her, but she is no longer at the address on her letters. His journey takes him across Argentina. Along the way he makes new friends, encounters great dangers, and

begins to grow up. This series has many echoes in the later *Porco Rosso*.

1977
Rascal the Raccoon
Araiguma Rascal

TV series, part of the *World Masterpiece Theater* series

Fifty-two episodes, screened from January to December 1977

Based on the stories of Sterling North

Director: Hiroshi Sato

Character design: Masaharu Endo

© Nippon Animation

- Miyazaki did key animation on episodes 4–6, 10, 12–22, and 24–28.

SYNOPSIS

Based on autobiographical stories of his youth at the turn of the century by an American writer. The author's pet and friend, Rascal the raccoon, accompanied him everywhere and helped him get into (and sometimes out of) many boyhood scrapes and adventures. The little raccoon is still a very popular character with Japanese audiences.

1978
Future Boy Conan
Mirai Shonen Conan

TV series

Twenty-six episodes, screened from March to October 1978

Based on the novel *The Incredible Tide* by Alexander Key

Director, episodes 9 and 10: Tatsuo Ayakawa, Isao Takahata

Character design: Yasuo Otsuka

Director, character design, mechanic design, layout, and storyboards: Hayao Miyazaki

© Nippon Animation

SYNOPSIS

In the years following a devastating nuclear war, mankind has dwindled to a few scattered colonies struggling for survival. Conan grows up on a lonely island with his grandfather, the last survivor of his people. A young girl, Lana, reaches their island while fleeing from the soldiers of Industria, an island that still holds to the old militaristic ways. When she is taken by the soldiers, Conan sets out on an epic journey to find her and set her free. The series is seminal in the development of many of Miyazaki's key themes and ideas about industrialization, balance, and the oppression of the weak by the powerful, and echoes strongly in *Castle in the Sky*.

1979
Anne of Green Gables
Akage no An

(literally, Red-Haired Anne)

TV series, part of the *World Masterpiece Theater* series

Fifty episodes, screened from January to December 1979

Based on the novels by Lucy Maud Montgomery

Director: Isao Takahata

Character design: Yoshifumi Kondo

Layout, scene design, and scene organization of episodes 1–15: Hayao Miyazaki

© Nippon Animation

SYNOPSIS

In the early 1900s, spirited orphan Anne Shirley dreams of having a family of her own. When she comes to live in Green Gables, an old house on Prince Edward Island, she has to settle into a new life, make friends, and learn to fit into a small community. Episodes 1–6 were edited by the director into a feature for theatrical release in 1990, and the series was broadcast on Canadian station CBC in a French-dubbed version in the mid-1990s.

1979
Lupin III: Castle of Cagliostro
Lupin III: Cagliostro no Shiro
Theatrical feature, premiered December 1979
1 hour, 40 minutes
Based on the manga by Monkey Punch and the
original stories of Maurice LeBlanc
Director, cowriter, and storyboards: Hayao Miya-
zaki
Animation director: Yasuo Otsuka
© Tokyo Movie Shinsha

- Special U.S. premiere in September 1980 at
  the World Science Fiction Convention in
  Boston. Further special U.S. screenings in
  March 1982 at the Los Angeles International
  Film Exposition, and in January 1989 at the
  3rd Los Angeles International Animation Cel-
  ebration. U.S. theatrical release in 1991 by
  Streamline Pictures in subtitled format. U.S.
  video release in 1992 by Streamline Pictures.
  U.K. video release in 1996 on Manga Video.
  U.S. video re-release scheduled for 1999 on
  Manga Video.

SYNOPSIS
A beautiful young woman is being forced into a
marriage of convenience to serve the ends of a
sinister Count. As the world's press and the TV
cameras converge on the tiny European country
of Cagliostro for the wedding, Lupin III revisits
his own past, pays a long-due debt, and helps un-
cover a treasure beyond even his wildest imaginings. (See chapter 2.)

1980
Lupin III (episodes 145 and 155)
TV series
One hundred fifty-five episodes, screened from
October 1977 to October 1980
Based on the manga by Monkey Punch

Director, screenplay, storyboards: Teruki Tsutomu,
Telecom (a.k.a. Hayao Miyazaki)
© Tokyo Movie Shinsha

- Miyazaki worked on episodes 145, *Shi no Tsu-
  basa Albatross* ("Albatross Wings of Death"),
  and 155, *Saraba Itoshiki Lupin Yo* ("Aloha
  Lupin").
- U.S. video release of these two episodes by
  Streamline Pictures in 1993 and 1994.

SYNOPSIS
More adventures of the lovable rogue Lupin and
his friends and foes. Miyazaki brings his distinctive style to two episodes that feature a classic Miyazaki heroine, a Laputa prototype robot, and a
marvelously eccentric flying ship. These two
episodes are available on video in the U.S. from
Streamline Pictures/Orion Home Video.

1980
New Adventures of Gigantor (episode 8)
Tetsujin 28 Go
TV series
Fifty-one episodes screened from October 1980 to
September 1981
Director: Tetsuo Imazawa
© Hikari Productions, TMS, NAS, NTV

- Miyazaki did key animation on episode 8.

SYNOPSIS
Mitsuteru Yokoyama's beloved giant robot and his
young master returned in full color for an updated
adventure series, also screened in the U.S.

1981
Little Nemo
Theatrical feature
1 hour, 30 minutes
Director: William T. Hurtz and Masami Hata
Story: Jean (Moebius) Girard and Yutaka Fujioka
Producer: Yutaka Fujioka

© TMS/Hemdale

- Released in 1989 in Japan, 1991 in the U.S.
- Miyazaki worked as a scene designer, but he and Takahata (who was in charge of the Japanese preproduction operation) left the project at a very early stage because of artistic differences. Kondo later storyboarded the pilot.

1981
Great Detective Holmes (episodes 1–6)
Meitantei Holmes
(a.k.a. *Sherlock Hound*)

TV series

Twenty-six episodes, screened from November 1984 to April 1985 (a break in production occurred with two episodes completed and two more partially completed; the series was finally finished for airing in 1983)

Based on the novels of Sir Arthur Conan Doyle

Director, episodes 1–6: Hayao Miyazaki

Character design: Yoshifumi Kondo

© RAI/TMS

- Shown in Italy from 1983–85 as *Il Fiuto di Sherlock Holmes* (Sherlock Holmes's Intuition). Also screened on British and American TV.
- Fourteen episodes were released on videotape in the U.S. in 1988, as *Sherlock Hound*, on Celebrity Home Entertainment's Just for Kids label. The first three tapes contain the six Miyazaki episodes, entitled "The Blue Ruby"; "The White Cliffs of Dover"; "The Little Client"; Treasure under the Sea"; "Where Did the Sovereigns Go?"; and "The Abduction of Mrs. Hudson."

SYNOPSIS

The adventures of the great detective Sherlock Holmes, his loyal friend Dr. Watson, and the evil criminal genius Moriarty were the basis for this charming series in which the Edwardian world of the original was populated entirely by anthropomorphic dogs.

1982
Zorro
Kaiketsu Zorro
TV series, never released in Japan

- Miyazaki assisted with key animation.

1982
Space Adventure Cobra
Theatrical release

1 hour, 39 minutes

Based on the manga and TV series by Buichi Terasawa

Director: Osamu Dezaki

© Buichi Terasawa, Tokyo Movie Shinsha

- U.K. video release 1994.
- Miyazaki helped out with key animation.

SYNOPSIS

Cobra is a futuristic space mercenary with an eye for a pretty girl and a knack of getting into dangerous situations. When he comes out of a premature "retirement" with a new face, he falls foul of a powerful criminal organization and must go on the run to stay alive and learn what their unearthly leader is seeking.

1982
Nausicaä of the Valley of the Winds
Kaze no Tani no Nausicaä
Manga

- Serialization began in *Animage* magazine in February 1982. The manga is available in an English translation from Viz Comics.

1983
The Journey of Shuna
Shuna no Ryoko

All-watercolor single volume comic published by *Animage*'s AM JUJU imprint in June 1983.

• Some critics consider the androgynous prince Shuna to be a sketch for the character and philosophy of Nausicaä , while there are also traces of its influence on *Princess Mononoke*. Yakkle, Ashitaka's steed, appears here.

1984
Nausicaä of the Valley of the Winds
Kaze no Tani no Nausicaä

(a.k.a. *Warriors of the Wind* in the U.S.)
Theatrical feature, premiered March 1984
1 hour, 56 minutes
Based on the manga by Hayao Miyazaki
Director, screenplay, and storyboards: Hayao Miyazaki
© Nibariki, Tokuma Shoten

SYNOPSIS

A young princess living in a post-holocaust world is faced with a terrible choice when her tranquil homeland is disrupted and her father killed by invasion. Does she join the forces of destruction or try to find a peaceful solution to the struggle for survival? (See chapter 3.)

1984
Great Detective Holmes
Meitantei Holmes

Theatrical short feature, edited from the TV series episodes directed by Miyazaki

1986
Warriors of the Wind

U.S. theatrical feature
1 hour, 30 minutes
Edited from the original film by Hayao Miyazaki
Director: Hayao Miyazaki
© Nibariki, Tokuma

• Released on video in the U.S. by New World Video in December 1985. Limited U.S. theatrical release in New York City, June 1985 by New World Pictures. Grand Prize winner at the First Los Angeles International Animation Celebration in September 1987. This edited version is widely considered to be a travesty of the original, but retains much visual splendor despite the destruction of much of the logic of the story. (See chapter 3.)

1986
Castle in the Sky
Tenku no Shiro Laputa

Theatrical feature, premiered August 1986
2 hours, 4 minutes
Loosely inspired by Jonathan Swift's novel *Gulliver's Travels*
Director, screenplay, and storyboards: Hayao Miyazaki
© Nibariki, Tokuma Shoten

• U.S. theatrical premiere at the Second Los Angeles International Animation Celebration, July 1987.
• U.S. video release (Buena Vista Home Entertainment), tentatively scheduled for 2000

SYNOPSIS

Pazu is an orphan who dreams of following his father in his quest for the legendary flying city of Laputa. Sheeta, also an orphan, is linked to the city and its power by the mysterious necklace she wears. The government wants Laputa's rumored wealth and mysterious powers. The Dola Gang is after treasure. When the city finally reveals its secrets, Sheeta and Pazu realize that there is a terrible price to be paid for ultimate power. They alone can save the world from paying that price. (See chapter 4.)

1987
The Story of Yanakawa Canal
Yanakawa Horiwari Monogatari
TV documentary, screened April 1987
2 hours, 45 minutes
Director: Isao Takahata
Producer: Hayao Miyazaki
Available on videotape in Japan since 1992.
A live-action documentary with a short animated sequence showing how the canal works.

1988
My Neighbor Totoro
Tonari No Totoro
Theatrical feature, premiered April 1988
1 hour, 23 minutes
Original story by Hayao Miyazaki
Director, screenplay, and storyboards: Hayao Miyazaki
© Nibariki, Tokuma
• Limited theatrical release in a few major cities in the U.S. in 1993 and videotape release in the U.S. by Fox Video in 1994. Screened on U.K. satellite TV in 1997 and 1998.

SYNOPSIS
Satsuki and her little sister Mei move with their father to the country to be nearer their mother, who is in hospital recovering from a long illness. In the peace and beauty of their surroundings the two sisters find a magical world full of wonders. (See chapter 5.)

1989
Miscellaneous Notes: The Age of Seaplanes

Zasso Note Hikotei Jidai
Manga
• Full-color comic published in Model Graphix monthly from March to May 1989; it served as a prototype/precursor of Porco Rosso
• Two parts appeared in U.S. publication Mangazine in 1992 and all three parts were translated in U.S. publication Animerica in 1993. (See chapter 7.)

1989
Kiki's Delivery Service
Majo no Takkyubin
(literally, Witch's Special Express Delivery)
Theatrical feature, premiered July 1989
1 hour, 42 minutes
Based on the novel by Eiko Kadono
Director, screenplay, storyboards, and producer: Hayao Miyazaki
Producer and musical director: Isao Takahata
Animation director: Yoshifumi Kondo
© Kadono, Nibariki, Tokuma Shoten
• Released on video in the U.S. in 1998 by Buena Vista Home Entertainment. U.K. and European release dates have not yet been announced as this book goes to press.

SYNOPSIS
At thirteen, all witches must leave home to live alone in a strange city for a year, using their powers to make their living. Kiki's only power is flying, so she sets up a courier service. All the troubles, dreams, and delights of growing up are wrapped in a magical package to touch the hearts of every little girl and everyone who loves children. (See chapter 6.)

1991
Only Yesterday
Omoide Poro Poro

Theatrical feature, premiered July 1991
1 hour, 59 minutes
Director: Isao Takahata
Character design: Yoshifumi Kondo
Producer: Hayao Miyazaki
© Nibariki, Tokuma Shoten
• U.S. release dates not yet announced.

SYNOPSIS

Looking back at her childhood, a young woman realizes that her life is at a crossroads and she must decide which path to take. How can those long-ago events and memories help her now?

1992
Porco Rosso
Kurenai no Buta
(literally, The Crimson Pig)
Theatrical feature, premiered July 1992
1 hour, 33 minutes
Original story by Hayao Miyazaki
Director and screenplay: Hayao Miyazaki
© Nibariki, Tokuma Shoten
• U.K. screenings on satellite TV in 1997 and 1998. French video and theatrical release in 1997. U.S. release dates not yet announced.

SYNOPSIS

The skies above the Adriatic are buzzing with activity as mercenaries and sky-pirates fight it out. On the ground, fascism is gathering force and political events are about to change the world forever. Caught up in a mystery no one can fathom, a man with the head of a pig and the heart of a hero must face up to his past before he can move into the future. (See chapter 7.)

1992
Sky-Colored Seed
Sorairo no Tane
TV station identity spot, screened November

1992
1 minute, 30 seconds
Director: Hayao Miyazaki
• Commemorating the fortieth anniversary of Nihon TV Network.

1992
What Is It?
Nandaro
Five TV station identity spots, screened November 1992
One is 15 seconds; four are 5 seconds each
Director and key animation: Hayao Miyazaki
• More anniversary celebrations for Nihon TV. Nandaro is an NTV mascot.

1994
Modern-Day Raccoon War Ponpoko
Heisei Tanuki Gassen Ponpoko
Theatrical feature, premiered July 1994
1 hour, 58 minutes
Director: Isao Takahata
Planning (idea): Hayao Miyazaki
© Nibariki, Tokuma Shoten
• U.S. release date yet to be announced.

SYNOPSIS

When modern development threatens to encroach on the last remaining territory of a group of raccoons, they decide to fight back, and demonstrate that they have richly earned their reputation as mythical tricksters and masters of disguise!

1995
Whisper of the Heart
Mimi o Sumaseba
Theatrical feature, premiered July 1995
1 hour, 51 minutes

Director: Yoshifumi Kondo
Screenplay, storyboards, and producer: Hayao Miyazaki
© Nibariki, Tokuma Shoten
- U.S. release date yet to be announced.

SYNOPSIS

A young girl who dreams of being a writer finds that she and a boy she hardly knows at school share many of the same tastes in reading. Then she meets his grandfather and is drawn in to a world of creative effort and endeavor.

1995
On Your Mark

Music video for Japanese rock duo Chage and Aska
Premiered in theaters July 1995
6 minutes, 40 seconds
Original story, screenplay, and director: Hayao Miyazaki
© Nibariki, Tokuma Shoten

SYNOPSIS

The near future: two young officers stumble on a mysterious winged girl during a police raid on a cult headquarters. Can they save her from the madness of their world and set her free? (See chapter 9.)

1997
Princess Mononoke
Mononoke Hime

Theatrical feature, premiered July 1997

2 hours
Director, original story, screenplay: Hayao Miyazaki
Animation director: Yoshifumi Kondo
© Nibariki, Tokuma Shoten
- U.S. release planned for autumn 1999, worldwide release to follow.

SYNOPSIS

The far past: a young girl raised in the primeval forests by ancient wolf gods fights for the survival of her adopted family and their world. A boy from a faraway land is on a quest for answers. A woman struggles to set her people free. The powers of nature are challenged for the first time by the powers of mankind—the beginning of a conflict that still resonates today. (See chapter 8.)

1998
Tiger in the Mire
Doromamire no Tora

Manga
- Published by *Model Graphix* magazine in December 1998, based on a book by World War II German tank commander Otto Carius about his experiences in Estonia, where he and a small company held off a Russian advance with just two Tiger tanks.

2000

A new film by Hayao Miyazaki is already in the planning stages as I write early in 1999. Its heroine is Chieko, a ten-year-old girl, based on a real child.

Notes

PREFACE

1 See my earlier book, *The Erotic Anime Movie Guide*, co-authored with Jonathan Clements and published by Titan Books in 1998, for a more detailed examination of the profile of Japanese products in the English-language market

1: HAYAO MIYAZAKI

1 McCarthy, "The House That Hayao Built," *Manga Max*, 5 April 1999.

2 Miyazaki, "Tezuka Was a Combative Partner," reprinted in Miyazaki's 1996 collection *Shuppatsuten 1979–96* (Points of Departure, 1979–96), Tokyo: Tokuma Shoten, 1997.

3 Miyazaki, "The Current Situation of Japanese Movies," in *Course on Japanese Movies 7*, Iwanami Shoten, January 1988.

4 "Manga Manga" interview transcript, reprinted in *Manga Mania* 20, March 1995. Miyazaki is still enthusiastic about the work of writers like Philippa Pearce and Arthur Ransome and spoke of them in glowing terms when I interviewed him in January 1999.

5 Miyazaki, interviewed in *Kinejun Special Issue*, no. 1166, Kinema Junpo Sha, 16 July 1995.

6 Reprinted in Miyazaki, *Shuppatsuten*.

7 Oshiguchi, "The Whimsy and Wonder of Hayao Miyazaki," *Animerica* 1, nos. 5 and 6, July/August 1993.

ANIMATION TECHNIQUE

1 One such is Bob Thomas, *Disney's Art of Animation*, New York: Hyperion, 1997. See also McCarthy, "How Anime Is Made" in *Anime UK* 3, no. 2, April 1994.

2 McCarthy, "The Adjuster: Interview with Toshio Suzuki," *Manga Max* 6, May 1999.

3 Ms. Yasuda, one of the senior animators at Studio Ghibli, kindly showed me her superb new workstation when I toured the studio in January 1999. She said, "We're still learning what it can do. Every spare minute we have, we do tests. But it can't replace human animators, only enhance their work."

4 McCarthy, "Adjuster."

5 *Asia Pulse*, 16 May 1997.

6 Interview in *A-Club* 19.

8 Toren Smith, "Interview with Masamune Shirow," *Manga Mania* 1, no. 8, February 1994.

9 Lafine et al., "Interview: Moebius," *Animeland* 1, April 1991.

10 McCarthy, "The Adjuster: Interview with Toshio Suzuki," *Manga Max* 6, May 1999.

11 "Interview with Hayao Miyazaki," *A-Club* 19, June 1987.

12 Over twenty-five minutes of material was cut from the original print. The characters were also renamed to be more "acceptable" for

Western audiences, an established practice in the U.S. animation market at the time.

13 To place this event into a clearer context for Western readers, this was the same year that Katsuhiro Otomo's *Akira* premiered in Tokyo.

14 In his English-language essay on the history of Studio Ghibli (*Archives of Studio Ghibli* 1, Tokyo: Tokuma Shoten, 1995–), Toshio Suzuki jokes that it's the "Miyazaki way" to try and achieve a breakthrough with a big problem by dreaming up an even bigger problem.

15 Most anime is made by widely scattered teams of people—often even on different land masses. Obviously this leads to less hands-on control for the director and producer, but it also gives rise to astronomical bills for couriers as cels, scripts, and key drawings shuttle all over Tokyo and as far afield as Korea and Thailand.

16 Suzuki, *Archives of Studio Ghibli* 1.

17 This quest for quality had been recognized much earlier by audiences; in 1968 a reviewer for *Taiyo* magazine wrote, after seeing both *The Jungle Book* and *The Great Adventure of Hols*, "in one corner of the world there now exists a commercial animation that has surpassed Disney and started to make rapid advances." Quoted in Mark Schilling, *The Encyclopedia of Japanese Pop Culture*, New York: Weatherhill, 1997.

18 Oshiguchi, "Whimsy and Wonder."

19 In an interview about her work on DreamWorks' series *Invasion America*, in *Manga Max*, 2 January 1999, Kuni Tomita commented that one of the differences between American and Japanese management was the way people at a high level in the production company with no real understanding of the anime style were able to make changes to the work of the creative team.

20 Ishii, "Interview with Mamoru Oshii," *Kinejun Special Issue*, no. 1166.

2: CASTLE OF CAGLIOSTRO

1 Artist and writer Kazuhiko Kato's agent and editor chose this pen name for him because they wanted something that was offbeat, memorable, and not specifically Japanese-sounding.

2 Miyazaki, *Shuppatsuten*.

3 Ilan Nguyen's excellent article in *Animeland* 25 illustrates this beautifully with images from both works.

3: NAUSICAÄ OF THE VALLEY OF THE WINDS

1 Oshiguchi, "Whimsy and Wonder."

2 Valery and Bounthy Warrior, "Nausicaä de la Vallee du Vent," *Animeland* 24, July 1996.

3 Miyazaki and Callenbach, "Discarding the Future?" *Asahi Journal*, 7 June 1985, reprinted in Miyazaki, *Shuppatsuten*.

4 Miyazaki, "Making of an Animation?" *Asahi Journal*, 20 April 1987, reprinted in Miyazaki, *Shuppatsuten*.

5 Miyazaki, "The Japanese Were at Their Happiest During the Jomon Era," in *Heibon Punch*, 9 July 1984, reprinted in Miyazaki, *Shuppatsuten*.

6 Ibid.

7 Interview in *A-Club* 19.

8 Lafine et al., "Interview: Moebius."

9 Interview in *YOM*, June 1994.

10 Littardi, "Interview: Isao Takahata," *Animeland* 6, July/August 1992.

11 Interview in *A-Club* 19.

12 Miyazaki and Callenbach, "Discarding the Future?"

13 Littardi, "Interview: Isao Takahata."

14 Information from Emmanuel Ohajah, who or-

ganized the screening at London's Institute of Contemporary Arts for the Building Bridges film festival, part of the No More Hiroshimas festival.

15 "Interview with Hayao Miyazaki," *Young*, 20 February 1984.

16 "Interview with Ryu Murakami," *Animage*, November 1988, reprinted in Miyazaki, *Shuppatsuten*.

17 Interview in *A-Club* 19.

18 Sertori, "Just Desserts," *Anime U.K.* New Series, vol. 1, no 2, April 1995.

19 Sato, *Godzilla, Yamato and Our Democracy*, quoted by Jonathan Clements in "Book Reviews: The Real Thing," *Anime FX* 10, January 1996.

20 Ishii, "Interview with Mamoru Oshii."

21 Lafine et al., "Interview: Moebius."

22 *Heibon Punch*, 9 July 1984, reprinted in Miyazaki, *Shuppatsuten*.

4: CASTLE IN THE SKY

1 Miyazaki, "Making of an Animation?"

2 McCarthy, "House That Hayao Built."

3 Miyazaki, "Making of an Animation?"

4 Perhaps in the early days of the bubble economy Japan was not in the proper frame of mind to question the virtues of ever-increasing technological control.

5 Littardi, "Interview: Isao Takahata."

6 Interview at Buta-ya, 20 January 1999

7 Ishii, "Interview with Mamoru Oshii."

8 As already noted (chapter 1) the style had been pioneered by Yasuji Mori on *World Masterpiece Theater* and other Nippon Animation productions.

9 Academic and writer Paul Wells sees this as a transition to adulthood, but I think he has confused the ritual elements of cutting the hair—a sacrificial act preceding renunciation of this world—with the social ritual of putting up the hair, indicating entry into adult society and marriage in many societies.

10 According to Jo Hisaishi's webpage, the rescoring and re-recording work was almost complete at the end of May 1999.

5: MY NEIGHBOR TOTORO

1 The former quote is from Oshiguchi, "Whimsy and Wonder," and the latter quote is from Shiba, "A Walk in Totoro's Forest," *Weekly Asahi*, January 1996, reprinted in Miyazaki, *Shuppatsuten*.

2 McCarthy, "Adjuster."

3 Shiba, "A Walk in Totoro's Forest."

4 McCarthy, "Adjuster."

5 See chapter 9 for more on merchandising.

6 Thanks to Fred Patten of Streamline Pictures for clarifying the sequence of events.

7 Miyazaki, liner notes to *Tonari no Totoro Image Songs* CD, quoted by Clements in "If You Go Down to the Woods Today: CD Reviews," *Anime FX* 11, February 1996.

8 Miyazaki, *Shuppatsuten*.

9 Miyazaki has expressed his concerns about overuse of television in a number of interviews, e.g. *Manga Mania* 20, March 1995, and *Manga Max* 5, April 1999.

10 Interview in *A-Club* 19.

11 Bloom, Harold, in *Shakespeare: The Invention of the Human*, London: Fourth Estate, 1999.

12 As transcribed by his daughter in *Bungei Shunju*, April 1999.

6: KIKI'S DELIVERY SERVICE

1. Miyazaki, Hayao, "The Hopes and Spirit of

Contemporary Japanese Girls," *The Art of Kiki's Delivery Service,* Tokyo: Tokuma, 1989.

2. Ibid.

3. I am grateful to Fred Patten of Streamline Pictures for clarifying the misinformation that has grown among Western fans around the topic of the Macek dubs of Miyazaki films.

4. Eisner, Ken, "Kiki Delivers the Goods," *Variety* (Seattle), 17 July 1998.

5. Burr, Ty, "Special Delivery," *Entertainment Weekly,* 4 September 1998.

6. nausicaa.net FAQ, quoted by Ryoko Toyama.

7. Quoted in Eisner, "Kiki Delivers the Goods."

8. Miyazaki, "Hopes and Spirit."

9. Vincentelli, Elisabeth, "Tooning In: Disney Imports a Japanese Auteur-Animator," *Village Voice,* 2 September 1998.

7: PORCO ROSSO

1 McCarthy, "House That Hayao Built."

2 Contrary to fan mythology, Carl Macek and Streamline Pictures had no hand in this dub.

3 Oshiguchi, "Whimsy and Wonder."

4 Ishii, "Interview with Mamoru Oshii."

5 "Hayao Miyazaki Interview: Reasons Why I Don't Make Slapstick Action Films Now," *Comic Box,* October 1989.

6 Oshiguchi, "Whimsy and Wonder."

7 In Miyazaki's manga, "Folgore" is the name of Porco's plane, not its engine.

8 Interview at Buta-ya, 20 January 1999.

9 Schilling, Mark, "The Red Pig Flies to the Rescue," *Japan Times* (Tokyo), 28 July 1992.

10 McCarthy, "House That Hayao Built."

11 Ibid.

12 Ibid.

13 Schilling, "Red Pig."

8: PRINCESS MONONOKE

1 "Reasons Why I Don't Make Slapstick Action Films Now," *Comic Box.*

2 "Miyazaki and Oshii around the End of Patlabor 2," *Animage* (Tokyo), October 1993.

3 Oshiguchi, "Whimsy and Wonder."

4 "Manga Manga," BBC2, February 1994.

5 *Asia Pulse,* May 1997.

6 Miyazaki, Hayao, "Proposal for Mononoke Hime," 19 April 1995.

7 Seno, "Alexandra Princess with a Mission," *Asiaweek,* 21 November 1997.

8 "Worldwide Video Markets: the End of the Beginning?" *Screen Digest,* November 1998.

9 "Manga Manga," BBC2, February 1994.

10 Interview at Buta-ya, 20 January 1999.

11 Miyazaki, "Proposal."

12 *Asia Pulse,* May 1997.

13 CNN *Today,* 3 October 1997.

14 "Manga Manga," BBC2, February 1994.

15 Shiba, "A Walk in Totoro's Forest." Miyazaki specifically refers to Ashitaka as an Emishi boy here and elsewhere.

16 Princess Mononoke Japanese theater program, July 1997.

17 "Manga Manga," BBC2, February 1994.

18 *The Art of The Princess Mononoke* lists the following programs used:

SoftImage 3D: 3D CG creation—3D character and landscape creation

SoftImage Eddie: Image processing—CG screen composites

SoftImage Toonz: Digital painting—used to paint the cels

MentalRAY: Shadow calculation—Inoshishigami and Tatarigami scenes

Media Illusion: Image processing and painting—used for the morphing scenes

Flint: Digital composition—multilayer composition; used in all scenes

19 Shiba, "A Walk in Totoro's Forest."
20 Sertori, Julia, "Twilight of the Gods," *Manga Mania* 46, July/August 1998.

9: THE MIYAZAKI MACHINE

1 *Visionaire*, no. 24 (New York) appeared in spring 1998. The issue consisted of twenty-four specially commissioned long format transparencies by a range of artists from many nations and disciplines, and a special light box on which to view them. An almost complete listing of Miyazaki's various activities is maintained and updated on nausicaa.net by members of the Miyazaki Mailing List.

2 McCarthy, "Adjuster."
3 The figure was confirmed to me by Haruyo Moriyoshi of Tokuma International a few days after the screening.
4 McCarthy, "Adjuster."
5 *Archives of Studio Ghibli* 1.
6 In conversation in Koganei, 20 January 1999.
7 Kanta Ishida in *Yomiuri Shimbun* (Tokyo), 28 August 1997.
8 Collins in conversation on 22 January 1999, Suzuki as above.
9 McCarthy, "Adjuster."
10 Interview with Andrew Stanton, *GaZO!* 2, March 1999.
11 McCarthy, "House That Hayao Built."
12 Ibid.

Bibliography

All the materials listed below have been very useful in my research and I gratefully acknowledge my debt to their authors and editors. (I have included my own works for the sake of completeness.) Many publications from Tokuma, in particular the *Art of Studio Ghibli* books and storybooks available both in English and Japanese, have also been indispensable in helping me to appreciate the artistry and intelligence which guided the creation of these movies. The Web sites of Studio Ghibli and Jo Hisaishi have been most informative.

There is a very useful and easily accessible online resource for those seeking more information on Miyazaki: nausicaa.net, the mine of information on the Internet maintained by the owners and members of the Miyazaki Mailing List, an international fan group devoted to spreading information and discussion on the works of Studio Ghibli. I would also like to acknowledge an enduring debt of gratitude to my own translators in Japan and London, and to the many, often nameless, authors of material in fan publications whose early determination to introduce Japanese animation to a wider audience has proved inspirational.

BOOKS

Archives of Studio Ghibli. Vols. 1–5. Tokyo: Tokuma Shoten, 1995–.

Baricordi, Andrea, et al. *Cartoonia Anime: Guida al Cinema di Animazione Giapponese.* Bolgona: Granata Press, 1991.

Bendazzi, Gianalberto. *Cartoons: One Hundred Years of Animation.* Bloomington: Indiana University Press, 1996.

Brophy, Philip, ed. *Kaboom! Explosive Animation from America and Japan.* Sydney: Museum of Contemporary Art, 1994.

Groensteen, Thierry, and Harry Morgan. *L'univers des mangas: une introduction a la bande dessinée japonaise,* 2d ed. Tournai: Casterman, 1996.

Ledoux, Trish, and Doug Ranney. *The Complete Anime Guide: Japanese Animation Directory and Resource Guide.* 2d ed. Issaquah, Washington: Tiger Mountain Press, 1997.

Levi, Antonia. *Samurai from Outer Space: Understanding Japanese Animation.* Chicago: Open Court, 1996.

McCarthy, Helen. *Manga Manga Manga: A Celebration of Japanese Animation at the ICA.* London: Island World Communications Ltd., 1992.

———. *Anime! A Beginner's Guide to Japanese Animation.* London: Titan Books, 1993.

———. *The Anime Movie Guide: Japanese Animation Since 1983.* London: Titan Books, 1996.

Miyazaki, Hayao. "The Hopes and Spirit of Contemporary Japanese Girls." In *The Art of Kiki's Delivery Service.* Tokyo: Tokuma Shoten, 1989.

————. *Shuppatsuten 1979–96* (Points of Departure, 1979–96). Tokyo: Tokuma Shoten, 1997.

Richie, Donald. *The Japanese Movie: An Illustrated History.* London: Ward Locke and Co. and Kodansha International, 1966.

Schilling, Mark. *The Encyclopaedia of Japanese Pop Culture.* New York: Weatherhill, 1997.

Schodt, Frederik L. *Dreamland Japan: Writings on Modern Manga.* Berkeley: Stone Bridge Press, 1996.

Suzuki, Toshio. "Ten Years of Studio Ghibli." In *Archives of Studio Ghibli* 1. Tokyo: Tokuma Shoten, 1995.

Wells, Paul, ed. *Art and Animation.* London: Academy Group, 1998.

PRESS, WIRE, AND ONLINE ARTICLES/INTERVIEWS

Where articles have appeared in U.S. or U.K. publications, I have not cited a place of publication as bibliographic search should be straightforward. Where articles have appeared in overseas publications the place of publication is included. Where no author or interviewer is credited, or where I have no reliable source for names, the article title alone is cited. These articles are grouped at the beginning of the bibliography, and are arranged in date order.

Interview with Hayao Miyazaki. *A-Club* 19 (Hong Kong), 10 June 1987.

"Ciclo en el Malda de cine japones de animacion." *Vanguardia* (Spain), 3 December 1993.

"Analysis: Digitization Zooms in on Japan's Film Industry." *Asia Pulse,* 16 May 1997.

"Hit Japanese Animation Film Breaks Box Office Record." *Japan Economic Newswire* , 25 August 1997.

"Japanese Princess Beats Steven Spielberg's Dinosaurs." *Agence France Presse,* 26 August 1997.

"Cartoon Japanese Princess Set to Beat Spielberg's E.T." *Agence France Presse,* 29 October 1997.

"'Mononoke' Pushes Box Office Record to 10 bil. Yen." *Japan Economic Newswire,* 17 November 1997.

"Hayao Miyazaki, Mononoke Hime and Studio Ghibli." *Kinejun Special Issue,* no. 1233. Kinema Junpo Sha (Tokyo), February 1998.

"Miyazaki Hits the Arthouse Circuit." *Manga Mania* 46, July/August 1998.

"Worldwide Video Markets: The End of the Beginning?" *Screen Digest,* November 1998.

Adam. "London Film Fest Reviews: Tenku No Shiro Laputa." *Variety,* 2 December 1987.

Akira and Shinobu, "Hayao Miyazaki: Le Cochon Volant." *Animeland* 6 (Paris), July/August 1992.

Baricordi, Andrea, and Massimiliano de Giovanni. "Hayao Miyazaki." *Mangazine* (Bologna), May 1991.

Burr, Ty. "Special Delivery." *Entertainment Weekly,* 4 September 1998.

Clements, Jonathan. "Book Reviews: The Real Thing." *Anime FX* 10, January 1996.

————. "If You Go Down to the Woods Today: CD Reviews." *Anime FX* 11, February 1996.

————. "Zen and the Art of Academic Research." *Foundation* 73, Summer 1998.

Colpi, Federico, "Portfolio Hayao Miyazaki." *Mangazine* (Bologna), June 1994.

De Giovanni, Massimiliano. "Il Ghibli Che Soffia dall'Este." *Kappa Magazine* (Bosco), August 1992.

Ebert, Roger. "Japanese Film 'Mononoke' Causes a buzz." *Minneapolis Star Tribune*, 21 December 1997.

Eisner, Ken. "Kiki Delivers the Goods." *Variety*, 17 July 1998.

Eng, Christina. "Kidding Around: More Than Typical Teen, Kiki Delivers at Asian-American Film Festival." *Oakland Tribune*, 12 March 1999.

Evans, Peter J. "Flights of Fancy." *Manga Mania* 20, March 1995.

Evans, Peter, and Helen McCarthy. "Kurenai no Buta." *Anime U.K.* 4, September 1992.

Fallaix, Olivier, and Pierre Giner. "Hommage a Yoshifumi Kondo." *Animeland* 39 (Paris), March 1998.

Geier, Thom et al. "Blood and Guts in Ancient Japan." *U.S. News and World Report*, 6 October 1997.

Giner, Pierre. "Interview: Hayao Miyazaki." *Animeland* 10 (Paris), March 1993.

Havis, Richard James. "Twelve Months of Turning Points." *Asiaweek* (Tokyo), 26 December 1997.

Herskovitz, Jon. "Japan's Towering Animator." *Variety*, 4–10 August 1997.

———. "'Princess' Rules Japan B.O." *Daily Variety*, 26 August 1997.

Ishii, Rika. "Interview with Mamoru Oshii." *Kine-jun Special Issue*, no. 1166. Kinema Junpo Sha (Tokyo), July 1995.

Kanta, Ishida. "The Future of Animation Illustrated by the Master." *Yomiuri Shimbun* (Tokyo), 28 August 1997.

Karrfalt, Wayne. "'Princess' Crowned King of Japanese Box Office." *The Hollywood Reporter*, 2 September 1997.

———. "'Princess' Is No Fairy-Tale Sell: Disney May Find It Hard to Market Violent Japanese Ani Hit." *The Hollywood Reporter*, 30 September 1997.

———. "'Mononoke' Japan's All-Time B.O. Champion." *The Hollywood Reporter*, 31 October 1997.

Klady, Leonard. "My Neighbor Totoro." *Variety*, 10 May 1993.

———. "Japan's 'Princess' Set for Royal Reception." RTve (Reuters/Variety Entertainment) wire service, 30 January 1998.

Kurosawa, Akira. "Akira Kurosawa's 100 Best Movies List." *Bungei Shunju* (Tokyo), April 1999.

Lafine, Pascal; Vincent Osee Vu; and Yvan West Laurence. "Interview: Moebius." *Animeland* 1 (Paris), April 1991.

Littardi, Cedric. "Interview: Isao Takahata." *Animeland* 6 (Paris), July/August 1992.

———. "Porci Con Le Ali." *Kappa Magazine* (Bosco), October 1992.

Lubich, David. "Japanimation." *The Guardian*, 20 January 1995.

Makino, Keiji, et al. "Why Has Literature Lost to Manga?" In *Kino Review*, Kyoto Seika University (Kyoto), 1998.

Mallory, Michael. "Princess Goes West." *Daily Variety*, 13 February 1998.

McCarthy, Helen. "Porco Rosso." *Anime U.K.* 12, February 1994.

———. "Lupin III: The Secret Files." *Anime U.K.*, new series 1 and 2, March/April 1995.

———. "The House That Hayao Built." *Manga Max* 5, April 1999.

———. "The Adjuster: Interview with Toshio Suzuki." *Manga Max* 6, May 1999.

Miyazaki, Hayao. "The Current Situation of Japanese Movies." *Course on Japanese Movies* 7, Iwanami Shoten (Tokyo), 28 January 1988.

———. "Reasons Why I Don't Make Slapstick Action Films Now." *Comic Box* (Tokyo), October 1989.

———. Interview in *Pacific Friend* 18, no. 9 (Tokyo), January 1991.

———. "Your Special Story: Now Nausicaä Has Finished." *Yom* (Tokyo), June 1994.

———. "Here Comes Animation." *Kinejun Special Issue*, no. 1166 [transcript of a talk given 22 May 1988 at Nagoya Animation Festival]. Kinema Junpo Sha (Tokyo), 16 July 1995.

Moisan, David. "*Nausicaä* and *Dune*: The Intertwined Worlds of Frank Herbert and Hayao Miyazaki." *Japanese Animation News and Review: The Official Newsletter of Hokubei Anime-Kai*, vol. 1, no. 4, July 1991.

Nguyen, Ilan. "Miyazaki Lupin III." *Animeland* 25 (Paris), September 1995.

———. "Aux sources du Studio Ghibli." *Animeland* 24 (Paris), July 1996.

———. "Mononoke Hime: Une ultime realisa-

tion en forme de retour." *Animeland* 32 (Paris), May 1997.

———. "The Princess Mononoke." *Animeland* 35 (Paris), September 1997.

Nichols Peter. "At Mickey's House, a Quiet Welcome for Distant Cousins." *New York Times*, 1 February 1998.

Oshiguchi, Takashi. "The Whimsy and Wonder of Hayao Miyazaki," *Animerica* 1, nos. 5 and 6, July/August 1993.

Pierre and Olivier. "Disney-Tokuma: L'alliance de David et Goliath." *Animeland* 25 (Paris), September 1995.

Prioux, Francois. "Nausicaa: du manga a l'anime." *Animeland* 24 (Paris), July 1996.

Schilling, Mark. "*Majo* Delivers Innovative World of Animation." *Japan Times* (Tokyo), 29 August 1989.

Schoenberger, Karl. "Japan's Motion Picture Industry Is Learning That the Sun Also Sinks." *Los Angeles Times*, 4 April 1990.

Seno, Alexandra A. "Princess with a Mission." *Asiaweek* (Tokyo), 21 November 1997.

Sertori, Julia. "Just Desserts: Eco-Anime." *Anime U.K.*, 2 April 1995.

———. "Twilight of the Gods." *Manga Mania* 46, July/August 1998.

Shiba, Ryutaro. "A Walk in Totoro's Forest." *Weekly Asahi* (Tokyo), 5 and 12 January 1996. Reprinted in Hayao Miyazaki, *Shuppatsuten 1979–96*. Tokyo: Tokuma Shoten, 1997.

Smith, Toren. "Masamune Shirow," *Manga Mania*, 8 February 1994.

Takahata, Isao. "The Fireworks of Eros." Reprinted in Hayao Miyazaki, *Shuppatsuten 1979–96*, Tokyo: Tokuma Shoten, 1997.

Teto and Bounthavy. "Kiki's Delivery Service." *Animeland* 24 (Paris), July 1996.

Trashorras, Antonio. "Presente Imperfecto, Futuro Incierto: Sitges 93." *Fantastic Magazine* (Madrid), July 1993.

Valery and Bounthy. "Nausicaä de la Vallee du Vent." *Animeland* 24 (Paris), July 1996.

Vidal, Jaume. "Barcelona acogera la primera muestra espanola de animacian japonesa." *el Pais* (Madrid), 26 November 1993.

Vincentelli, Elizabeth. "Tooning in: Disney Imports a Japanese Auteur-Animator." *Village Voice*, 2 September 1998.

Watts, Jonathan. "Japan in Grip of Blood-Soaked Cartoon Film: E.T. Sent Packing." *The Guardian*, 5 November 1997.

West Laurence, Yvan. "Mon Voisin Totoro: Miyazaki au naturel." *Animeland* 41 (Paris), May 1998.

———, and Alexandra Foucher. "Conan le Fils du Futur." *Animeland* 24 (Paris), July 1996.

BROADCAST MEDIA

Allen, Natalie, and John Lewis. "Animated Film Breaks Box-Office Records in Japan: 'Phantom Princess' Sets Japanese Record." Broadcast on CNN, U.S., 30 October 1997.

Hayao Miyazaki interview in "Dope Sheet." Broadcast on Channel 4, U.K., 8 January 1999.

"Manga Manga" documentary on Japanese animation broadcast on BBC2, U.K., February 1994.

PROMOTIONAL MATERIALS

Fox Lorber. Promotional material for U.S. video release of *My Neighbor Totoro*, 1994.

Manga Entertainment. Promotional material for U.K. video release of *Castle of Cagliostro*, 1995.

Streamline Pictures. Promotional material for original U.S. release of *The Castle of Cagliostro*, 1992.

Tokuma Shoten. Japanese theater program for *Princess Mononoke*, July 1997.

Tokyo Movie Shinsha (now TMS-Kyokuichi Corporation). Promotional materials for the following titles: *Castle of Cagliostro*, *Sherlock Hound*, *Panda Kopanda*, release dates as noted in the filmography.

Ucore S.A. "Hayao Miyazaki Filmographie." Promotional material for French release of *Porco Rosso*, spring 1994.

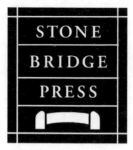

STONE BRIDGE PRESS

Quality Books & Software
About Japan

OTHER TITLES OF INTEREST FROM STONE BRIDGE PRESS

Obtain any of the following books by visiting your local bookseller.
Or call toll free 1-800-947-7271

sbp@stonebridge.com • www.stonebridge.com

THE ANIME COMPANION
What's Japanese in Japanese Animation?

GILLES POITRAS
The otaku's best friend, an encyclopedic reference to all the Japanese cultural details in anime you don't want to miss! Fully indexed with regular Web updates by the author.
176 pp, 50+ b/w illustrations, $16.95

DREAMLAND JAPAN
Writings on Modern Manga

FREDERIK L. SCHODT
A collection of insightful essays on the current state of the manga universe, the best artists, the major themes and magazines, plus what it means for the future of international visual culture. By the author of the acclaimed *Manga! Manga! The World of Japanese Comics*.
360 pp, 8 pp color, 100+ b/w/ illustrations, $16.95

THE FOUR IMMIGRANTS MANGA
A Japanese Experience in San Francisco, 1904–1923

HENRY (YOSHITAKA) KIYAMA
TRANS. FREDERIK L. SCHODT
The true adventures of four young guys who come from Japan to California at the turn of the century. Told in comic-strip format, with a detailed introduction and commentary on what the comic tells us about early Asian-American history. Privately published in Japanese in 1931, and available now in English for the first time.
144 pp, illustrated throughout, $12.95

KANJI PICT-O-GRAPHIX
Over 1,000 Japanese Kanji and Kana Mnemonics

MICHAEL ROWLEY
Want to get serious about *kanji* and learning Japanese? Use the visual cues in this book to get a handle on basic meanings of common Japanese characters. Entertaining, clever, and visually stunning art makes the *kanji* easy to memorize. Includes *hiragana* and *katakana* too!
208 pp, illustrated throughout, $19.95